A Reader of Pashto

by

HERBERT PENZL

with a New Introduction by Ismail Sloan

ISHI PRESS
INTERNATIONAL

A Reader of Pashto

by Herbert Penzl

with a New Introduction by Ismail Sloan

This work was developed pursuant to a contract with the United States Department of Education

Library of Congress Catalog Card No. 65-21769

First Printed in 1962 by
University of Michigan Press,
Ann Arbor, Michigan

Current Printing in November, 2009
by Ishi Press in New York and Tokyo

ISBN 0-923891-71-4
978-0-923891-71-8

Ishi Press International
1664 Davidson Avenue, Suite 1B
Bronx NY 10453-7877
USA

917-507-7226

Printed in the United States of America

Introduction by Ismail Sloan

INTRODUCTION

Herbert Penzl, (born **September 2, 1910** in **Neufelden, Austria**, died **September 1, 1995** in Berkeley, California), wrote this book. It, along with "***A Grammar of Pashto A Descriptive Study of the Dialect of Kandahar, Afghanistan***", is the definitive works on the **Pashto Language**.

Pashto is a language spoken by at least 40 million people in Southern and Eastern Afghanistan and in the Northwest Frontier Province of Pakistan.

Pashto is regarded as a tremendously difficult language to learn, perhaps the most difficult Indo-European Language. Just about nobody learns it except for those born into the language. The main reasons for this include the gender system. It is comparable to German. In German, Das Mädchen meaning "the woman" is neuter even though is should logically be feminine. A bigger problem is that in Pashto the verb does not go along with the subject (such as in I am, you are, he is). In Pashto, the verb is modified by the object.

Pashto is an S-O-V language. Adjectives come before nouns. Nouns and adjectives are inflected for two genders and four cases (direct, oblique I, oblique II and vocative). The verb system is very intricate with the following tenses: present, subjunctive, simple past, past progressive, present perfect and past perfect. In any of the past tenses (simple past, past progressive, present perfect and past perfect), Pashto is an ergative language; i.e., transitive verbs in any of the past tenses agree with the object of the sentence

Linguists say that there are six major dialects of Pashto. However, the main concern should be with the two big dialects. Here again, there is a similarity with German. The word "Ich" meaning "I" in German is pronounced "ick" in Northern Germany but "ish" in Southern Germany. (It is my theory that Penzl, a noted Germanic scholar, was interested in Pashto because of these similarities between Pashto and German.)

Similarly, in **SouthEastern Afghanistan**, the word for the name of the language is pronounced "Pashto", but across the border in Pakistan it is pronounced "Pukhtu". There is a uniform sound change across the language, where the /sh/ in the West becomes /kh/ in the East. This does not seem to cause local speakers much trouble, because they are used to it and can understand each other, although sometimes only with great difficulty.

Estimates of the number of Pashto speakers range from **40 million to 60 million**, which should make it among the most widely spoken languages in the world. One source ranks it as number 20 in the world in the number of speakers of the language. Another source ranks it as number 35. However, most sources do not rank it at all. The language seems to be virtually unknown except among those in contact with it.

This is at least in part due to the nature of the people who speak Pashto. At one time, Pashto was spoken primarily by desert tribal people. The **Kuchi** tribes, nomads who live out in the desert with their herds of sheep and camels, all speak Pashto. The Kuchis have little need for reading and writing and almost all are illiterate. As a result, there is little Pashto literature, except for songs and poetry. In Afghanistan, there are few if any books and newspapers in Pashto. In Pakistan, the situation is a bit better, but not much.

All this began to change with the **Wars in Afghanistan.** Prior to 1978, when Afghanistan was at peace, it was rare to see even a single Pashto speaker far from his homeland. Few Afghans ever ventured out of Afghanistan, not even to neighboring Pakistan.

All that changed with the Soviet invasion of 1979. An estimated five million Afghans were forced to leave their country to get away from the war. Three million went to Pakistan and two million went to Iran. Almost all of them were Pashto speakers, as the war was concentrated in Pashto speaking areas.

As a result, vast tracts of land west of Peshawar that had been empty prior to the war, became filled with hundreds of thousands of tents that had to be provided to house the refugees. As far as the eye could see, there were tents set up, whereas there had been nothing but barren land there previously.

Meanwhile, many of the Kuchis, the desert nomads, had been put out of business by the war. Their livelihood depended on free trade. They could no longer travel long distances, carrying their goods from market to market. One of the first things the new Marxist government of **Nur Muhammad Taraki** did in **1978** was fix the price of basic goods, including foodstuffs, in the markets. Shopkeepers were no longer allowed to sell their goods in the market for what they had been accustomed to receiving. Therefore, they could no longer pay the Kuchis for their sheep. In short order, one could no longer buy even a chicken in the central market place in **Kabul**.

In 2002, the situation improved for the better, with the **US Invasion of Afghanistan** in retaliation for the attacks on **9/11** against the **World Trade Center**. The **Taliban** were quickly driven from power. **King Zahir Shah** returned to Afghanistan, after having spent 29 years in exile in Italy since 1973.

As a result, many of the three million refugees in Pakistan returned to their homes in Afghanistan. This was in part because Afghanistan was more or less at peace and also because their presence in Pakistan was no longer welcome or tolerated.

Meanwhile, many Afghan refugees had reached America and had become citizens here. There are now big enclaves of Pashto speaking Afghans in Northern Virginia, California and Queens, New York, among other places. There is an entire generation of new Afghans born here. Many of them are highly educated and literate. Some are returning to their country. One of these is **Hamid Karzai**, a Pashto speaker who is the current **President of Afghanistan**.

I am a member and in some cases even the moderator of several Afghan and Pashto language email groups. Most of the members of these groups are highly literate and well educated. They usually write to each other in English, but some of them write in Pashto. As Pashto language fonts are not readily available, they write in Pashto using the **Roman ABC alphabet**.

Introduction by Ismail Sloan

I have long believed since I first became familiar with Pashto that the key to the development of Pashto is to drop the **Arabic alphabet** and use the Roman alphabet instead. The Arabic alphabet is unsuitable for Pashto because there are many sounds in Pashto that do not have an equivalent in Arabic and at the same time there are many sounds in Arabic that do not have an equivalent in Pashto.

Take the word "Pashto", for example. There is no "p" in Arabic. There is also no "o" in Arabic. There is an /sh/ type sound in Arabic but it is not really the same as the /sh/ in Pashto. Thus, new letters have to be created to write Pashto in Arabic. Yet, the word Pashto can easily be written using the Roman ABC alphabet.

I met **Herbert Penzl** in 1981 at the annual meeting of the **Linguistic Society of America** held in **New York City** on **December 27-30, 1981**. I went to that meeting specifically to meet Herbert Penzl because I was aware of his fame for his study of Pashto. I had already written and published my **Khowar-English Dictionary** and was hoping to do similar work with Pashto.

I told Professor Penzl that I had shown the book "***A Dictionary of the Pukhto, Pushto, or Language of the Afghans***" by **H. G. Raverty** (first published in **1859**) to several of my Pashto speaking friends from the **Kandahar** area, and none of them could recognize the words in the book. Professor Penzl seemed surprised at this and said that those were real words, and that Raverty had not made them up.

Herbert Penzl was not as up-to-date as I was on the current developments in Afghanistan. However, he told me that he had been an invited official guest of the **Government of Afghanistan** in **November 1979**, only one month before **President Hafizullah Amin** had been killed by the **Soviets** on **December 27, 1979**. Penzl told me that Hafizullah Amin had personally invited him to **Kabul** for the celebration of some event. The reason for the Invitation was, of course, recognition for the work Herbert Penzl had done in writing this book, "***A Grammar of Pashto***".

As this had been only one month before Hafizullah Amin had been **killed** during the **Soviet Invasion of Afghanistan**, I asked Dr. Penzl if Hafizullah Amin had had any idea of what was about to happen. Dr. Penzl said that no, Amin had been "very optimistic" about the future of Afghanistan and about his own future.

I told Professor Penzl that I had been a political prisoner in Afghanistan (basically for being suspected of being an American CIA Agent) and that I believed that Hafizullah Amin had probably personally ordered my release. (Boy! Was that ever a big mistake!) The reason I thought so was that my release had been ordered by **Syed Daod Taroon, the Security Chief of Afghanistan** and **Hafizullah Amin's right hand man**. I had been released from prison in Afghanistan on **September 3, 1978**. Thereafter, on **February 14, 1979**, the **United States Ambassador to Afghanistan Adolph "Spike" Dubs** was killed on orders of **Syed Daod Taroon**, the same man who had ordered my release. Then, on **September 14, 1979** Syed Daod Taroon was killed in a shoot-out in which **President Nur Muhammad Taraki was also killed.**

The result was that Herbert Penzl and myself were still alive, but everybody else was dead.

Also, during my meeting with Professor Herbert Penzl I brought up my situation with the **University of California at Berkeley,** where Herbert Penzl was a full professor. I had been a student there in the Math Department. However, in the aftermath of the **Free Speech Movement** in the mid-1960s, I had been blacklisted by one **Dean Lemmon** because of my leadership of a small but controversial student club on the campus. This I felt was unfair since I had not been arrested in **Sproul Hall** or anything like that. I had not done anything illegal.

Professor Penzl knew Dean Lemmon, who was still a Dean in spite of the passage or 14 years, and agreed to talk to him. I later called Professor Penzl who told me that he had in fact spoken to Dean Lemmon about me. Dean Lemmon remembered me and said that as they had even let back in Mario Savio, the leader of the student revolution, he would consider letting me back in.

I think that I am just about the only non-Afghan and non-Pakistani **Native Born American** (meaning that I can become President) who can speak Pashto. I am by no means entirely fluent, but at least I can tell the taxi driver where I want to go. (**Sloan's Law**: All Taxi Drivers speak Pashto!)

Whenever asked how I came to speak Pashto, I explain that I was enrolled in an intensive language training course at Afghan Government expense.

Most do not get it, so then I need to explain that I was in jail there. Since most of my fellow prisoners were Pashto speakers, I had to learn Pashto to get along in jail. Also, my study of Pashto gave me something useful to do during my time in jail. It was obvious that many of my fellow prisoners were being executed. So, this was not a case of spending time in prison **until** I got out. Rather, the question was **IF** I would get out, rather than being lined up in front of a ditch and then shot, as many of my fellow prisoners were.

Anyway, knowing Pashto would certainly improve my chances of getting out alive. This was a good motivator.

About four years ago, I applied for a job as a Pashto Translator with a company that supplies support staff for the American military in Afghanistan. They gave me a Pashto Language translation test over the telephone. I must confess that I failed the test. Later, I met a young boy about 19 who had gotten one of these jobs as a Pashto translator. I tried to speak to him in Pashto and I quickly realized that my Pashto was much better than his. So, I asked him how he had gotten a job as a Pashto translator, when his Pashto was so weak. He explained that he had grown up in America but his parents spoke Farsi at home, not Pashto. He had not been able to get a job as a Farsi translator, as the US Military already had lots of them, so he had obtained a job as a Pashto Translator. By the way, he had already served a tour of duty in Afghanistan and was back in Queens for a holiday. He was due to return to Afghanistan in a few days. These jobs pay over $100,000. Of course, the Army grunts would not know if he was giving them a good translation or not, so what difference would it make? Our tax dollars at work!!

Introduction by Ismail Sloan

Read this book!!!!

I was in a total of seven jails and prisons in Afghanistan in 1978 but the main ones were Jalalabad Mahbas, Demazang and Puli Charki. None of my fellow prisoners in Demazang and Puli Charki ever got out alive, or at least I never saw any of them again, but I did later meet three of my former fellow prisoners from Jalalabad in Pakistan. So, anybody in Jalalabad Prison had at least some chance to survive, whereas those in Demazang and Puli Charki had almost no chance at all.

However, even in Jalalabad Prison, the chances were not that good. The former prisoners whom I met gave me the names of many other prisoners who had been executed there.

The two United States Consular Officers whom I credit with getting me out of Jail and out of Afghanistan alive were Warren Marrick and David Bloch. There were others who helped, but I do not know their names. One who helped get me out later wrote that he remembered seeing me in police custody and that my glasses had been broken. He sent me an email in 1996 but I lost it when my email account got canceled.

Two of my fellow prisoners from Jalalabad Prison became famous later on. One was Anwar Amin of Nuristan, whose case is discussed extensively on Richard Strand's Nuristan website.

The other was Akhtar Jan, who is now known in the press as Akhtar Jan Kohistani.

Five years after I had been released from jail in Afghanistan, I met Akhtar Jan in University Town Peshawar. He was working for an organization called SERV, that was providing help for the Afghan Refugees. He was working with Abdul Khaleq, a Kalash man I knew from Bumboret Chitral. It was amazing to meet two old friends together, especially since I did not know that they knew each other.

Later on, Akhtar Jan wrote me and said that he wanted to attend university in England and he asked me to write a letter of recommendation. I wrote the letter and mailed it to the university. However, after that I did not hear from Akhtar Jan again for more than twenty years. I feared the worst.

Then, his name came in the news. Turns out that he had made it to England and had spent more than 15 years as a BBC radio broadcaster making Pashto Language broadcasts.

After the American invasion of Afghanistan in 2002, Akhtar Jan like many Afghans returned to his country. Recently, he had gotten married in Village Kalkatak in Chitral. This is another amazing coincidence. Village Kalkatak is directly across the Chitral River from Village Damik in Jinjoret which is the residence of my Chitrali wife, Honzagool. They can see each other across the river (but that is about all. The river is strong and fierce there. Anybody who tries to swim it will probably drown. Better to walk seven miles to the nearest bridge.)

According to one news report, Akhtar Jan had married a niece of Prince Mohay-ud-Din, former Minister of State of Pakistan. If true, this makes Akhtar Jan a sort-of in-law of mine, because Prince Mohay-ud-Din is a second cousin of my Chitrali wife Honzagool and thus is 2nd cousins 3 times removed from our daughter, Shamema. Their common ancestor is Mehtar Aman-ul Mulk.

http://www.royalark.net/Pakistan/chitral7.htm

On November 2, 2008, while he was approaching his wife's home in Kalkatak, Akhtar Jan was kidnapped by the Taliban and taken to Nuristan in Afghanistan. This became a major item in the news, because it was reported that Akhtar Jan is now an Adviser in the Government of Hamid Karzai. The kidnappers demanded a prisoner exchange for one of their top commanders. The details are still sketchy but it appears that from there Akhtar Jan was taken to Upper Dir. The local Mullahs in Upper Dir tried to broker a deal with the Taliban to secure his release. It was reported that Akhtar Jan had been released on January 2, 2009, but this report proved to be false. At one point, Akhtar Jan escaped in a vehicle, but he was recaptured by the Taliban, who drove a faster vehicle.

After verifying that the Akhtar Jan who had been kidnapped by the Taliban was the same man who had been in jail with me in 1978, I had to decide whether to publicize this fact. Knowing his connection with me might help him get out or, on the other hand, it might seal his doom.

Finally, I decided that the Taliban does not read the Internet anyway, so it can only help him. I wrote on the Internet:

On November 8, 2008 I wrote on my Chitrali email group:

> "I have been reading about Akhtar Jan Kohistani, an Afghan Government official who was kidnapped in Drosh, Chitral on November 2, 2008 and I just realized that this is almost certainly the same man who was in prison with me in Jalalabad in 1978.
>
> http://www.afgha.com/?q=node/9558
> http://www.thenews.com.pk/updates.asp?id=59141
>
> On or about June 4, 1978 I was arrested in Nawzad, Helmand Province, Afghanistan and taken to jail in Lashkar Gah, Afghanistan. After two weeks I escaped from jail, but then I was arrested again at Torkam while trying to cross the border into Pakistan. I was taken to Jalalabad Mahbas Prison and later transferred to Demazang Prison and then to Puli Charqi Prison in Kabul.
>
> Fortunately, on September 3, 1978 I was released into Pakistan with the help of US Consular Officers Warren Marrick and David Bloch.
>
> One man I met in Jalalabad Prison was Akhtar Jan. In fact, he helped me mail the letter to the US Embassy in Kabul that eventually got me out of jail.
>
> A few years later, I met this same Akhtar Jan in Peshawar. I was happy to see him because at least half of the prisoners in Jalalabad Prison with me had been executed by firing squad.

Akhtar Jan later asked me to write a letter of recommendation to help him obtain a visa and admission to a university in England. After sending him the letter of recommendation, which must have been in 1981 or 1983, I never heard from him again.

I am almost certain that the Akhtar Jan Kohistani who was kidnapped in Chitral on November 2, 2008 is the same Akhtar Jan who was in prison with me in Jalalabad in July August 1978. If not, he is someone with a remarkably similar biography.

I will do anything I can to help him, as he definitely helped me when we were in prison together in 1978.

Very few prisoners got out of that prison alive. The only two others I know of who survived were Jalaladin from Nuristan whom I later met in a refugee camp in Chitral and Muhammad Anvar Amin, with whom I played many games of chess, Indian style, in Jalalabad Prison. (I won all the chess games, but what do you expect from a mountain man from Nuristan.) I developed my "Jalalabad Defense" (1. e4 e5 2. Nf3 c5) there.

Muhammad Anvar Amin was later killed in Pakistan. This is described in Richard Strand's Nuristan site:

`http://users.sedona.net/~strand/Nuristani/Kamkata/Kom/KomTexts/Anvar3.html`

So, at least four prisoners survived Jalalabad Prison. However, none of the prisoners I met in Demazang or Puli Charqi prisons were ever seen alive again.

Ismail Sloan

I received the following reply back from a Chitrali named Muhammad Abeer Khan:

“very intersting story. dun tell any body if Akhtar Jan is the same one who helped you in Afghanistan prison otherwise American CIA will again put u in prison not in Jalalabad this time but in Guntanamo. Hahaha

“this is unbelivbale your attachment with Chitral is still alive despite your broken marriage with KHONZA GUL. (i *was in School when this story of yours and KG took place*.)

“Thanks!!

“MAK, Chitral”

I can take a joke, if it was intended to be one, and if it was not intended to be one that is OK too because I am not intending to go back there any time soon.

The story continued to be in the news. Abdul Khaleq reported that Akhtar had been released on payment of ransom of 14 million rupees (about $17,190). This report proved to be false,

Former Afghan official shifted to Dir Wednesday, January 28, 2009

DIR KHAS: A former BBC radio broadcaster and one-time Afghan government official Akhtar Kohistani who was kidnapped from Chitral last November has been shifted to Dhog Darra area in Dir Upper district and a local jirga of elders was now trying to secure his release.

There were reports that villagers in the area have warned the kidnappers to free the man or face action. Kohistani, who is an Afghan national and belongs to Nuristan province in Afghanistan, was visiting his in-laws in Chitral when he was kidnapped by a group of armed men. Initial reports, also verified by the Chitral Police, said he had been taken across the border to Nuristan. But on Monday, Kohistani was seen in Dhog Darra near Sheringal in Dir Upper and since then hectic efforts are afoot to secure his release.

A jirga has been talking to the kidnappers, who are said to be Taliban militants and include Afghans living in the area. The kidnappers were reportedly demanding release of their men held in Afghanistan and Rs 20 million as ransom money.

Sources said Nuristani, who is in his 50s, tried to escape and managed to cover a distance of nine kilometres in a vehicle but a fast-moving Taliban pick-up chased him and took him into custody again. He was near Sheringal when he rearrested and thrashed. The militants drove him back to their mountain hideout.

Police officials have visited the area and senior cops were said to have threatened action against the kidnappers if Kohistani wasn't freed. The kidnappers had also sought advice from local clerics before deciding Kohistani's fate. They alleged that Kohistani and members of his family used to work for the Afghan government and its Western allies. Kohistani at one time was employed at the BBC Pashto service in London. He had served as an adviser to the local government ministry in Kabul in recent years.

Militants to leave Dir in 2 weeks, Kohistani released Tuesday, February 10, 2009

DIR: Achieving a major breakthrough, a grand jirga in Doog Darra, Upper Dir, secured the release of former BBC broadcaster Akhtar Kohistani and convinced the Afghan militants to leave the area within two weeks.

The jirga meeting was held on Monday at Bara Doog for the second consecutive day while it would continue today (Tuesday) to announce a final decision.

Jirga sources told 'The News' that Kohistani had been handed over to the jirga on

February 8 but the development was kept secret till the all-encompassing decision, The handover of Kohistani to the jirga will be formally announced today (Tuesday), the sources said.

People in Miana Doog of the district and Afghan militants and their local supporters had picked up arms against each other over the capture of Kohistani and militant presence in the peaceful area.

The locals in Miana Doog had been asking the militants to free the kidnapped person unconditionally and leave the area at once, but the militants flatly refused.

The refusal led the people to take positions against the militants at Miana Doog and to establish a checkpost to stop movement of the militants from and to five villages where militants had hideouts.

Akhtar Kohistani was kidnapped in Chitral when he was visiting his in-laws and was shifted to Doog Darra through mountains.

The issue came to the fore when Kohistani staged an abortive escape attempt on January 24.

Following the revelation of militants' presence in Doog Darra, tension there was heightened in the area. A grand local jirga has been trying for the last more than two weeks to secure the release of Kohistani and evict the militants from the area without fighting with them.

The sources said that the jirga would give two weeks to the militants today (Tuesday) to leave the area. The people of Miana Doog, who have been offering armed resistance to the militant, were demanding the eviction of the militants within 24 hours but the Afghan militants demanded a safe passage. They said the mountains were covered by snow, denying a safe passage to them.

Earlier, the people of Miana Doog were refusing to give an unconditional written authority to the jirga to make any decision and pressed for their demands. However, later in the day they agreed to delegate an unconditional authority.

Sources said the jirga would announce to the militant to leave the area within two weeks, or maximum 20 days. The sources also said the militants would shut down their illegal FM channel as well.

http://www.groundreport.com/World/Militants-demand-their-Al-Qaeda-member-for-safe-r_1

Introduction by Ismail Sloan

Militants demand their Al-Qaeeda member for safe release of Afghan media advisor

PESHAWAR: Militants operating in the Upper Dir-150 miles away from Peshawar, capital of North West Frontier Province, near to Pak-Afghan border-demanded their Al-Qaeeda member for safe release Akhtar Kohistani, the media advisor of Ministery of Rural Rehabilitation and Development Social Production Department of Afghanistan. A high police official told this correspondent on the condition of not disclosing his name that a jirga held between militants and a delegation of local elders led by Aman Ullah, an influential Myer of union council Doog Dara. "Militants demanded their colleague Qari Mohaee din known as Abdullah for the safe release of Akhtar Kohistani", police official said.

This story is still developing. However, the latest news seems to be that the militants did not keep their end of the agreement and stayed. The local villagers got fed up with the militants and decided simply to kill them. Some of the militants reportedly surrendered to the police, but the police turned the militants over to the villagers who promptly killed them.

I see this as a positive development. The militants are from Afghanistan but were forced across the border into Pakistan by action of the US Military on the Afghan side of the border. As a result, all of NWFP except for Chitral has been under siege by the militants. Only if the local people stop harboring the militants will the fighting end in Pakistan.

The main reason why this discussion is included in this book is that all of these people, both the militants and the local residents, speak Pashto.

After a brief introduction to the use of this reader and a summary of the Pashto language, the author presents 25 units of reading selections and correlated exercises. A typical lesson consists of-- (1) a short Pashto text in typewritten **Arabic-Persian** form, (2) a **Romanized** transcription of this text indicating pronunciation, (3) a glossary of new words in Romanized transliteration, (4) short notes on grammar and pronunciation, (5) an English translation of the text, and (6) short exercises in writing in Pashto (in units 1-10 only). The texts chosen for this beginning reader represent current usage in the three major Pashto dialectal regions and include a variety of styles and levels of difficulty. An appended "Pashto word-index" lists the Pashto forms and the unit and sentence in which they are presented. The author assumes that most users of this text have completed the equivalent of a one-semester, non-intensive course in the Pashto language. This reader and other instructional materials in Pashto were prepared at the University of Michigan at Ann Arbor, Department of Near Eastern Studies.

Ismail Sloan
Bronx NY USA
November 5, 2009

PREFACE

The General Introduction explains the purpose and arrangement of this Reader, which was completed in 1961 as part of a research project of the Department of Near Eastern Languages and Literatures at a time when the author was on the faculty of The University of Michigan.

Nine of the thirty-one textual selections contained in the twenty-five units of the Reader were originally edited under the auspices of the Program in Oriental Languages of the American Council of Learned Societies with the assistance of A. Ahad Yari of the University of Kabul. All units were developed with the aid and assistance of Noor Ahmad Shaker of the University of Kabul and of Abdul Ghafoor of Kohdaman, Afghanistan. The last two units were contributed by Khayal Bokhari and Jehanzeb Niaz of the Pashto Academy of Peshawar, West Pakistan.

The author gratefully acknowledges the help in obtaining Pashto texts from the following: the President of the Department of Press in Kabul; the U. S. Joint Publications Research Service; Maulana Fazl-i-Manan, the owner of the University Book Agency in Peshawar; and Mr. Qalander Momand and Mr. Rashid Ali Dehqan of Peshawar. Finally, the author (and The University of Michigan's Department of Near Eastern Languages and Literatures) pays tribute to the Inter-University Summer Program of Middle Eastern Languages, whose financial assistance made possible the final publication of this book.

Herbert Penzl

Berkeley, California

January 1965

CONTENTS

GENERAL INTRODUCTION

I. PURPOSE OF READER

The Pashto Reader is intended to provide a graded introduction to the reading of Pashto texts, and not only material for classroom use but also for self-study. It is hoped that the stylistic and dialectal range of the texts and the detailed implementation accompanying them will aid the readers of the book in acquiring a steadily increasing skill in reading Pashto, and besides encourage a more intensive study and ensure a better understanding of the grammatical structure of Pashto.

We must assume that most users of the book will possess at least an elementary knowledge of Pashto; i.e., one that might correspond to one semester's non-intensive work in the language. But it can by no means be excluded that under favorable circumstances exceptional individuals can benefit from the Reader even after less formal work in Pashto.

II. CONTENTS OF READER

The Reader contains besides this General Introduction a brief chapter on the Writing of Pashto; a Grammatical Summary; 25 units (see III below); a Pashto Word-index.

(a) The chapter on the WRITING OF PASHTO cannot and does not provide systematic instruction in the Persian-Arabic alphabet and its special Pashto additions. The proper place for this is a basic course. Only the general principles of Roman transcription and Roman transliteration of the Pashto texts as adopted for this reader are explained, and the existing sound types and phonemes of Pashto are listed in their relation to the prevalent orthography.

(b) The GRAMMATICAL SUMMARY cannot take the place of a reference grammar. To avoid lengthy grammatical explanations but to suggest further study, throughout the 25 units frequent references to this writer's A GRAMMAR OF PASHTO: A DESCRIPTIVE STUDY OF THE DIALECT OF KANDAHAR, AFGHANISTAN (Washington (D.C.): American Council of Learned Societies, 1955) can be found. The Grammatical Summary is only intended to explain the classification of words used in the glossaries and to provide some convenient reference tables for Pashto morphology.

(c) The PASHTO WORD-INDEX at the end with entries in the Pashto alphabet only is just a "finder-list". A word is usually given only once in the unit glossaries at its first appearance. Afterwards the reader can consult the word-index to find references by unit and sentence for up to three previous and later occurrences. The entries of the word index have been arranged exactly in the order of a Pashto dictionary.

III. CONTENTS OF THE 25 UNITS

Each unit comprises the Pashto text, the Roman transcription, the glossary, the notes, the translation; units 1-10 have also exercises.

(a) Each unit contains one or several (e.g., 10a, 10b; 14a, 14b, 14c; 15a, 15b, 15c; 22a, 22b) PASHTO TEXTS in typewritten form. They are graded as to complexity of contents and style, and have been selected to provide samples of many kinds of written Pashto. We find simple stories and anecdotes (1 2, 6, 7); simple expository and descriptive prose (3, 4, 5, 8); literary prose (11, 12, 13); advertisements and announcements (14); simple newspaper stories (10, 15); more complex expository prose (9, 16, 17); newspaper reports and editorials (18, 19); historical prose (20); folk poetry (21); classical poetry (22); poetry in archaic style (23); excerpts from prose fiction (24, 25). Some of the authors of the texts are anonymous, some belong to the best-known writers of Afghanistan and Peshawar: e.g., Gul Pacha Olfat (12, 13), Abdul Rauf Benawa (20), Sadiqullah Rishteen (8), Qalandar Momand (24), Rashid Ali Dehqan (25). Four texts were written especially for the Reader: 4, 5 by A. Ahad Yari; 16, 17 by Noor Ahmad Shaker.

Three main dialectal types of Pashto are presented in the texts: the Eastern dialects; the Kandahar dialect (1, 16, 17, 20); the Peshawar dialects (24, 25).

(b) Each text is followed by a ROMAN TRANSCRIPTION which indicates the pronunciation of the author or of speakers from the same region as the author. Thus the "Eastern" (East.) texts show essentially the pronunciation of Abdul Ghafoor (Kohdaman); the Kandahar (Kand.) texts that of Noor Ahmad Shaker (Kandahar); the Peshawar (Pesh.) texts that of Khayal Bokhari and Jehanzeb Niaz (Peshawar district).

(c) The GLOSSARY lists the new words in Roman transliteration only in the order of their occurrence in the numbered sentences of the transcribed text. In units 1-10 the occurring forms, if not identical with the usual citation forms, are identified, and up to unit 13 also the direct plural of nouns, the direct sing.fem. form of adjectives, the past stems of verbs are given. In units 11-25 mostly just classification labels are provided for nouns, adjectives, verbs. The Pashto Word-index serves as the index to the unit glossaries. The Pashto script was not included for production reasons.

(d) The NOTES call attention to the discrepancies between orthography and pronunciation and, where necessary, to the differences between Kandahar or Peshawar features and the Eastern type of Pashto. They often offer factual comments, and regularly grammatical explanations and references to A GRAMMAR OF PASHTO (GP). References to the sentences of each unit are made by numbers in parentheses.

(e) The ENGLISH TRANSLATION is neither intended to be literal nor too free. Its main purpose is to aid the reader in understanding the Pashto constructions perfectly. It has no merit by itself.

(f) EXERCISES of various type are provided for units 1 to 10. They are intended to encourage the acquisition of an active command of the Pashto writing system and orthography. They are also designed to lead to a use of the texts as samples of Pashto structure which should be constantly and intensely studied and drilled on. For this reason one grammatical feature was taken up in each of the first ten units: nouns (unit 1); adjectives (2); pronouns (3); forms of verb (4); use of cases (5); sentence structure (6); use of tenses (7); use of imperfective present (8); passive phrase (9); optative (10).

THE WRITING OF PASHTO

I. THE TRANSLITERATION OF PASHTO

The users of the Reader will have to learn how to recognize and, it is hoped, also how to write the letters of the Arabic-Persian alphabet and the special Pashto letters. For each letter of the Pashto alphabet a Roman letter is used in the glossaries; only hamza and final h are not transliterated. We can list the following equivalents in the order of the Pashto alphabet (which is also the order of the entries in the Pashto Word-index). Read down the right column and then the left column:

	s	س	ā	آ	u̲, i̲, ə, a	ا
	š	ش			b	ب
	ṣ	ښ			p	پ
	s̤	ص			t	ت
	z̤	ض			ṭ	ټ
	t̲	ط			s̲	ث
	z̄	ظ			j	ج
	ʿ	ع			č	چ
	ǥ	غ			h̲	ح
	f	ف			ts	څ
	q	ق			dz	ځ
	k	ك			x	خ
or ګ	g	گ			d	د
	l	ل			ḍ	ډ
	m	م			z̲	ذ
	n	ن			r	ر
	ṇ	ڼ			ṛ	ړ
u, o,	w	و			z	ز
	h	ه			ž	ژ
	y	ى			ẓ	ږ
əy ـى	e ې	i ي				

In this list the following symbols are Pashto innovations:

ټ ṭ a loop below added to ت

څ ts three dots above added to ح

ځ	dẓ	a hamza above added to ح
ډ	ḍ	a loop at the right added to د
ړ	ṛ	a loop at the right added to ر
ږ	ẓ	one dot below, one dot above added to ر
ښ	ṣ	one dot below, one dot above added to س
ڼ	ṇ	a loop below added to ن
ې	e	two dots, one above the other, added to ى
ۍ	ey	a small extension added at the left to ى

The new Pashto symbols modify their shapes and connect (or do not connect) like the basic symbols ت ح د ر ن ى. ۍ occurs only finally and is not used in Peshawar.

The following symbols occur only in Arabic (or Persian) loan words in Pashto:

ث	s̲	ط	t̲
ح	h̲	ظ	z̄
ذ	z̲	ع	ʿ
ص	s̤	ف	f
ض	z̤	ق	q

The transliteration used in the Reader differs from the one used in A GRAMMAR OF PASHTO (GP) in some respects (cf. § 2, Introd. § 4). Instead of geminate and cluster writing, diacritics have been freely used in the Reader. The only digraphs, which also suggest the pronunciation, are ts for څ and dz for ځ .

II. THE TRANSCRIPTION OF PASHTO

(a) TRANSCRIPTION AND TRANSLITERATION. The transcription part of each unit renders the phonemes of the respective dialects. The transcription symbols used are, on the whole, identical with the transliteration symbols except that in the transcription always

s replaces s̤ s̲

z replaces z̤ z̲ z̄

t replaces t̲

< s̤ s̲ z̤ z̲ z̄ t̲ > are merely transliteration symbols for the Arabic letter without any phonemic significance in Pashto; e.g., násər for نثر nas̲ər 'prose'; wazifá for وظیفه waz̄ifa 'duty'; lutf for لطف lut̲f 'kindness'.

Usually the aspirate /h/ will replace h̲ of the orthography: hāl for حال h̲āl 'state'. Sometimes /h/ itself is lost after a vowel: e.g., merabāní for مهرباني mi̲hrbāni 'kindness'; pālawāní for پهلواني pahlawāni 'wrestli̲ng'.

Among educated speakers only in very informal speech will the bilabial stop /p/ replace the labiodental spirant /f/: pékər for فكر fí̲kər 'thought'. The glottalized, pharyngealized or uvular stop /q/ is more commonly replaced by the velar stop /k/: kalám for قلم qalam 'pen'. /ʕ/ is rarely pronounced as a pharyngeal fricative or glottal stop but e.g., faā́l for فعال faʕāl 'active', mālúm for معلوم maʕlum 'known', etəbā́r for اعتبار i̲ʕti̲bār 'esteem, value' (Cf. GP §§ 37-40)

(b) TRANSCRIPTION AND PHONEMES. The symbols used in the transcription refer to the following vowel, diphthong, and consonant phonemes:

Vowels:

	front	central	back (rounded)
high	i (ī Kand.)		u (ū Kand.)
lower high	i̲		u̲
mid (long)	e		o
lower mid	e̲ (Pesh.)	ə	
low		a ā	

Diphthongs:

ay aw əy ai (Pesh.), etc.

Consonants:

	labial	dental	alveolar	pre-palatal	velar	glottal
semivowels	w			y		
liquids			l r	ṛ		
nasals	m	n		ṇ		
stops	p b	t d		ṭ ḍ	k g	q
spirants	f		s z		x ǥ	
			š ž	ṣ ẓ (Kand.)		
affricates		ts dz	č j			

ṛ is a retroflexed lateral flap, ṇ its nasalized counterpart (GP §§ 15, 19). ṭ and d are voiceless and voiced retroflexed fortis prepalatal stops (GP § 24f.) x and ǥ are voiceless and voiced velar spirants, respectively. ts dz č (=tš) j (=dž) are phonetically, and probably phonemically as well, clusters of dental stops and sibilants (GP §§ 22.2a, 23.2a)

ṣ and ẓ are the symbols that seem to indicate the transliteration of some kind of sibilant. Actually only in Kandahar are they voiceless and voiced fortis retroflexed prepalatal spirants (GP § 34f.).

ṣ in most Eastern dialects represents a voiceless mediopalatal fricative, and in Peshawar it has merged with the velar spirant /x/.

ẓ has merged with /g/ in most Eastern dialects and in Peshawar.

The consonant symbols < w y l r m n p b t d k g f s z h j > even < ts dz > are used in this Reader with the sound-values of English conventional orthography. If we use the other transcription symbols for vowels and consonants of English, we could write them with approximately the same sound-values as follows:

i (Kand. ī) for the vowel(s) of English m<u>ea</u>t (really iy)

u (Kand. ū) p<u>oo</u>l (really uw)

i	it
u	pull
e	gate (really ey!)
o	coat (really ow!)
e (Pesh.)	dare
a	carnation
ā	father
ə	sofa
ay	pie
aw	cow
š	for the consonant of English fish
ž	measure
č	cheer

(c) PHONEMES AND ORTHOGRAPHY. The short vowel phonemes /a ə i u/ are usually not indicated by the Pashto orthography; final /a/ or /ə/ is written ه < h >.

The phonemes /u o w/ are all written و . The distinction between i ي and the Pashto e ې is not as yet systematically carried through in all Pashto publications: medially يـ is still often written for /e/ instead of the correct ېـ and finally ی stands for /ay e i /. If /əy/ is not a feminine ending, ئ is generally used instead of the Pashto symbol ۍ : e.g., kawə́y کوئ 'you (pl.) do'.

The dialectal mergers of /ts/ and /s/, /dz/ and /z/, /ẓ/ and /g/, /ṣ/ and /x/ or /š/ are not indicated by the orthography. Local variants with /s/ instead of /š/ are occasionally written: سته sta instead of شته šta 'there is'.

The position of the loud, medium, and weak stresses within words and phrases is not marked by the orthography. Our transcription differentiates between them; e.g., wàrṣkārá (medium-weak-loud) ورښکاره 'appearing to them'. The glossaries show the stress of words as pronounced in isolation; this may differ slightly from the stress as shown in the transcription of the text where the forms may have relatively less or more stress in context.

Pashto publications show increasingly western punctuation symbols (، • ؟ ! ؛ ") with the same syntactic and intonational significance.

Word division is not always clearly marked in Pashto publications, as any glance in a Pashto newspaper will show.

GRAMMATICAL SUMMARY

A complete study of the structure of the Pashto language as revealed by the 31 texts necessitates the grammatical identification and analysis of morphemes, words, phrases, sentences. The glossaries identify the occurring word forms as to part of speech and morphological and grammatical subclasses. For syntactical patterns and questions of word formation frequent references to A GRAMMAR OF PASHTO (GP) are provided in the Notes.

I. WORD CLASSES.

Pashto has the following main classes of words (parts of speech): nouns (substantives), adjectives, pronouns, particles, verbs. Nouns, adjectives, pronouns are the nominal word classes.

(a) Substantives (nouns) have inflectional endings indicating case (direct, oblique, oblique II, vocative), number (singular, plural), gender (masculine, feminine). They appear in particle phrases and as centers of nominal phrases: kitā́b in də dé kitā́b 'of this book', dā́ ṣè kitā́b 'this fine book'; and as subject, object, actor (agent) in sentences.

Also adjectives indicate case, number, gender. They appear in nominal phrases but not as their center. They do not function by themselves as subject, object, actor.

Pronouns, a closed word class of restricted membership, indicate case, number, gender, but not as consistently as most substantives or even adjectives. They appear in sentences like the nouns as subject, object, actor, but never as center, and only some as parts, of nominal phrases.

(b) Particles have no inflectional endings, but they occupy various syntactic slots. They can accordingly be subdivided into: interjections (ho! 'yes'), prepositions (də 'of'), conjunctions (aw 'and'), modal particles (ba), pronominal particles (ye 'of him, by him'), and adverbs (də́lta 'here).

(c) Verbs and verbal phrases in Pashto indicate person (1st, 2d, 3d), number (singular, plural), tense (present, past; perfect, past perfect phrases), mood (indicative, imperative, optative), aspect (imperfective, perfective), voice (active; passive phrase). Some forms indicate gender (masculine, feminine).

Verbal phrases consist of the auxiliary (yəm, past wəm) and the perfect participle: e.g., rāǵə́lay yə̀m '(I) have come' (perfect I phrase); the auxiliary kéẓəm 'to become' and the passive participles: e.g., lidə̄l kéẓi '(he) is being seen' (present I passive phrase); the auxiliary šəm 'to be able to' and the optative: lidə́lāy (or lidə́lay) šəm '(I) can see' (potential phrase). The verbs kéẓəm and kawə́m combine also with noun and adjective forms to other verbal phrases: e.g., faysalá kawə́m '(I) decide'; wàrskāra kéẓi '(he) appears'. Vërbs or verbal phrases constitute the predicates in all complete sentences.

II. NOUN SUBCLASSES

Nouns (substantives) can be subdivided according to their plural formation which is determined by gender and singular ending. The glossary entries show the labels m 1 ("masculine first class") m 2 m 3 m 4 m 5, f 1 ("feminine first class") f 2 f 3 f 4 f 5 f 6. Aside from irregular formations (m 5, f 6) the following morphemes are involved:

		direct singular		direct plural
m 1		----		--úna
m 2		----		--ā́n
m 3		--áy		--í
	(Pesh.)	--é̲ (-é)		
m 4		´--ay		´--i
	(Kand.)	´--əy		
	(Pesh.)	´--e̲ (-e)		
f 1		´--a		´--e
	(Kand.)	´--ə	(Kand.)	´--i (obl.. ´--u)
f 2		--á		--é

f 3	--ấ; --ó	--ấwe; --ówe
		(Kand.) --ấwi; --ówi
f 4	--í; --ə́y (Pesh.) --ái (--é̱)	--ə́y (Pesh.) --ái (--é̱)
f 5	--ấ, etc.	--āgấne (Kand.) --āgấni

The following table shows examples and the various case forms:

	dir. sing.		obl.sing.	obl. II, voc.	dir.pl.	obl.pl.
m 1	kor	'house'	kor	kóra	korúna	korúno, koró
m 2	dost	'friend'	dost	dósta	dostấn	dostấno
m 3	saṛáy	'man'	saṛí	saṛə́ya	saṛí	saṛó, saṛə́yo
m 4	kə́lay	'village'	kə́li	kə́lya!	kə́li	kə́lo (kə́lyo)
f 1	ṣə́dza	'woman'	ṣə́dze		ṣə́dze	ṣə́dzo
f 2	špá	'night'	špé		špé	špó
f 3	ǵwā	'cow'	ǵwấ		ǵwấwe	ǵwấwo
f 4	badí	'feud'	badə́y		badə́y	badə́yo
f 5	ǵwā		ǵwā		ǵwāgấne	ǵwāgấno

III. ADJECTIVE SUBCLASSES

Adjectives can be subdivided according to their formation of the feminine. The glossary entries show the labels adj. I, adj. II, adj. III, adj. IV, adj. V. The following morphemes are involved:

	masculine	feminine
adj. I	----	´--a (Kand.) ´--ə
adj. II	----	--á
adj. III	--áy (Pesh.) --é	--ə́y (Pesh.) --ái (--é̱)
adj. IV	´--ay (Kand.) ´--əy (Pesh.) ´--e	´--e
adj. V	masc. = fem.	

The following table shows examples and the various case forms:

				obl.sing.	dir.pl.	obl.pl.
		dir.sing.				
adj.I	m	spin	'white'	spin	spin	spíno
	f	spína		spíne	spíne	"
adj.II	m	uẓd	'big'	uẓdé	uẓdé	uẓdó
	f	uẓdá		uẓdé	uẓdé	"
adj.III	m	kučnáy	'little'	kuční	kuční	kučnéyo(kučnó)
	f	kučnéy		kučnéy	kučnéy	"
adj.IV	m	stéṛay	'tired'	stéṛi	stéṛi	stéro
	f	stéṛe		stéṛe	stéṛe	"
adj.V	m,f	ʿi̲lmí	'scientific'	ʿi̲lmí	ʿi̲lmí	ʿi̲lmí

IV. PRONOUNS

Pronouns have usually not been included into the glossaries. We can differentiate between personal pronouns, demonstrative pronouns, and indefinite-interrogative pronouns, and list the following forms:

(a) PERSONAL PRONOUNS

direct		oblique	possessive
zə	'I'	mā́	zmā (dial.zəmā́,də mā́, etc.)
tə	'you'	tā	stā (dial. də tā, etc.)
mu(n)ẓ	'we'	mu(n)ẓ	zmu(n)ẓ
tā́se, tā́so	'you' (pl.)	tā́se, tā́so	stā́se, stā́so

(b) DEMONSTRATIVE PRONOUNS.

	dir.sing	obl.sing.	dir. pl.	obl.pl.
only in substantive function:	day (m) (Pesh.de̱)	dә́ (m) 'he'	duy (m,f)	duy (m,f) 'they'
			daǵuy	daǵuy (m,f)
			haǵuy	haǵuy (m,f)
	dā	de	dā	de 'this'
	daǵa	daǵa, deǵe	daǵa	daǵo, 'this' deǵo
		daǵe (f)		
	haǵa	haǵa heǵe	haǵa	haǵo, 'that' heǵo
		haǵe (f)		

(c) INDEFINITE-INTERROGATIVE PRONOUNS.

	dir.	obl.	
sing., pl.	tsok	čā	'someone; who?' (substantival only)
	tse	tse	'some; what? which?'
pl.	tso	tso	'some; how many?'

Other forms: dzíne, obl. dzíno 'some, several'; tsóna, tsómra 'how much'; nor, fem. nóre 'other(s)'.

V. VERBAL SUBCLASSES

(a) All Pashto verbs can be syntactically subdivided into intransitive and transitive verbs. A few verbs are transitive-impersonal; i.e., their 3rd plural masculine past forms can appear without subject: e.g., saṛí wә́wayel,'The man said' (GP § 83.3a). Transitive verb forms in past and perfect tenses agree with the subject (here the goal of action!) in person, number, gender, and the agent (actor) has to be expressed by a nominal form in the oblique case or by a pronominal particle (me, (Kand. mi); de (Kand. di); mo (Kand. mu); ye): e.g., wéna ye karéla, 'He was planting a tree', constructed like a passive sentence 'A tree (wéna, sing. fem.) by him (ye) was being planted (karéla past I, sing.fem.)'.

(b) Verbs can be subdivided according to their stem formation in their present and past tenses. The following forms are formed from the present stem: present I (imperfective present), present II (perfective present), imperative I (imperfective imperative), imperative II (perfective imperative). These forms are formed from the past stem: past I (imperfective past), past II (perfective past), a perfect participle ending in -ay (Kand. -əy, Pesh. -e), fem.-e (like adj. IV); the passive participles (like adj. I); the optative, ending in -éla̅y (a̅y); the verbal noun, ending in -él (masc.pl.); the verbal adjective in -úṅkay, fem. -úṅke (adj. IV).

The glossary entries show these class labels: verb I, verb II, verb III, verb IV, verb IV-A. In the first verbal class present and past stems are alike; in the second class the past stem can be considered a modification of the present stem; in the third class the two stems are completely different; in the fourth class we have four stems: the present I, present II, past I, past II stems; class IV-A contains the numerous compounds of the class IV verbs kawə́m and kéẓəm which become verbal phrases in the perfective forms (present II and past II). Examples of the five verb classes are as follows:

	present I	present II	past I	past II	
verb I	taṛə́m		taṛ-		'to tie'
verb II	raséẓəm		rased-		'to reach, arrive'
verb III	górəm		kat-		'to look at'
verb IV	kawə́m	k(ṛ)-	kaw-	kṛ-	'to do'
	kéẓəm	š-	ked-	šw-	'to become'
	dzəm	(w)láṛ š-	tl-	(w)láṛ-	'to go'
	ra̅dzə́m	rá̅š-	ra̅tl-	rá̅ǵl-	'to come'
	(i̲)ẓdə́m	k(ṣ)éẓd-	i̲ṣow- i̲ṣod-	k(ṣ)éṣow- k(ṣ)éṣod-	'to put'
	wṛəm	yós-	wṛ-	yówṛ-	'to carry off'

verb IV-A	joṛawə́m	jóṛ k(ṛ)-	joṛaw-	jóṛ kṛ-	'to build, cure' (trans.)
	joṛə́ẓəm	jóṛ š-	joṛed-	jóṛ šw-	'to become built' (intrans.)

(c) The auxiliary has the following forms:

				Kand.	Pesh.	optative
present	sing.	1st	yəm '(I) am'			
		2d	ye			
		3d	day, fem. da	dəy, fem. də	de, fem. da	
	pl.	1st	yu			
		2d	yəy	yast	yai (ye̱)	
		3d	di			
present II sing. pl.		3d	wi (yi)	wi	wi	
past	sing.	1st	wəm '(I) was'		om	
		2d	we			
		3d	we, fem. wa	wu, fem. wə	o(wo), fem. wa	way (Kand. wāy, Pesh. we)
	pl.	1st	wu		(w)u	
		2d	wəy	wāst	wai (we̱)	
		3d	we, fem. we		(w)u, fem. we	

(d) Below we list all the forms and phrases of a transitive verb:

		present I	present II	imperative I	imperative II
sing.	1st	taṛə́m '(I) tie'	wə́taṛəm	taṛá!	wə́taṛa!
	2d	-ẹ́	-ẹ		
	3d	-í	etc.	'keep on tying!'	'tie!'
pl.	1st	-ú			
	2d	-ə́y			
	3d	-í			

		past I		past II		verbal noun
sing.	1st	taṛéləm	'(I)was	wə́taṛələm	'(I)	taṛel (m.pl)
	2d	-éle	being	-ele	was	'the tying'
	3d	tāṛə́	tied by...'		tied	
	f.	taṛéla	(Kand.taṛéy;	etc.	by...'	
			Pesh. taṛélo)			verbal adj.
pl.	1st	taṛélu				taṛúnkay,f.-únke
	2d	-éləy	(Kand.-élāst)			'tying'
	3d	-él, fem.-éle				

optative:
taṛ(él)ay (taṛ(él)ay)

		perfect I phrase		past perfect phrase	perfect participle
sing.	1st	taṛélay yə̀m	'(I) have	taṛélay wə̀m	taṛélay,fem.
	2d	" yè	been	" we	taṛéle
			tied		
		etc.	by...'	etc.	

		perfect II phrase	perfect optative
sing.	3d	taṛélay wì	taṛélay wày (taṛélay wày)

PASSIVE PHRASES

		present I	present II	passive participles
sing.	1st	taṛél kéẓəm	wə́taṛəl šəm	taṛél, fem. taṛéla
		f.taṛéla "	wə́taṛəla "	wə́taṛəl, fem.
		'(I) am being tied'	'(that I) be tied'	wə́taṛəla 'tied'

		past I	past II	optative
sing.	1st	taṛél ked(él)əm	wə́taṛəl šwəm	taṛél ked(él)āy
	2d	" ked(él)e	" šwe	
		etc.	etc.	
		'(I) was being tied,' etc.	'(I) was tied,' etc.	

		perfect I	past perfect	perfect optative
sing.	1st	taṛə̀l šéway yəm	taṛə̀l šéway wəm	taṛə̀l šéway wāy
		etc.	etc.	(way)

	perfect II
3d	taṛə̀l šéway wi (yi)

POTENTIAL PHRASES

present	taṛélāy (taṛélay) šem	'(I) can tie'
past	taṛélāy (taṛélay) šwem	'(I) could be tied by...'
passive present	taṛĕl ked(él)āy šem	'(I) can be tied'
passive past	taṛĕl ked(él)āy šwem	'(I) could be tied'

UNIT 1

ټوکه

د یوه مدیر ټیلفون خراب شوی و ، په دې حال کښې یو سړی ورته راغی مگر مدیر نه پېژاندی —

نو مدیر د دې د پاره چه و دې سړي ته ځان فعال ښکاره کي د مخه تر پوښتني یې ټیلفون پورته کی ، بږغ یې کړه : — کېبل — مرکز ۰۰۰ !

د مطبوعاتو ریاست راکه : — (وروسته تر پنځو ثانیو)
رئیس صاحب یې ؟ — سلام علیکم ! ۰ جوړ یې په خیر یې ؟
زه یم ۰۰۰ ما تاسی ته پنځه مقالې تقدیم کړی وې ،
دوې مقالې می نوری و انیس او اصلاح ته لیکلی دي ،
ماپښین به یې ستاسی حضور ته وړاندی کم — یو بل
کتاب می له انگلیسي ژبې په پاړسي ترجمه کړی ۰ دی ۰
بلي — مهرباني ده ، تشکر — ستاسی لطف دی ۰

بیرته ټیلفون ایږدي د دې سړي څخه پوښتنه کوي :
ستاسی څه کار و — ؟

سړی : — زه ټیلفوني یم — د دې د پاره راغلی
یم چه ستاسی ټیلفون جوړ کم — !!!

TRANSCRIPTION

ṭóke

(1) de yewè mudír ṭilifún xarā̀b šéwey wu, (2) pe dé hā́l kṣi yaw saṛáy werte ráǵey mágar mudír né pežāndéy-

(3) nò mudír de dé de pā́re či we dé seṛí te dzā́n faā́l ṣkārá ki de máxa ter puṣténi ye ṭilifún pórte key, (4) ẓáǵ ye kṛè;-

kebél - markā́z . . . !

de matboā́tu riyāsā́t rā́ke: - (5) (wrúste ter pindzó sāniyó)

reís sāìb yé-? salā́m alā́ykum! jóṛ ye, pe xáyr ye?

zé yem . . . (6) mā tā́si te pindzé maqālé·taqdìm kéṛi wè,

(7) dwé maqālé mi múri we Anī́s aw Islā́ te likéli di,

(8) māpṣín be ye stā́si huzúr te wṛā́ndi kem- (9) yaw bél kitā́b mi le inglisí tsexe pe paṛsí tarjumà kéṛey dey.

(10) bále- merabānī́ de, tašakúr- stā̀si lútf dey. . ."

(11) bírte ṭilifún iẓdí, (12) de dé seṛí tsexe puṣténe kewì:

(13) stā́si tsé kā́r wu-?

(14) saṛáy: - zé ṭilifuní yem- (15) de dé de pā́re raǵéley yèm či stā́si ṭilifún jóṛ kem - - - !!!

GLOSSARY

ṭóke, pl. ṭóki f 1 'joke, funny story'

(1) de prep. 'of'

yewé obl.masc.sing. of yaw, fem. yawá adj.II 'one'

mudír obl.sing. of mudír, pl. mudirā̌n m 2 'director'

ṭilifún, pl. ṭilifumíne, ṭilifunā́n m 1, m 2 'telephone'

xarā̀b šéwey wu 3d sing.masc.past perf. of xarābéẓem, pres. II xarā́b š-. past I xarābed-́, past II xarā́b šw- verb IV-A (intrans.) 'to get bad, spoiled, out of order' (xarā́b, fem. xarā́be adj.I)

(2) pe . . . . kṣi prep. 'in, on'

de obl. of dā dem. pron. 'this'

ẖāl, pl. ẖālúne, ẖālā́t m 1 'condition, state'

saṛáy, pl. saṛí m 3 'man'

wérte pron.prefix 3d pers. wer- and part. te 'to him'

rā́ǵey 3d sing.masc.past II of rādzém, pres. II rā́š-, past I rātl-́, past II rā́ǵl-, verb IV (intrans.) 'to come'

mágar conj. 'but'

ne neg. 'not'

pežāndéy 3d sing.masc.past I of péženem, past pežānd- verb II (trans.) 'to know, be acquainted with'

(3) no adv. 'then, so, thus'

de . . . de pā̌re prep. - adv. phrase 'for the sake of, for' či conj. 'that'

seṛí obl.sing. of saṛáy (2 above)

we . . . te prep. 'to'

dzān, pl. dzānúne m 1 'oneself'

faˁā́l, fem. faˁā́le adj. I 'active'

ṣkārá adj. V 'clear, evident'

ki 3d sing.pres.II of kawə́m, pres.II kṛ- (k-), past I
kawə́l-, past II, kṛ́- verb IV (trans.) 'to make, do'

ṣkārà kawə́m 'to make clear, reveal'

de máxa ter prep. phrase 'before'

puṣténi obl.sing. of puṣténe, pl. puṣténi f 1 'question'

ye pron.part. 3d pers. 'by him'

pórte adv., adj.V 'upward'

key 3d masc.sing. past II of kawə́m verb IV (as above)

pórte kawə́m 'to lift, raise'

(4) ẓaǵ, pl. ẓaǵúne m 1 'sound'

kṛe like key (3 above)

ẓáǵ kawə́m verb IV 'to shout, call, speak (to)'

kebə́l, pl. kebelúne m 1 '(telephone) exchange: cable'

maṯboˁā́t Arab. pl. 'publications'

riyāsát, pl. riyāsatúne m 1 'department, division'

rā́ke imp.II of rākawə́m, pres. II rā́k-, past I rākawə́l-,
past II rā́kṛ- verb IV (trans.) 'to give to me'
(prefix ra-)

(5) wrústə adv. 'afterwards'

tər prep. 'over, to'

wrústə tər prep. phrase 'after'

pindzó obl. of pindzə́ '5'

s̲āniyó obl.pl. of s̲āniyá, pl. s̲āniyé f 2 'second'

rəís, pl. rəisā́n m 2 'president'

s̤āh̲íb, pl. s̤āh̲ibā́n m 2 'master; Mr.'

yé 2d sing. of yəm aux. 'I am'

salā́m ʕaláykum (Arabic greeting common among muslims)

joṛ, fem. jóṛə adj. I 'well, healthy'

pə prep. 'in, on'

xayr m 1 'state of grace, virtue'

zə pers.pron. 'I'

(6) mā obl. of zə 'I'

tā́si obl. 'you' (pl.)

tə part. 'to' (wə́rtə 2 above, wə . . . tə 3 above)

pindzə́ num. (5 above)

maqālé pl. of maqālá, pl. maqālé f 2 'article'

taqdìm kéṛi wè 3d pl.fem.past perf. of taqdimawə́m, pres. II taqdím kṛ-, past I taqdimawə́l-. past II taqdím kṛ- verb IV-A (trans.) 'to submit'

(7) dwe fem. of dwa num. 'two'

nū́ri dir.fem. of nor 'others'

mi pron.part. 1st pers. 'by me'

aw conj. 'and'

likə́li di 3d pl.fem.perf. of likə́m verb I (trans.)'to write'

(8) māpṣín, pl. māpṣinúnə m 1 'afternoon'

bə modal part.

ye pron.part. 'them' (3, 4 above)

stā́si poss. of tā́si 'you'

h̲uẓúr m 'presence'

wṛā́ndi adv. 'ahead, in front'

wṛā́ndi kəm 1st sing.pres. II of wṛā́ndi kawə́m verb IV 'to submit'

(9) bəl, fem. bə́la adj. I 'other'

kitā́b, pl. kitābúnə m 1 'book'

lə . . . tsə́xə prep. 'from'

inglisí f 'English'

pāṛsí f 'Persian'

tarjumá, pl. tarjumé f 2 'translation'

kə́ṛəy dəy 3d masc.sing.perf. of kawə́m verb IV 'to do, make'

tarjumá kawə́m verb IV 'to translate'

(10) bále adv. 'yes'

mihrabāní, pl. mihrabānə́y f 4 'kindness'

də (da) 3d sing.fem.aux. 'is'

tašakúr m 'thanks'

lut̲f m 'kindness'

(11) bírtə adv. 'back'

iẓdí 3d sing.pres. I of iẓdə́m, pres.II kṣéẓd-, past I iṣowə́l-, past II kṣ̈éṣowəl- verb IV (trans.) 'to place, put'

(12) də . . . tsə́xə prep. 'from'

kawí 3d sing.pres. I of kawə́m verb IV

pușténə kawə́m verb IV 'to ask, question'

(13) tsə pron. 'what; some'

kār, pl. kārúnə m 1 'work, business'

(14) ṭilifuní, pl. ṭilifunyā́n m 2 'lineman'

(15) rā́gə́ləy yəm 1st sing.masc.perf. of rādzə́m 'to come' (2 above)

jóṛ kəm 1st sing. pres. II of joṛawə́m, pres. II jóṛ kṛ- (k-), past I joṛawə́l-, past II jóṛ kṛ- verb IV-A 'to repair, fix, heal'

NOTES

This story was taken from <u>də paștó kelí</u>, vol. IV, p 74f., by Abdul Rauf Benawā (Kabul: paștó ṭoléna, 1941); these volumes were largely used in Pashto classes for Persian-speaking officials. The transcription indicates a Kandahar pronunciation (Mr. Noor Ahmad Shaker's).

In the Grammatical Summary some forms show the differences between the Kandahar dialect and the Eastern (or Northern) dialects. [1] Observe in this text the variation between loud-stressed á áy and weak-stressed ə əy : ṭókə but tarjumá, maqālá; šə́wəy (1)*, rā́gəy (2) but saṛáy (2); yaw but yəwə́ (1). With some speakers of the Kandahar dialect, /a/ tends to be preserved even in weak-stressed position, if the loud-stressed

*Numbers in parentheses refer to sentence numbers in the text.

stem syllable has a or ā: saṛáy, but obl. seṛí, máxa (3), xaráb (1). Kandahar e (ey) thus often corresponds to Eastern a (ay): ṭóka, wérta (2), pórta (3), raís (5), ráka (4) wrústa (5), ḫälúna (2), da (10).

[2] Notice the variation between loud-stressed é and ó and weak-stressed i u, respectively: maqālé (6,7) but puṣténi (3); ṣāniyó (5) but maṯboˁátu (4). Often Kandahar i and u correspond thus to Eastern e and o: tási (East. táse) (6), wṛándi (East. wṛánde) (8), bírte (East. bérta) (11), stási (East. stáse) (8), ṭilifún (East. ṭelefún) (3), táqdīm kéṛi (East. kéṛe) (6), likéli (East. likéle) (7), matboátu (East. matboáto) (4); múri (East. nóre) (7) (GP § 9.2).

(2) -ey in pežāndéy and in key (3) is a typical Kandahar ending; elsewhere -e, -, -o (Peshawar) is found: pežāndé and keṛ or kṛe (in 4).

hāl for ḫāl (GP § 37.2). rágey is a past II form of an intransitive, pežāndéy a past I form of a transitive verb; saṛáy (dir.sing.) is the subject, mudír (obl.sing.) the actor. To imitate the agreement of verb-subject with past tenses of transitive verbs, the translation would have to be: "The man was not known by the mudir." (See also 3, 4, 6, 7, 9 below.)

(3) faál for faˁāl (GP § 40)

ye refers back to mudír (obl.) and indicates the actor: "By him the telephone was lifted."

(4) matboā́tu for maṯboᶜātu (GP § 22.3: ṯ; see faā́l above)

The Department of Press has the rank of a ministry.

"Sound by him (ye) was made."

(5) sāniyó for s̱āniyo, saī́b for ṣāhib (GP §§ 30.3, 36.1)

aláykum for ᶜalaykum (see faā́l above)

(6) "By me (mā) . . . five articles have been submitted."

(7) "Two articles . . have been written by me (mi)."

Anís and Islāẖ are two Kabul dailies.

Islā for Iṣlāẖ (GP § 37.2)

(8) huzúr for ẖuẕur (GP §§ 31.2, 37.2)

(9) "Another book . . . has been translated by me (mi)."

pāṛsí, usually fārsí

(10) merabāní for mihrbāni (GP § 8.3), lutf for luṯf (§ 22.3)

TRANSLATION

A Joke

(1) The telephone of a director had gotten out of order.

(2) At this time a man came to him, but the director did not know him.

(3) Then the director, in order to reveal himself to this man as active, before (any) question lifted the telephone (receiver):

(4) He shouted: " Operator, operator! Give me the Press Department!"

(5) After five seconds: "Mr. President, is it you? Good morning! Are you well, are you in good shape? It's me.

(6) I submitted to you five articles.

(7) Two articles more I have written for 'Anis' and 'Islah'.

(8) I will submit them to you ("to your presence") in the afternoon.

(9) I have translated another book from English into Persian.

(10) Yes, this is a kindness, thanks, very kind of you."

(11) He puts the telephone back.

(12) He asks that man a question:

(13) "What was your business?"

(14) Man: "I am a telephone repairman.

(15) I have come (in order) to fix your telephone."

EXERCISES

I. WRITING:

A. Copy the Pashto text.

B. Write the Pashto text from the Roman transcription. Check for correctness afterwards and note the words where transcription and Pashto orthography disagree. The Glossary offers the exact transliteration.

II. QUESTIONS ON THE TEXT:

Write suitable answers to the following ten questions:

A. In the Roman alphabet.

B. In the Pashto alphabet.

1. də čā ṭilifun xarāb šəwəy wu? ۱. د چا ټیلفون خراب شوی و؟

2. mudir saṛay pežāndə kə* nə? ۲. مدیر سړی پېژانده که نه؟

---

* kə (East. ka) conj. 'or, if'.

3. mudir də seṛi tsəxə puṣtənə wəkṛə?	۰۳ مدير د سړي څخه پوښتنه وکړه ؟
4. čā ṭilifun portə kəy, mudir kə* səṛi?	۰٤ چا ټيلفون پورته کی مدير که سړي ؟
5. wrustə tər tsonə waxt** ye salām ʿalaykum wəwāyə**?	۰٥ وروسته تر څونه وخت يې سلام عليکم ووايه ؟
6. tsumrə maqāle ye taqdim kəṛi we?	۰٦ څومره مقالې يې تقديم کړی وې ؟
7. Anis pə pāṛsi dəy kə pə inglisi?	۰۷ انيس په پارسی دی که په انگليسي؟
8. mudir tərǰuma lə kumi*** žəbi tsəxə kəwi?	۰۸ مدير ترجمه له کومې ژبې څخه کوي؟
9. saṛay tsok wu?	۰۹ سړی څوك و ؟
10. saṛay wali*** rāǵələy wu?	۱۰ سړی ولی راغلی و ؟

tsok, obl. čā; tsóna (tsóne), tsómra (tsúmre) are indefinite-interrogative pronouns (see Grammatical Summary and GP § 79).

---

* kə (East. ka) conj. 'or, if'.

** waxt see 3.4; wə́wāyə see 2.1.

*** kum see 2.4; wáli (East. wále) see 6.4.

III. GRAMMAR:

A. Write the following nouns and their respective plural forms (in the Pashto alphabet):

mudír, markáz, ṭilifún, puṣténe, saṛáy,

reís, riyāsát.

B. Write the oblique singular and oblique plural forms (in the Pashto alphabet) of:

maqālá, ṣāniyá, kitā́b, kār.

C. Why are mudír, ṭilifuní, markáz masculine and

why are mērabāní, pāṛsí, maqālá feminine?
(for gender rules see GP § 50)

D. What does m 1, m 3, f 1, f 2, etc., after substantives (nouns) in the Glossary mean? (Cf. GP §§ 51, 53, 57, 58, also Table III, p. 61)

IV. PRONUNCIATION:

A. Add indications of stress to the Roman transcription of the questions on the text.

B. If your instructor speaks an "Eastern" dialect or you are familiar with an "Eastern" pronunciation, rewrite the transcription of the Pashto text and questions with its Kandahar pronunciation accordingly. Study the comments on the Kandahar pronunciation in the Notes first.

UNIT 2

طالبان او شیخ

وایي د یوه کلي په یو مسجد کښې څو تنه طالبان اوسېدل. طالبان په مسجد کې مسافر نه پرېږدي او بیا په تېره شپخان. یوه شپه جماعت ته ناوخته یو مسافر راغی، دغه مسافر د کوم بزرگ او ماذون شیخ و، اوږدې تسبې یې په لاس کښې وې او سپین څادر یې پر سر و. چه جماعت ته راننووت، طالبانو ترې پوښتنه وکړه چه مېلمه، د کوم ځای یې؟ ده ورته وویل چه د پلاني ځای. طالبانو ورته وویل چه څوک یې؟

نو ده ورته د خپل پیر نوم واخیست چه زه د صاحب مبارک سپی یم. طالبانو ورته وویل چه کورې شه، وزه! دا جماعت دی. مونږ دلته د خدای سپي نه پرېږدو پاتې لا د صاحب مبارک سپی. ټول ورپسې راپورته شول او شیخ په بلا پېښ یې له جماعت نه وویست.

TRANSCRIPTION

tāləbā́n aw šéx

(1) wā̌yi də yawə́ kéli pə yàw masjí̱d ke tsó tàna tāləbā́n osedə́l.

(2) tāləbā́n pə masjí̱d ke mu̱sāfér né predī́ aw byā pə téra šexā́n.

(3) yawà špá jumā́t ta nāwā́xta yaw musāfér rā́gay.

(4) dā́ga musāfér de kùm bezérg aw māzún šéx we.

(5) uzdé tasbé ye pe lā́s ke wĕ aw spín tsādár ye per sár we.

(6) či jumā́t ta rānénawòt tālebā́no trè pusténa wékra či melmá de kúm dzā̀y yè?

(7) dé wèrta wéwayel či de plāní dzā́y.

(8) tālebā́no wèrta byā́ wéwayel či tsók yĕ.

(9) no dé wèrta de xpĕ́l pír múm wā́xist či zé de sāhíb i mubārák spáy yèm.

(10) tālebā́no wèrta wĕ́wayel či kwére ša, wéza! dā́ jumā́t day.

(11) múnz délta de xwdā́y spí né predŭ pā́te lā́ de sāhíb i mubārák spáy.

(12) tól wérpese rāpórta šwél aw šéx pe balā̀ pés ye le jumā́t na wéwest.

GLOSSARY

tālebā́n pl. of tāléb m 2 'student (of theology)'

šex, pl. šexā́n m 2 'pious man, mystic'

(1) wā́yi 3d pl.pres.I of wā́yem verb I 'to say'

yawé obl.masc.sing. of yaw, fem, yawá adj. II 'one'

kéli obl.sing. of kélay m 4 'village'

masjíd obl.sing. of masjíd, pl. masjidúna m 1 'mosque'

tso indef. -interrog.pron. 'some; how many?'

tána dir.pl. of tan m 'person'

osedə́l 3d pl.masc.past I of ósəm (osézəm), past osed- verb II (intrans.) 'to live, reside'

(2) mu̲sāfə́r (mu̲sāfí̲r), pl. mu̲sāfərā́n m 2 'traveller'

prezdí 3d plur.pres.I of prezdə́m, past presod- verb III (trans.) 'to leave, let'

byā (bi̲yā́) adv. 'again'

pə téra adv. 'especially, particularly' (ter adj.I 'past')

šexā́n (see above)

(3) špa, pl. špe f 2 'night'

ju̲māˁát obl.sing. of ju̲māˁát, pl. ju̲māˁatúna m 1 'mosque'

nāwáxta adv. (adj. V) 'late'

rā́ǥay 3d sing.masc.past II of rādzə́m, pres. II rā́š- past I rātl-́, past II rā́ǥl- verb IV (intrans.) 'to come'

(4) dáǥa dir.sing.masc.dem.pron. 'this'

kum, fem. kúma adj. I 'some; which?'

bəzə́rg (bzərg) obl.sing. of bəzə́rg, pl. bəzərgā́n 'holy man, saint' m 2

mā̲zún obl.sing. of mā̲zúń, pl. mā̲zunā́n m 2 'religious leader'

wə 3d sing.masc.past of yəm aux. '(I) am' (unit 1: wu (1.1, 1.13))

(5) uzdé dir.pl.fem. of uzd, fem. uzdá adj. II 'big, long'

tasbé pl. of tasbá, pl. tasbé f 2 'bead'

ye pron.part. 'of him'

lās, pl. lāsúna m 1 'hand'

we 3d pl.fem.past of aux.

spin, fem. spína adj. I 'white'

tsādár, pl. tsādarúna m 1 'sheet, shawl'

per prep. 'on'

sar, pl. sarúna m 1 'head, top'

(6) rānénawot 3d sing.masc.past II of rānenawézem, past rānénawat- verb II (intrans.) 'to enter' (prefix rā-)

tre contracted from prep. ter and pron.part. ye 'from him'

puṣténa, pl. puṣténe f 1 'question' (see 1.12)

wékṛa 3d sing.fem.past II of kawém verb IV 'to do, make'

melmá, pl. melmāné m 5 'guest'

dzāy, pl. dzāyúna m 1 'place'

(7) dé obl.sing.masc. of day dem.pron. 'he, this one'

wérta 'to them' (see 1.2)

wéwayel 3d pl.masc.past II of wáyem verb I (trans.-impers.) (1 above)

plāní obl.sing.masc. of plānáy, fem. plānéy adj. III 'a certain'

(8) tsok indef.-interrog.pron. 'who?; somebody'

(9) dé dem.pron. (7 above)

xpel obl.sing.masc. of xpel, fem. xpéla adj. I 'one's own'

pir obl.sing. of pir, pl. pirán m 2 'saint'

num, pl. numúna m 1 'name'

wáxist 3d sing.masc.past II of ǎxlem, past axist- verb II (trans.) 'to take'

s̤āh̲íb i̲ mu̲bārák "holy master" (Persian phrase) s̤āhíb
m 2, mu̲bārák adj. I

spay, pl. spi m 3 'dog'

(10) kwére interj. (used to chase dogs away)

ša imp. II of kéẓəm verb IV (intrans.) 'to become, get'

wéza imp. I of wézəm, past wat- verb II (intrans.) 'to go out'

day (Kandahar: dəy, see 1.9) 3d sing.masc. 'is'

(11) munẓ pers.pron. 'we'

délta adv. 'here'

xwdāy obl. of xwdāy m 2 'God'

pā́te lā́ adv. 'let alone, especially (not)' (pā́te adj. V 'remaining', lā adv. 'yet, still')

(12) ṭol dir.pl.masc. of ṭol, fem. ṭóla adj. II 'all, whole'

wérpəse adv. "after him" (prefix wər-)

rāpórta adv. 'upward, up' (prefix rā-)

šwəl 3d pl.masc.past II of kéẓəm verb IV 'to become'

balā́, pl. balā́we f 3 'misfortune'

peṣ, fem. péṣą adj. I 'facing, confronted with'

le . . . na prep. 'from'

wéwest 3d sing.masc.past II of bā́səm, (w)est-(ist-) verb III (trans.) 'to take off, take out'

NOTES

This story is taken from <u>də</u> <u>paṣtó</u> <u>qisé</u>, p. 69f., edited by Sadiqulla Riṣtin (Sadiqullah Rishteen) (Kabul, 1952).

tālebā́n for ṯālebān (GP § 22.3)

(1) tána plural form after tso (GP § 63.1a,2)

ke for kṣe (Kandahar: kṣi, see 1.2) (also 2,5)

(2) predí for preẓdí

(3) ju̱mā́t for ju̱māʕat (GP § 40) (also 6, 10, 12)

(4) māzún for māẕun (GP § 31.2)

(5) tasbé, usually pronounced taspé (or tazbé)

(6) "By the students (ṯālebā́no obl.) the question was made."

či̱ also introduces direct speech (in 7, 8, 9, 10 too).

(7) "By him (də́ obl.) to them was said." (also 8, 10)

(9) "By him . . . his saint's name was taken (told)."

(10) wéza! The original source has the form وځه, wédza, a common hyperform (in dialects where z and dz have coalesced) which suggests a connection with dza 'go!'

(11) predú (see 2 above)

munẓ in almost all Eastern dialects ẓ is pronounced like g: mung

(12) "The pious man . . . was thrown out by them (ye)."

TRANSLATION

THE THEOLOGY STUDENTS AND THE PIOUS MAN

(1) The story goes ("they say") that in a mosque of a village some theology students were living.

(2) The students do not let travellers into the mosque and particularly no pious men.

(3) One evening a traveller came late to the mosque.

(4) This traveller was the pious follower of some holy man and religious leader.

(5) His strings of big beads were in his hand and his white shawl was on his head.

(6) When he entered the mosque, the students asked him: "Guest, where are you from?"

(7) He told them from such and such a place.

(8) The students said to him again: "Who are you?"

(9) Then he told them the name of his saint: "I am the dog of the holy master."

(10) The students said to him: "Beat it, get out! This is a mosque.

(11) We don't let God's dogs (in) here, let alone the dog of the holy master."

(12) All got up after him and threw the pious man, beset by misfortune, out of the mosque.

EXERCISES

I. WRITING:

Write the Pashto text from the Roman transcription, checking for correctness afterwards.

II. QUESTIONS ON TEXT:

Write suitable answers in Pashtọ to the following ten questions:

A. In the Roman alphabet.

B. In the Pashto alphabet.

1. pə yaw masjid kşe tsok osedə?	۰۱ په يو مسجد کښې څوك اوسېده ؟
2. musāfir kəla* masjid ta rāğay?	۰۲ مسافر کله مسجد ته راغی ؟
3. tālebāno šex pežāndə ka nə?	۰۳ طالبانو شيخ پېژانده که نه ؟
4. tālebāno wə šex ta salām wəwāyə?	۰٤ طالبانو و شيخ ته سلام ووايه ؟
5. də šex pə lās kşe tsənga** tasbe we?	۰٥ د شيخ په لاس کښې څنگه تسبې وې ؟
6. də šex pər sar tsənga tsādar wə?	۰٦ د شيخ پر سر څنگه څادر و؟
7. musāfir də kum dzāy wə?	۰۷ مسافر د کوم ځای و ؟
8. šex də xwdāy spay wə?	۰۸ شيخ د خدای سپی و ؟
9. tālebān tsok pə masjid ke nə preẓdi?	۰۹ طالبان څوك په مسجد کښې نه پرېږدي ؟
10. šex ta wale*** pə balā peş wāyi?	۰۱۰ شيخ ته ولې په بلا پېښ وايي ؟

* kə́la adv. 'when?'

** tsə́nga see 6.13

*** wále see 6.4

III. GRAMMAR:

1. (a) Identify all adjectival forms in the text as to case, number, gender.

   (b) To which of the five adjectival classes extant in Pashto do they belong? (see GP § 68.2, table IV on p. 79.)

2. (a) Fill in the adjectival forms with the correct endings.

   (b) Write the resulting sentences in the Pashto alphabet.

   (c) What is the English meaning of the sentences?

   1. ______(plānay) mudir ______(xarāb) ṭelefun porta kəṛ.

   2. ______(yaw) ṭoka ye wə ______(faᶜāl) mudir ta taqdim kəṛe da.

   3. tāse ______(jōṛ) yəy? ______(bəl) ṭōka ham pežanəy?

   4. pə ______(yaw) ri̠yāsat kṣe ______(kum) raís kār kawi.

   5. stāse maqāle ______(uẓd) di. ______(xpəl) ki̠tāb tarjuma kawəy?

3. (a) Form meaningful Pashto sentences by using correct adjectival and verbal forms with the following nouns and adjectives:

yaw	dzā́y	úẓd	dày
(plānáy, kum, bel)	(masjíd, tsādár, maqālá, puṣténa, maqālé, dzāyúna, tasbé)	(spin, xarā́b, peṣ)	(da, di)

e.g., yawá maqālá xarā́ba dà.

(b) Write the resulting sentences in the Pashto alphabet.

(c) Add indications of stress to the Roman transcription of the questions (II above) and the fill-in exercises (2 above).

UNIT 3

جرګه

د پښتنو په ملي عنعناتو کښې جرګه خورا اهمیت لري. پخوا پښتنو ټول مهمات په جرګه فیصله کول.

وایي چه سلطان بهلول لودین د هندوستان پاچا به د پښتنو سردارانو جرګه درلوده. هر وخت به چه دا جرګه تشکیل شوه، دی به د پاچاهۍ د تخت نه راکوز شو. د نورو سره به یوازې د پښتانه په ډول کښېناست. په دې جمعیت کښې ده هېڅ امتیاز نه درلود.

د پښتنو جرګې خورا مشهورې دي. ځینې مدققین وایي چه دا جرګې د پخوانو آریانانو له رسومو څخه په دوی کښې پاته دي. اوس هم د آزادو سرحدو پښتانه د جرګې پابند دي. هر وخت چه یو مهم کار پېښ شي، پښتانه په کښې جرګه کوي. د پښتنو جرګه ځانته اصول او مخصوص قوانین لري؛ د جرګې ځای معلوم دی چه یا حجره یا دېره یا چوتره او یا لوی مسجد وي. په پښتنو کې د جرګې او ټولنې خلق فطرتاً معلوم وي چه په هغوی کښې څوک اختلاف نه لري. نو دوی سره راغونډېږي او په موضوع باندې بحث کوي.

TRANSCRIPTION

jergá

(1) de paṣtanó pe mi̲lí ananā́to kè jergá xorā́ amyát larì.

(2) pexwā́ paṣtanó ṭól mu̲hi̲mā́t pe jergá faysalà kawél.

(3) wā́yi či̲ su̲ltā̀n Bālól Lodín de hi̲ndu̲stā́n pāč̣ā́ ba de paṣtanó sardārā́no jergá derlóda.

(4) hár wáxt ba či̲ dā́ jergá taškíl šwa, dáy ba de pāčāhéy de táxt na rākúz šu.

(5) de nóro sara ba yawā́ze de paṣtāné pe ḍáwl kénāst.

(6) pe dé jami̲yát kè dè héts i̲mti̲yā́z né derlòd.

(7) de paṣtanó jergé xorā́ mašhúre di.

(8) dzíne mu̲daqi̲qín wā́yi či̲ dā́ jergé de pexwānó āri̲yānā́no le ru̲súmo tsexa pe dúy ke pā́ta di.

(9) ós hám de āzā́do sarhadó paṣtāné de jergé pābánd di.

(10) hár wáxt či̲ yaw mu̲hí̲m kā́r péṣ ši, paṣtāné pe ké jergá kawì.

(11) de paṣtanó jergá dzā́nta u̲súl aw maxsús qawānín larì;

(12) de jergé dzā́y mālúm day či̲ yā hu̲jrá yā derá yā čotrá yā lóy masjí̲d wi.

(13) pe paṣtanó kè de jergé aw ṭoléne xálq fi̲tratán mālúm wì či̲ pe hagúy kè tsók i̲xtelā́f né lari.

(14) no dúy sara rāgu̲nḍéẓi aw pe mawzó bānde bā́s kawì.

GLOSSARY

jergá, pl. jergé f 2 '(tribal) council'

(1) paṣtanó obl.pl. of paṣtún, pl. paṣtāné m 5 'Pashtun, Afghan'

milí̲ obl.pl. of milí̲ adj. V 'national'

ʕanʕanā́to obl.pl. of ʕanʕaná, pl. ʕanʕané (f 2), Arab. ʕanʕanā́t m 'tradition'

xorā́ (xwarā́, xwerā́) adj. V, adv. 'very, very much'

ahmyát (ahmi̲yát), pl. ahmyatúna m 1 'importance'

larí 3d sing.pres. I of larém, past derlod- verb III (trans.) 'have, possess'

(2) pexwā́ adv. 'formerly, previously'

paṣtanó (see 1) 'by the Pashtuns'

mu̲hi̲mā́t Arab. pl. of mu̲hí̲m m 'important event' (mu̲hí̲m adj. I 'important')

fays̤alá, pl. fays̤alé f 2 'decision'

kawél 3d pl.masc.past I of kawém verb IV (trans.) 'to do, make'

fays̤alà kawém verb.IV 'to decide'

(3) su̲lt̲ān, pl. su̲lt̲ānān m 2 'king, sultan'

hi̲ndu̲stā́n m 'India'

pā́čā, pl. pāčāhā́n m 2 'king'

ba mod.part.

paṣtanó obl.pl. of paṣtún, fem. paṣtaná adj. II 'Pashtun, Afghan' sardārā́no obl.pl. of sardā́r, pl. sardārā́n m 2 'chief'

derlóda 3d sing.fem.past of larém (see 1 above)

(4) har, fem. hára adj. I 'every,each'

waxt, pl. waxtúna m 1 'time'

taškíl šwa 3d sing.fem.past II of taškiléẓem, pres. II taškíl š-, past I taškiléd-, past II taškíl šw- verb IV-A (intrans.) 'to become formed, be assembled'

pāčahéy obl.sing. of pāčāhí, pl. pāčāhéy f 4 'royalty, being king' (pāčā́ 3 above)

de . . . na prep. 'from'

taxt, pl. taxtúna m 1 'throne'

rākúz šu 3d sing.masc.past II of rākuzéẓem, pres. II rākúz š-, past I rākuzéd-, past II rākúz šw- verb IV-A (intrans.) 'to get down' (prefix rā-)

(5) de . . . sara prep.-adv.phrase 'with'

nóro obl.pl. of nor, fem. nóre 'others'

yawā́ze adv. (adj. V) 'only'

paṣtāné obl.sing. of paṣtún (see 1 above)

ḍawl (ḍáwel), pl. ḍawlúna m 1 'manner, way'

kṣénāst 3d sing.masc. past II of kṣeném (kenem), past kṣenāst- verb II (intrans.) 'to sit'

(6) jamʿi̱yát, pl. jamʿi̱yatúna m 1 'gathering, assembly'

dé dem.pron.

hets (Kandahar: hits) adj. V 'no, none'

i̱mti̱yā́z, pl. i̱mti̱yāzúna (Arab. i̱mti̱yāzā́t) m 1 '(special) privilege, distinction'

(7) mašhúre dir.pl.fem. of mašhúr, fem. mašhúra adj. I 'famous'

(8) dzíne indef.pron. 'some, several'

mu̱daqi̱qín Arab.pl. of mu̱daqí̱q m 'research scholar'

pexwānó obl.pl. of pexwānáy, fem. pexwānéy adj. III 'former, previous' (pexwā́ adv., 2 above)

āri̱yānā́no obl.pl. of āri̱yā́n, pl. āri̱yānā́n m 2 'Aryan'

ru̱súmo obl.pl. of rasm, pl. rasmúna, Arab. ru̱súm m 1 'custom'

duy dem.pron. 'they, them, these'

pā́ta also pā́te adj. V 'remaining, left over'

(9) os adv. 'now'

ham adv. 'also'

āzā́do obl.pl. of āzā́d, fem. āzā́da adj. I 'free, independent'

sarẖadó obl.pl. of sarẖád, pl. sarẖadúna m 1 'frontier', border'

pābánd dir.pl. of pābánd, fem. pābánda adj. I 'attached to'

(10) mu̱hí̱m, fem. mu̱hí̱ma adj. I 'important' (see 2 above)

kār, pl. kārúna m 1 'work, task, problem, business'

péṣ ši 3d sing.masc.pres. II of peṣéẓem, pres. II péṣ š-, past I peṣed-́, past II péṣ šw- verb IV-A (intrans.) 'to occur, turn up' (peṣ adj. I)

(11) dzā́nta adj. V 'special'

uṣúl Arab. pl. m 'rules, regulations'

maxṣúṣ dir.pl. of maxṣúṣ, fem. maxṣúṣa adj. I 'special, particular'

qawānín Arab. pl. of qānún m 1 'law, rule'

(12) maʕlúm, fem. maʕlúma adj. I 'known, familiar'

yā . . . yā conj. 'either . . . or'

ḥujrá, pl. ḥujré f 2 'public guest house'

derá, pl. deré f 2 'reception hall'

čotrá, pl. čotré f 2 (raised open area, platform)

loy, fem. lóya adj. I 'big, large'

wi 3d sing.pres. II of yəm aux.

(13) ṭolə́ne obl.sing. of ṭolə́na, pl. ṭolə́ne f 1 'assembly, gathering, society' (ṭol adj. 2.12)

xalq (also xáleq, xalk) m pl. 'people'

fi̱tratán adv. 'incontrovertibly, naturally, evidently'

haǵúy dem.pron. 'these, those, they'

tsok indef.-interrog.pron. 'someone; who?'

i̱xti̱lā́f, pl. i̱xti̱lāfúna (Arab. i̱xti̱lāfā́t) m 1 'disagreement, difference'

(14) sará adv. 'together'

rāǵunḍéẓi (rāǵwənḍéẓi) 3d pl.pres.I of rāǵunḍéẓəm, pres. II rāǵúnḍ š-, past I rāǵunḍed-́, past II rāǵúnḍ šw- verb IV-A (intrans.) 'to gather, assemble' (prefix rā-)

pə . . . bā́nde prep.-adv. phrase 'on, upon'

mawzṓʿ, pl. mawzoʿgā́ne f 5 'topic, subject'

ba<u>hs</u>, pl. ba<u>hs</u>úna m 1 'discussion'

NOTES

This selection was taken from <u>paṣtunwalí</u> ("Pashtoonhood") by Qyāmuddin Xādi̱m (Kabul: paṣtó ṭolə́na, 1952), p. 52f.

(1) paṣtún m 5 (see GP § 55.4b)

ananā́to for ʿanʿanāto   ke for kṣe

amyát for ahmyat

(2) faysalá for fayṣ̤ala

"All important matters (mu̱hi̱mā́t dir.pl.masc.) were being decided (fayṣ̤alà kawə́l pl.masc.) by the Pashtoons (paṣtanó obl.pl.)."

(3) Bālól for Bahlol

(4) taškíl šwa here for taškíla šwa

(5) kə́nāst for kṣə́nāst past II. kenā́st would be past I 'was sitting'

(6) jami̱yát for jamʿi̱yat

(8) pəxwānó for pə́xwānə́yo

(11) u̱súl for u̱ṣ̤ul

maxsús for maxṣ̤uṣ̤

(12) mālúm for maʿlum

hu̱jrá for hu̱jra

(13) fi̲tratán for f<u>it</u>ratan

(14) mawzó for maw<u>z</u>o̤ʿ

bā̃s less formally for ba<u>hs</u>

TRANSLATION

(1) Among the national traditions of the Pashtoons, the (tribal) council has great importance.

(2) Formerly the Pashtoons were deciding all important matters by council.

(3) The story goes that Sultan Bahlol Lodin, the King of India, would have a council of the Pashtoon chiefs.

(4) Every time the council was assembled, he would come down from the throne of royalty.

(5) With the others he would sit only in the manner of a Pashtoon.

(6) In this gathering he had no (special) privilege.

(7) The councils of the Pashtoons are very famous.

(8) Some research scholars say that these councils have remained among them from the customs of the ancient Aryans.

(9) Now also the Pashtoons of the free frontiers are attached to the council.

(10) Every time an important task turns up, the Pashtoons meet on it in council.

(11) The council of the Pashtoons has special rules and particular laws.

(12) The place of the council is known: it may be a guest-house or a reception hall or a raised open area or a large mosque.

(13) Among the Pashtoons the people of council and assembly

are clearly known so that nobody has any different opinion about them.

(14) Then they meet together and have a discussion on a topic.

EXERCISES

I. QUESTIONS ON TEXT:

Write suitable answers in Pashto to the following questions:

A. In the Roman alphabet.

B. In the Pashto alphabet.

1. sult̲ā̀n Bahlól Lodín tsók wù?
۱. سلطان بهلول لودين څوك و؟

2. sult̲ā̀n Bahlól Lodín de čā́ pe ḍáwel kṣ̌ènāstə́?
۲. سلطان بهلول لودين د چا په ډول کښېناسته ؟

3. sult̲ā̀n Bahlól de sardārā́no pe jergá kṣe kúm i̲mti̲yáz derlṓd?
۳. سلطان بهلول د سردارانو په جرگه کښې کوم امتياز درلود ؟

4. dzíne mu̲daqi̲qín de paṣtanṓ de jergṓ pe bā́b* kṣe tsé wā́yi?
۴. ځيني مدققين د پښتنو د جرگو په باب کښې څه وايي ؟

5. paṣtāné tsé wàxt ǰergà kawí?
۵. پښتانه څه وخت جرگه کوي ؟

6. ǰergá pe kùm dzā́y kṣ́e kéẓi?
۶. جرگه په کوم ځای کښې کېږي ؟

---

* de ... pe bā́b see 10b.

7. tsók də ɟərgé pābánd dì? ۰۷ څوك د جرګې پابند دي ؟

8. də ɟərgé xáləq tsə́nga maˁlúm wì? ۰۸ د جرګې خلق څنګـــه معلوم وي ؟

9. də paṣtanó ɟərgé wále mašhúre dì? ۰۹ د پښتنو جرګې ولې مشهورې دي ؟

10. tāləbā́n də ɟərgé xáləq dì? ۰۱۰ طالبان د جرګې خلق دي ؟

II. GRAMMAR:

A. Identify all pronominal forms including pronominal adjectives, pronominal prefixes and particles in Texts 1, 2, 3. If in doubt, consult GP, Chapter VI.

B. Insert the pronouns with the appropriate endings corresponding to the English forms and write the resulting sentences in the Pashto alphabet:

1. pə _____(this, that) masjī́d kṣe_____(no) mu̱lā́ nə́šta.

2. _____(they) mu̱sāfərā́n dì aw pə _____(this, that) dzā́y kṣe né òsi.

3. ṭili̱fún _____(he, I, we, they, she, somebody) pórta kə̆ṛ.

4. mā _____(to him, you, them) wə́wayəl: də_____(him, her, this one, them) mi̱hrabānī́ da.

5. _____ (your, my, his) ki̱tābúna lóy di.

UNIT 4

نوروز

له پخوانيو دا دود پاتې دی چه د نوروز په ورځ مېله کېږي. په ښارو کې ډېر اولس په يوه ټاکلي ځای کې سره راغونډېږي. دوکانونه هم موقتاً هلته جوړېږی. د ښار والي او مامورين دا ميله اداره کوي. څوک چه ښه حيوانات او مرغان لري او د ښودلو له پاره يې راوړي بخشش اخلي. سازونه او اتڼونه کېږي.

مېله په قولبه کولو او بېل وهلو او نيال کښېودلو شروع کېږي. پالوانان غېږې نيسي. هرڅوک له خپلو ملګرو سره هرې خوا ته ګرزي، او په پای کې کور ته له سوغات سره ځي. ښې ډوډۍ، نوي سابه او چرګان خوړل کېږي.

په مزار شريف کې تر هر ځايه لويه مېله کېږي. زرګونه زرګونه خلق ورځي. د سخي صاحب جنډه پورته کېږي. د سيلو شمار نه وي. بزکشي تر هر وخته زيات هلته جوش لري.

TRANSCRIPTION

nawróz

(1) lə pəxwānə́yo dā́ dód pā́te day či̲ də nawróz pə wrádz melá kéẓi.

(2) pə ṣāró ke ḍér u̲lə́s pə yawə́ ṭākə́li dzā́y ke sarà rāǥu̲nḍéẓi.

(3) dukānúna hám mawqatán hálta joṛéẓị.

(4) də ṣā́r wālí aw māmurín dā́ melá i̲dārà kawí.

(5) tsók či̲ ṣə́ haywānā́t aw mərǥā́n larĭ aw də ṣodə́lo lə pā́ra ye rāwṛí baxší̲š áxli.

(6) sāzúna aw ataṇúna kéẓi.

(7) melá pə qolbà kawə́lo aw bél wahə́lo aw ni̲yā́l keṣodə́lo šu̲rò kéẓi.

(8) pālawānā́n ǥéẓe nìsi.

(9) hártsok lə xpə́lo məlgéro sara háre xwā́ ta gə́rzi, aw pə pā́y ke kór ta lə sawǥā́t sara dzí.

(10) ṣé ḍoḍə́y, néwi sābə́ aw čərgā́n xwaṛèl kéẓi.

(11) pə Mazā́re šaríf ke tər hár dzā́ya lóya melá kéẓi.

(12) zərgúna zərgúna xálq wardzí. də saxí sāí̲b janḍá pòrta kéẓi.

(13) də sayló šmā́r nə́ wi.

(14) bu̲zkaší tər hár wáxta zyā́t hálta jóš larí.

GLOSSARY

nawróz m New Year's day (Persian)

(1) lə prep. 'from'

dōd, pl. dodúna m 1 'custom'

wradz, pl. wrádze f 1 'day'

melá, pl. melé f 2 'picnic, fair, festivity'

(2) ṣāró obl.pl of ṣār, pl. ṣārúna m 1 'city, town'

ḍer, fem. ḍéra adj. I 'much'

u̱lə́s, pl. u̱ləsúna m 1 'people, tribe'

ṭākéli obl.sing.masc. of ṭākélay, fem. ṭākéle perf. part. of ṭākə́m verb I (trans.) 'to determine, select'

(3) dukānúna dir.pl. of dukā́n m 1 'shop'

ham adv. 'also'

mawqatán adv. 'temporarily'

hálta adv. 'there'

joṛéẓi 3d pl.pres. I of joṛéẓəm verb IV-A (intrans.) 'to become built, cured, fixed'

(4) wālī́, pl. wālyā́n m 2 'mayor, ruler'

māmurī́n Ar.pl. of māmúr m 'official'

i̱dārá, pl. i̱dāré f 2 'administration'

i̱dārà kawə́m verb IV 'to administer, supervise'

(5) ṣə dir.pl.masc. of ṣə, fem. ṣa adj. II 'good, fine'

ẖaywānā́t Ar. pl. of ẖaywā́n m 2 'animal'

mərgā́n pl. of mərǵé m 2 'bird'

ṣodélo obl. of ṣodél m pl. verbal substantive of
ṣéyem, past ṣod- verb II (trans.) 'to show'

de . . . le pára prep.-adv.phrase 'for the sake of'

rāwṛí 3d sing.pres. I of rāwṛém verb I (trans.)
'to bring (something)'

baxšíš, pl. baxšišúna m 1 'gift, award'

áxli 3d sing.pres. I of áxlem, past axist- verb II
(trans.) 'to take'

(6) sāzúna pl. of sāz m 1 'music'

atanúna pl. of atáṇ m 1 'dance'

(7) qolbá, pl. qolbé f 2 'plow, plowing'

kawélo obl. of verbal subst. of kawém verb IV

qolbá kawém verb IV 'to plow'

bel, pl. belúna m 1 'spade'

wahélo obl. of wahél verb.subst. of wahém verb I
(trans.) 'to beat'

bél wahém verb I 'to spade'

niyál, pl. niyālúna m 1 'plant, bush'

keṣodélo obl. of verb.subst. of ẓdem verb IV
'to set, place, put' (for kṣeṣodélo)

šurúʕ, pl. šurúʕwe f 3 'beginning'

šurúʕ kéẓem verb IV 'to start, begin' (intrans.)

(8) pālawānān dir.pl. of pālawān or pahlawān m 2 'wrestler'

ǵéẓe dir.pl. of ǵeẓ f 1 'wrestling'

nísi 3d pl.pres. I of nísəm, past niw- verb II (trans.) 'to take, seize, grasp'

(9) hártsok indef.pron. 'everybody' (har and tsok)

məlgə́ro obl.pl. of məlgə́ray, pl. məlgə́ri m 4 'friend, companion'

xwā, pl. xwā́we, xwāgā́ne f 3, f 5 'side, direction'

gə́rzi, 3d sing.pres. I of gə́rzəm, past gərzed- verb II 'to stroll, walk around'

pāy m 'end'

kor, pl. korúna m 1 'house'

sawgā́t, pl. sawgātúna m 1 'gift, remembrance'

dzi 3d sing.pres. I of dzəm verb IV 'to go'

(10) ḍoḍə́y dir.pl. of ḍoḍə́y f 4 'bread, food, meal'

néwi dir.pl.masc. of néway, fem. néwe adj. IV 'new'

sābə́ m pl. 'vegetables'

čərgā́n dir.pl. of čərg m 2 'rooster, chicken'

xwaṛə̆l kéẓi 3d pl.pres. I of pass.phrase of xwrəm, past xwaṛ- verb II (trans.) 'to eat'

(11) tər prep. 'to, up to'

dzā́ya obl. II of dzāy

(12) zərgúna m pl. of zər 'thousand'

xalq m pl. 'people'

wardzí 3d pl.pres. I of wardzə́m verb IV 'to go (there)'

janḍá, pl. janḍé f 2 'flag, banner'

pòrta kẹ́ẓi 3d sing.pres. I of pòrta kẹ́ẓəm verb IV (intrans.) 'to get raised, lifted'

(13) sayló obl.pl. of sayl, pl. saylúna m 1 'show, entertainment'

šmār (also šmer), pl. šmārúna m 1 'number'

(14) bu̲zkaší, pl. bu̲zkašéy f 4 "buzkashi"

zyā́t (zi̲yā́t) adv. 'more' (also adj. I)

još, pl. jošúna m 1 'heat, boiling, climax'

NOTES

This selection was written by A. Ahad Yāri, a native of Surkhāb in the province of Kabul, during his stay in Ann Arbor, Michigan. Mr. Yāri now teaches Pashto at the University of Kabul.

(1) In Mr. Yāri's dialect the conj. či̲ is tse, the prep. də is de. The orthography and transcription as given do not show this pronunciation.

New Year's day is the 21st of March.

(5) rāwṛém is used with things, sometimes animals, never with human beings, where rāwəlém, past rāwast- (verb II trans.) has to be used.

(9) gérzəm sometimes gérdzəm, probably influenced by dzəm 'to go'.

(11) Mazār-e-Sharif is an important Afghan city. The name is Persian and means "holy shrine".

(12) saxí ṣāh̲íb, "generous master", is the name for the fourth calif whose tomb is believed to be in Mazār-e-Sharif.

(14) wáxta is like dzā́ya (11) an oblique II case (GP § 65.1b)
būzkaší is a tug of war between two teams performed on horseback with a butchered calf or goat as the object of contention.

TRANSLATION

The New Year's Day

(1) From the ancestors this custom has remained that on the day of the new year a fair is held.

(2) In the towns many people gather in one selected place.

(3) Shops are also built there temporarily.

(4) The mayor of the city and the officials supervise the fair.

(5) Anyone who has good animals and birds and brings them for showing receives an award.

(6) There is music and dancing.

(7) The fair begins with plowing, spading, and planting.

(8) Wrestlers wrestle.

(9) Everybody strolls with his friends everywhere and finally goes home with a gift.

(10) Good food, new vegetables, and chickens are eaten.

(11) In Mazar-i-Sharif there is a bigger fair than anywhere.

(12) Thousands and thousands of people attend; the banner of the 'Generous Master' is raised.

(13) There will be innumerable (kinds of) entertainment.

(14) 'Buzkashi' flourishes there more than ever.

EXERCISES

I. QUESTIONS ON TEXT:

Write answers in the Pashto alphabet to the following questions:

۱. د پخوانیو خلکو په وخت کښې د نوروز مېله کېدله که نه ؟

۲. په ښارو کې خلق *چېرې راغونډېږي ؟

۳. دا مېله څوک اداره کوي ؟

۴. په مېله کښې خلق د څه د پاره بخشش اخلي ؟

۵. مېله څنګه شروع کېږي ؟

۶. د پهلوانانو کار څه دی ؟

۷. لویه مېله په کوم ځای کښې کېږي ؟

۸. د مزارشریف مېلې ته څونه خلق ورځي ؟

۹. مدیران په مېله کښې اتڼ کوي ؟

۱۰. بزرګ یا پیر د بزکشۍ سیل ته ورځي ؟

II. GRAMMAR:

1. (a) Identify all the verbal forms, excluding nominal forms derived from verbs, in texts 1, 2, 3, 4 grammatically, and check yourself afterwards by consulting the glossaries. Example: kéẓi 3d sing.pres. I.

   (b) To which five types do these verbal forms in the texts belong? (see Grammatical Summary and GP §§ 84-88) Example: kéẓi verb IV.

   (c) Are the verbal forms transitive, intransitive, impersonal-transitive, auxiliary? (for definitions see GP §83) Example: kéẓi intransitive, also aux. (§83.4)

2. (a) Rewrite in the Pashto and Roman alphabets text 4 as

* čére adv. 'where'

if it were a report on last year's New Year's day festivity, using appropriate past tense forms instead of the present forms; e.g., . . .de nawróz pe wrádz melá wéšwa (4.1).

. . . ḍér u̱lés . . . . . rāǵu̱nḍ šwèl (4.2), etc.

(b) Rewrite text 2 in the present tense.

3. Write in the Roman and Pashto alphabets the corresponding present II (1st sing.) past I (1st sing., 3d sing. masc., 3d sing.fem.) past II (1st sing.) forms of the following verbs:

ṭākém, wardzém, áxlem, xwrém, ósem, joṛéẓem, joṛawém, ẓdem, rāǵu̱nḍéẓem

Example: kéẓem (pres. I) wéšem (pres. II) kedélem (past I) kedé (past I, 3d m) kedéla(kedá) (past I, 3d f)

wéšwem (past II)

4. List in the Pashto and Roman alphabets all the forms of the following verb tenses (3 or 4 singular, 3 or 4 plural forms):

present I of wā́yem, rāwṛém

present II of nísem, taqdimawém, larém

past I of kṣeném, yem, péžanem

past II of dzem, bā́sem, preẓdém

UNIT 5

کلی

څو کوره چه یوځای سره پراته وي کلی ورته وايي . کلي ښارو ته نژدې يا ترې لرې وي . په کليو کې د ځمکو خاوندان بزگر او همسايگان ساتي . خو کرا نه ځنې اخلي ، او څنگه چه رواج وي مزدوري ورکوي . کليوال په گډه ملا ، نجار ، آهنگر ، ډم ، او پاڼه‌وان نيسي . په غم او ښادي ، جماعت او ميلمه پاللو کې ټول برخه اخلي او دې ته کورگېلي وايي . جماعت کې پينځه وخته لمونځ کوي او د کلي کوچنيان له ملا نه سبق زده‌کوي . جماعت ته نژدې ډېره وي چه مسافر او د کلي ميلمانه هلته ورځي . د کلي اولس هرکلی ورته وايي ، ډوډۍ ورته راوړي ، او عزت ورکوي .

په کليوالو کې ملا او سپينږيرو ته په درنه سترگه کتل کېږي . دوی په کلي کې توپير نه کوي . په غم او ښادي کې حاضر وي . د خير لاس پورته کوي . خلق خوابدي ته نه سره پربږدي ، د دوی مرکه کوي او خلق يې هم مني .

له وړو کليو څخه هلکان لويو کليو او ښارو ته د مکتب له پاره ځي . د کلي خلق د ښاروالو سره معاملې کوي . خپل حاصلات پر خرڅوي او د کور احتياجات ځنې اخلي .

TRANSCRIPTION

kélay

(1) tsó kóra či̲ yą́w dzā̀y sara prāté wi kélay wèrta wā́yi.

(2) kéli ṣāró ta ni̲ždé yā trḕ lére wi.

(3) pe kélyo ke de mdzéko xāwandā́n bazgér aw hamsāyagā́n sātí.

(4) xò krā́ né dzi̲ne áxli,

(5) aw tsénga či̲ rawā́j wì mazdurí warkawí.

(6) keliwā́l pe gáḍa mu̲lā́, najā́r, āyingár, ḍém, aw pādawā́n nísi.

(7) pe ǥám aw ṣādí, jumā́t aw melmà pālélo ke ṭól bárxa áxli aw dé ta kòrgelí wā́yi.

(8) jumā́t ke pindzé wáxta lmúndz kawí aw de kéli kučnyā́n le mu̲lā́ na sabáq zdà kawí.

(9) jumā́t ta ni̲zdé derá wi či̲ mu̲sāpér aw de kéli melmāné hálta wardzí.

(10) de kéli u̲lés harkaláy wèrta wā́yi, ḍoḍéy wèrta rāwṛí, aw i̲zát warkawí.

(11) pe keliwā́lo ke mu̲lā́ aw spinẓíro ta pe draná stérga katèl kéẓi.

(12) dúy pe kéli ke topír né kawi, pe ǥám aw ṣādí ke hāzér wi.

(13) de xáyr lā́s pòrta kawí.

(14) xálq xwābadí ta né sara preẓdí, de dúy maraká kawì aw xálq ye hám maní.

(15) le waṛó kélyo tsexa halekā́n lóyo kélyo aw ṣāró ta de maktáb le pā́ra dzí.

(16) de kéli xálq de ṣārwā́lo sara māmilé kawì.

(17) xpél hāsi̱lā́t per xartsawí aw de kőr etyājā́t dzi̱ne ắxli.

GLOSSARY

(1) tso indef.pron. 'some'

kóra dir.pl. of kor, pl. korúna m 1 'house'

dzāy, pl. dzāyúna m 1 'place'

prāté dir.pl.masc. of prot, fem. pratá adj. II 'situated, located, lying'

(2) ni̱ždé (also ni̱zdé) adj. V 'near, close'

yā conj. 'or'

lére adj. V. 'far'

(3) mdzéko obl.pl. of mdzéka (also dzméka), pl. mdzéke f 1 'land, ground, earth'

xāwandā́n dir.pl. of xāwánd m 2 'owner'

bazgér dir.pl. of bazgár m 5 'farmer'

hamsāyagā́n. dir.pl. of hamsā́ya m 2 'neighbor; dependent, tenant'

sātí 3d pl.pres. I of sātém verb I 'to keep, support'

(4) xo adv. 'indeed, but'

krā́ (also ki̱rā́), pl. krāgā́ne f 5 'rent'

dzi̱ne part. 'from (them)'

(5) tsénga adv. 'how'

tsénga či̲ conj. 'how, as'

rawā́j, pl. rawājúna m 1 'custom'

mazdurī́, pl. mazduréy f 4 'wages; being a servant'

warkawī́ 3d pl.pres. I of warkawém verb IV 'to give (to them)' (prefix war-)

(6) keliwā́l dir.pl. of keliwā́l m 'villager'

pe gáḍa adv. 'in common, together'

mu̲lā́, pl. mu̲lāyā́n m 2 'muslim priest, mulla(h)'

najā́r, pl. najārā́n m 2 'carpenter'

āhingár, pl. āhingér, āhingarā́n m 5, m 2 'blacksmith'

ḍem, pl. ḍemā́n m 2 'barber'

pādawā́n, pl. pādawānā́n m 2 'herdsman'

(7) ğam, pl. ğamúna m 1 'grief, sad event, sorrow'

ṣādī́, pl. ṣādéy f 4 'happiness, happy event'

pālélo obl.verb.substantive of pālém verb I (trans.) 'to treat, entertain'

bárxa, pl. bárxe f 1 'part, share'

korgelī́ f 'being a good villager, neighborliness'

(8) lmundz, pl. lmundzúna m 1 'prayer'

lmúndz kawém verb IV 'to pray'

kučnyā́n (kučni̲yā́n) dir.pl. of kučnáy m 'little one, child' (also adj. III)

sabáq, pl. sabaqúna m 1 'lesson'

zda adj. V 'learned, acquired'

zda kawī́ 3d pl.pres. I of zda kawém verb IV 'to learn'

(9) hálta adv. 'there'

(10) harkaláy, pl. harkalí m 3 'welcome'

ˁi̲zát, pl. ˁi̲zatúna m 1 'honor'

(11) spinẓíro obl.pl.masc. of spinẓíray adj. IV 'old, "white-bearded"'

draná sing.fem. of drund adj. II 'heavy; respectful'

stérga, pl. stérge f 1 'eye'

katèl kéẓi 3d sing.pres. I passive of górem, past kat- verb III (trans.) 'to look'

(12) topír, pl. topirúna m 1 'differentiation, discrimination'

h̲āz̤ér dir.pl.masc. of h̲āz̤ér, fem. h̲āz̤éra adj. I 'present' (h̲u̲z̤úr 1.8)

(13) lās, pl. lāsúna m 1 'hand'

(14) xwābadí obl.sing. of xwābadáy, pl. xwābadí m 3 'dispute, conflict'

maraká, pl. maraké f 2 'judgment, council, arbitration'

maní 3d pl.pres. I of maném verb I 'to follow, accept'

(15) waṛó obl.pl. of woṛ, fem. waṛá adj. II 'small'

halekā́n dir.pl. of halék m 2 'boy'

maktáb, pl. maktabúna m 1 'school'

(16) ṣārwā́lo obl.pl. of ṣārwā́l m 'resident of a town' (ṣār m 4.2)

maʕāmilé dir.pl. of maʕāmilā́ f 2 'trade, business'

(17) ẖāṣiḻā́t Ar.pl. of ẖāṣī́l m 'crop, product'

xartsawí 3d pl.pres. I of xartsawə́m verb IV-A (trans.)
'to sell' (xarts m 1 'expense, price')

iẖtiyājā́t Ar.pl. of iẖtiyā́j m 'need, necessity'

NOTES

This text was written by Mr. A. Ahad Yāri.

(1) kóra, wáxta (8), previously tána (2.1), are plural forms
after tso or numerals (GP § 63.1a, 1b).

(3) bazgə́r (see GP § 55.2)

(6) āyingár for āhingar

(8) jumā́t for jumāʕat

ke for pə . . . ke

pindzə́ (pindzə́) wáxta refers to the required five
daily prayers.

(9) musāpə́r (dir.pl.) for musāfər; p informally for f
(see GP §§ 38, 20.3)

(10) izát for ʕizat

(12) hāzə́r for ẖāẕər

(16) māmilé for maʕāmile

(17) etyājā́t for iẖtiyājāt

pər here for pre (from pər ye)

TRANSLATION

A Village

(1) To a few houses that may be located together in one place, they say "village".

(2) Villages may be close to towns or far from them.

(3) In the villages the owners of the land keep farmers and tenants.

(4) But they don't get rent from them,

(5) and as the practice will be, they give them wages.

(6) The villagers together hire a priest, a carpenter, a blacksmith, a barber, and a herdsman.

(7) In sorrow and happiness, in the mosque and in entertaining guests all take part, and they call this "neighborliness".

(8) In the mosque they pray five times, and the children of the village learn their lessons from the priest.

(9) Close to the mosque will be a guest-house, where travellers and guests of the village go.

(10) The people of the village bid them welcome, bring them food, and honor them.

(11) Among the villagers the priest and old men are looked upon respectfully.

(12) They do not discriminate in the village; in grief and happiness they will be present.

(13) They raise the hand of grace.

(14) They do not leave people in disputes with each other; they arbitrate them and people accept this also.

(15) From small villages boys go to large villages and towns for school.

(16) The village people do business with the people of the towns.

(17) They sell their crops to them and get their house(hold) needs from them.

EXERCISES

I. QUESTIONS:

Write answers in Pashto to the following questions:

۱۰ کلي ښارو ته نژدې وي ؟

۲۰ کلیوال د نوروز میلې ته ولې مرغان راوړي ؟

۳۰ د ځمکو خاوندان همسایګانو ته *څه شی ورکوي ؟

٤۰ کورګېلي څه ته وایي ؟

۵۰ کلیوال څو وخته لمونځ کوي ؟

٦۰ په کلیو کې دېره چېرې وي ؟

۷۰ په کلیوالو کښې چا ته په درنه سترګه کتل کېږي ؟

۸۰ کوچنیان د چا څخه سبق زده کوی ؟

۹۰ هلکان د څه د پاره ښارو ته ځي ؟

۱۰۰ کلیوال د ښاروالو څخه *څه شی اخلي ؟

II. GRAMMAR:

A. Explain the use of oblique and direct case forms of nouns, adjectives, pronouns in texts 1, 2, 3, 4, 5: the use of direct case forms for the subject and object of sentences; the use of oblique case forms after prepositions or as the actor (agent) in sentences with a transitive verb in a past tense (e.g., Notes on text 1). (GP §§ 64-66)

---

* tsə́ š̃ay 'what?'; š̃áy see 8.1

B. Form sentences by using the appropriate forms in parentheses with the correct case endings and write them in the Pashto alphabet:

1. __________ (day, mudír, t̲āləbā́n, keliwā́l) wə __________ (məlgə́ray, raís, māmurín, nor, tsok) ta dā́se wə́wayəl.

2. pə __________ (dā́ kə́lay, maktáb, ṣārúna, maqālā́) kṣə hə́ts ______ (masj̲íd, haləkā́n, h̲aywā́n, dzāy) nə́šta.

3. lə __________ (kə́li, pír, jumāʕát, kučnyā́n) tsəxa rāgə́lay dày.

4. də ________ (kúm saṛáy, day, paṣtún, xāwáṇd) ki̲tā́b day.

5. __________ (mu̲lā́ ṣāh̲i̲b, spinẓíray, haləkā́n, məlmānə́) jóṛ yè (yèy or yā̀st)?

UNIT 6

سمدستي مېوه

وايي چه په يو ځای کښې يو زوړ سړی لگيا و د
ښووّن ونه يې کرله. يو پاچا وربانديې راغی، يو ساعت ورته
په فکر کښې ودرېد. اخر کښې يې ورته وويل چه سپين ږيريه!
دا وخت اوس ستا د ښووّن د کرنې نه دی، ولې چه ته
سپين ږيری سړی يې، د گور په غاړه ولاړ يې او ښووّن يوه
داسې ونه ده چه ډېره مده وروسته مېوه نيسي. نو خدای خبر
دی چه ستا به دومره عمر وي او که نه وي چه د دې
ونې مېوه وخورې. سپين ږيري ورته وويل چه پادشاه، قربان
دې شم، زه يې په دې نيت نه کرم چه زه به ژوندی
يم او زه به يې مېوه خورم. بلکه زه يې د دې له
پاره کرم چه زما نه وروسته نور خلك خو به يې مېوه
وخوري. د دنيا هم دا سلسله ده چه يو يې کري او بل
ته پاتې کېږي. پخوانو خلکو زمونږ د پاره کرلې وې او مونږ
به يې د وروستنيو د پاره کرو.

ده چه دا خبره وکړه، نو د پاچا ډېره خوښه شوه او
حکم يې وکړ چه ده ته دې انعام ورکړی شي. سپين ږيري
چه انعام واخيست نو پاچا ته يې وويل: وگوره چه زما
ونې څنگه زر مېوه ونيوله. پادشاه په دې خبره لا خوشحاله
شو او امر يې وکړ چه نور انعام هم ورکړئ.

چه نور انعام یې ورکړ   د ه بیا بادشاه ته وویل چه وګوره   نورې ونې
په کال کښې یو وارې مېوه   نیسي   او زما ونې په یوه   ساعت کښې دوه   واره
مېوه   ونیوله ٠ بادشاه ته دې خبرې لا خوند ورکړ او حکم یې   وکړ چه نور انعام
هم   ورکړی ٠ بیا پادشاه له ده نه روان شو او خپل ملګرو ته یې وویل :

ځئ چه ځو   که د دې   سپین ږیري   سره   نور هم   ودرېږو   نو
د   پیسو نه به   مو خلاص کړي !!

TRANSCRIPTION

samdestí mewá

(1) wā́yi či̲ pə yaw dzā́y kṣe yaw zóṛ saṛáy lagyā́ wə de ṣowə́n wə́na ye karə́la.

(2) yaw pāčā́ wə̀rbānde rā́g̸ay. yằw sāát wə̀rta pə fí̲kər kṣe wə́dared.

(3) axə́r kṣe ye wə́rta wə́wayəl či̲ spinẓírya! dā́ ẃáxt òs stā́ də ṣowə́n də karə́ne nə́ day,

(4) wále či̲ tə̀ spinẓíray saṛáy yé, də gór pə g̸ā́ṛa walā́ṛ yè,

(5) aw ṣowán yawà dā́se wə́na dà či̲ ḍéra mu̲dá wrústa mewá nìsi.

(6) no xwdā́y xabár day či̲ stā̀ ba dómra ú̲mər wì aw ka nə́ wi či̲ də dé wə́ne mewá wə́xwre.

(7) spinẓíri wə̀rta wə́wayəl či̲ pādšā́, qu̲rbā́n de šə̀m,

(8) zə̣́ ye pə də̀ ni̲yát nə́ karə̀m či̲ zə̀ ba žwandáy yəm aw zə́ ba ye mewá xwrə́m.

(9) bálke zə́ ye də dé lə pā́ra karə́m či̲ zmā́ na wrústa nór xā́lk xo ba ye mewá wə́xwri.

(10) də dunyā́ hamdā́ si̲lsi̲lá da či̲ yáw ye karí aw bə́l ta pā̀te kéẓi.

(11) pəxwānó xálko zmúnẓ də pā́ra karə́le wə̀ aw múnẓ ba yè də wrustanə́yo də pā́ra karú.

(12) dé či dā̀ xabéra wékṛa, no də pāčā́ ḍéra xwáṣa šwà
aw húkəm ye wékəṛ či dé ta de inā́m wárkṛay ši.

(13) spinẓíri či inā́m wā́xist, no pāčā́ ta ye wéwayəl:
wégora či zmā́ wéne tsénga zér mewá wéniwəla.

(14) pādšā́ pə dé xabéra lā̀ xušā́là šù aw ámər ye wékəṛ
či nór inā́m hám wárkṛəy.

(15) či nor inā́m ye wárkə̀ṛ, dé byā́ bādšā́ ta wéwayəl či
wégora, nóre wéne pə kā́l kṣe yáw wā̀re mewá nì̀si
aw zmā̀ wéne pə yawé sāát kṣe dwá wā́ra mewá
wéniwəla.

(16) bādšā́ ta dé xabére lā̀ xwánd wárkəṛ aw húkəm ye wékəṛ
či nór inā́m hám wárkṛəy.

(17) byā́ pādšā́ lə dé na rawā́n šu aw xpélo məlgéro ta ye
wéwayəl:

(18) dzéy či dzú, ka də dé spinẓíri sara nór hám wédareẓu
nò də paysó na ba mò xlā́s kṛi.

GLOSSARY

samdəstí adj. V 'immediate'

mewá, pl. mewé f 2 'fruit'

(1) zoṛ, fem. zaṛá adj. II 'old'

lagyā́ (lagiyā́) adj. V 'occupied, busy'

ṣowə́n obl.sing. of ṣowán, pl. ṣowə́n m 5 'olive tree'
(GP § 55.2)

wə́na, pl. wə́ne f 1 'tree'

karéla 3d sing.fem.past I of karə́m verb I (trans.) 'to plant, sow'

(2) wə́rbā̀nde adv. 'on him, upon him' (prefix wər-)

fí̱kər (fi̱kr), pl. fi̱krúna m 1 'thought, thinking'

sāʕát, pl. sāʕatúna m 1 'hour, while, clock'

wə́dared 3d sing.masc.past II of daréẓəm, past dared- verb II (intrans.) 'to stop, stand'

(3) axə́r, m 1 'end'

os adv. 'now'

karə́ne obl.sing. of karə́na, pl. karə́ne f 1 'planting, sowing'

(4) wále adv. 'why?'

wále či̱ conj. 'because'

gor, pl. gorúna m 1 'grave'

ǥā́ṛa, pl. ǥā́ṛe f 1 'edge, neck'

walā́ṛ, fem. walā́ṛa adj. I 'standing'

(5) mu̱dá or modá, pl. modé f 2 'time'

dā́se dem.pron. 'such'

wrústa adv. 'afterwards'

(6) ka conj. 'if, or'

xabár, fem. xabára adj. I 'aware, informed'

dómra (dú̱mra) dem.pron. 'this much, so much'

ʕú̱mer, pl. ʕu̱mrúna m 1 'age, life-time'

(7) qu̱rbā́n šəm 1st sing.pres.II of qu̱rbanéẓəm verb IV-A 'to become sacrificed'

de pron.part. (2d pers.sing.)

(8) ni̲yát (nyát), pl. nyatúna m 1 'intention, purpose'

žwandə́y, fem. zwandə́y adj. III 'alive'

(9) bálke conj. 'but'

(10) duɲyā̃ (duni̲yā́), pl. dunyāgā́ne f 5 'world'

hamdā́ dem.pron. 'this very, exactly this'

si̲lsi̲lá, pl. si̲lsi̲lé f 2 'chain of events, tradition'

pā́te kéẓəm verb IV (intrans.) 'to be left'

(11) wrustanéyo obl.pl. of wrustanáy, fem. wrustanéy
adj. III 'later, latter'

(12) xabə́ra, pl. xabə́re f 1 'talk, statement; matter'

xwáṣa šwa 3d sing.fem.past II of xwaṣéẓəm verb IV-A
(intrans.) 'to be approved, liked'

h̲ú̲kəm, pl. h̲u̲kmúna m 1 'order'

i̲nʿā́m, pl. i̲nʿāmúna m 1 'gift, prize, bonus'

de mod.part. (indicating a command)

(13) wə́gora imp. II of gó́rəm, past kat- verb III (trans.)
'to look' (5.11)

tsə́nga adv. 'how'

zər or žər adv. 'quickly'

(14) lā adv. 'still, yet'

xu̲šh̲ā́la adj. V or xu̲šh̲ā́l, fem. xu̲šh̲ā́la adj. I 'happy'

ámər, pl. amrúna m 1 'order, command'

(15) kāl, pl. kalúna m 1 'year'

jáw wā̀re adv. 'once, one time'

wār m 'turn, time'

(16) xwạnd, pl. xwandúna m 1 'taste, pleasure'

(17) rawā́n šu 3d sing.masc.past II of rawānéẓəm verb IV-A (intrans.) 'to move, start out' (rawā́n adj. I see 8.9).

(18) paysó obl. of paysé f 2 pl. 'money'

mo pron.part. (1st pers.pl.; 2d pers.pl.)

xlā́ṣ̈ kṛi 3d sing.pres. II of xlāṣ̈awə́m verb IV-A (trans.) 'to set free, finish, open'

NOTES

This story is (like text 2) taken from Sadiqulla Riṣtin's paṣtó qisé ("Pashto Tales") (Kabul: 1952), pp. 45-47.

(2) pāčā́ m 2 (also 12, 13 below). This word appears also here in the following written forms: pādšāh (7, 14, 17), bādšāh (15, 16).

wə́rbànde. The pronominal prefixes combine freely with particles and adverbs: rā́ta, rāpórta (2.12), də́rsara, wə́rta, wə́rpəse (2.12), wə́rtsəxa. (See GP § 78.1; for verbal composition, § 98.1b)

pə́kər for fi̱kr is informal Pashto.

(3) spinẓírya vocative form, see GP § 66.

karə́na is formed from karə́m, GP § 67.5a.

(5) mewá ǹisi "bears fruit"

(7) qu̱rbā́n de šə̀m here used as affectionate form of address.

(9) xalk here written for the more common xalq. k for q (see GP §§ 26.2, 39).

zmā, zmunẓ (11) possess. forms of pers.pron. (see GP §77.3)

(12) wárkṛay ši 3d sing.pres. II passive of warkawém verb IV Here the perfect participle is used instead of the passive participle (GP § 97).

(14) xu̱šā́la for xu̱šẖā́la

nor is adj. I when used with things rather than persons.

(18) mo pron.part. used as object.

TRANSLATION

Immediate Fruit

(1) The story goes that somewhere an old man was busy planting an olive tree.

(2) A king came upon him. For a while he stood thinking about him.

(3) Finally he said to him: "Old man! This is not the time for you to plant an olive tree.

(4) Because you are an old man, you stand at the edge of the grave.

(5) And an olive tree is a tree of a kind that bears fruit (only) after a long time.

(6) Thus god knows whether yours may be such a long life or not that you might eat the fruit of this tree."

(7) The old man said to him: "My dearest King ("may I be sacrificed for you"),

(8) I don't plant it with this intention that I shall be alive and shall be eating its fruit.

(9) But I plant it in order that indeed after me other people will eat its fruit.

(10) This is the very tradition of the world that one (man) plants it and it is left for another.

(11) People in the past had planted them for us, and we will be planting them for the sake of those who come after us."

(12) When he said this, it pleased the king a great deal, and he ordered that a prize be given to him.

(13) When the old man received the prize, he said to the king: "Look, how quickly my tree bore fruit."

(14) The king enjoyed this statement even more and commanded: "Give him another prize."

(15) When they gave him another prize, he said again to the king: "Look, other trees bear fruit once a year and my tree bore fruit twice in one hour."

(16) The king appreciated this speech even more and ordered: "Give him another prize."

(17) The king moved away from him and said to his friends:

(18) "Let's get going. If we stay still longer with this old fellow, then he will relieve us of all (our) money."

EXERCISES

I. QUESTIONS ON TEXT:

Write suitable answers in Pashto to the following ten questions. Formulate other questions on the text yourself and answer them.

۱. سړی په څه لگیا و؟

۲. بڼوون کوم *قسم ونه ده ؟

---

* qi̱səm see 9.8

٠٣ يو سپين ږيرى چېرى ولاړ وي ؟

٠٤ سپين ږيري په كوم نيت ونه كرله ؟

٠٥ موږ يې د چا د پاره كرو ؟

٠٦ د دنيا سلسله څه ده ؟

٠٧ پاچا ولې سپين ږيري ته انعام وركړ ؟

٠٨ سپين ږيري پاچا ته څه وويل ؟

٠٩ د سپين ږيري ونې په يو ساعت كې څو واره مېوه ونيوله ؟

٠١٠ پاچا ولې له سپين ږيري نه روان شو ؟

II. WRITING:

A. Write the following words in the Pashto alphabet and comment on the correlation between alphabet and pronunciation:

(a) faā́l, ju̲mā́t, ananā́t, jami̲yát, ú̲mer, mālúm, i̲zát, saát, i̲nā́m.

(b) merabānī́, ami̲yát, āyingár, hāl, saí̲b, Islā́, hu̲jrá, bās (3.14), hú̲kəm, xu̲šā́l.

(c) u̲súl, maxsús, hāsi̲lā́t, xlāsawə́m, sāni̲yá.

(d) tālə́b, matboā́t, lutf, sultā́n, fitratán.

(e) hāzə́r, huzúr, mawzó, māzún (2.4).

B. Look up some of the words of A above in the Word Index to familiarize yourself with the order of the Pashto alphabet.

III. GRAMMAR:

A. Study the agreement in number, case, gender, (person) between subject and verb in all pertinent sentences in texts 1, 2, 3, 4, 5, 6. Observe how the actor (in the oblique case!) who has to be expressed in all sentences with a transitive verb in one of the past tenses, is outside of this agreement: e.g., spinẓíri inʿā́m wā́xist (13 above) "The old man received the prize." is constructed like "By the old man (actor, obl.) the prize (subj.,dir.sing.masc.) was received (3d sing. masc. past II)." (GP §§ 100.2a, 103.3a)

B. Form sentences using the various actors and subjects indicated in the parentheses and make the verb form agree:

(a)	də́	də xpə̆l pír núm	wā́xist.
	(saṛáy, musāfí̲r, ze, spinẓíray)	(i̲nʿā́m, mewá, mewé, sawǵā́t, baxši̲šúna)	(wā́xistəla, wā́xistəle, wā́xistəl)
(b)	pāčā́	puṣtə́na	wə́kṛa.
	(day, ṯāləbā́n, keliwā́l, hártsok, tə)	(puṣtə́ne, ámər, melá)	(wə́kṛe, wə́kəṛ)
(c)	saṛí	mewé	wárkṛe.
	(paṣtún, pālawā́n, haləkā́n)	(mewá, i̲nʿā́m, čərgā́n, paysé)	(wárkṛa, wárkəṛ, wárkṛəl)
(d)	spí	zə́	wə́xwaṛələm.
	(spi pl., zə, muẓ, tə)	(muẓ, tə, mewá, mewé)	(verb form?)
(e)	mā̀	kitābúna	wayə́li wə̀.
	(raís, dā́ lóy saṛáy, etc.)		(forms of likə́m, warkawə́m, taqdimawə́m, tarjumà kawə́m, ẓḍəm, nísəm, áxləm)

C. Rewrite text 6 using the present tense for all past tenses.

D. Rewrite text 5 in the past tenses as if conditions described were a thing of the past: e.g., tśo kóra . . . prātə́ we (5.1), etc.

UNIT 7

ملا نصرالدين

وايي چه يوه ورځ ملا نصرالدين نادار و. د کور په خوا کې يې يو سخت سړی اوسېده چه له ملا هم ساده و. ملا بام ته وخوت او په زوره يې په دعاوو بريد وکه: "خدايه، سل روپۍ راکه، که يوه يې کمه يې نې اخلم."

موذي چه دا خبره واورېده، نه نوي روپۍ يې په دسمال کې وتړلې او د ملا بام ته يې ورواچولې.

ملا پيسې وشمېرلې او له ځان سره يې وويل: "خدايه، تا خو سل روپۍ راکړې، خو يوه روپۍ يې استاوزي په لارې کې پټه کړه." سخت سړي چه دا خبره واورېده، په منډه د ملا کره راغی او روپۍ يې له ملا نه وغوښتې.

ملا نصرالدين ورته وويل: "ما ته خدای روپۍ راکړې خو لکه چه يوه روپۍ يې تا پټه کړه. ځه، دا به ښه يي چه نه ته څه وايې او نه زه."

سخت سړی لاړ او د قاضي نه يې امر راووړ.
ملا نصرالدين ورته وويل: "نو خر او چپن دې راکه چه درسره لاړ سم."

چه محکمې ته ولاړل، قاضي ملا ته په غصه شو. ملا قاضي
ته وویل: "قاضي صاحبه، ته مه خپه کېږه، د دې سړي دا
خوی دی. زه ډاربږم چه اوس به ووایي چه دا خر او چپن
هم د ما دي."

سخت سړي چه دا خبره واورېده، بېخي لیونی سو او په
چپنې یې خپېړې ولګولې چه له ملا یې وباسي. قاضي یو ټبر
تند سړی و؛ سخت سړي ته یې وویل: "لاس دې له ملا لرې
که او تند ځه، که بیا دې په چا دعوا وکړه، سخته سزا به
درکم."

TRANSCRIPTION

mu̲lā̀ nasru̲dín

(1) wā́yi či̲ yawà wrádz mu̲lā̀ nasru̲dín nādā́ra wə.

(2) də kór pə xwā́ ke ye yaw sáxt saṛáy osedə́ či̲ lə mu̲lá hàm sā̈dá wə.

(3) mu̲lā́ bā́m ta wə́xot aw pə zóra ye pə dwā́wo bríd wəkə:

(4) "xwdā́ya, sə́l ru̲pə́y rā́ka, ka yawá ye káma yì né àxləm."

(5) mozí či̲ dā́ xabə́ra wā́wreda, nə́nawì ru̲pə́y ye pə du̲smā́l ke wə́taṛəle aw də mu̲lā́ bā́m ta ye wərwā́čawəle.

(6) mu̲lā́ paysé wə́šmerəle aw lə dzā́n sara ye wə́wayəl:

(7) "xwdā́ya, tā́ xo sə́l ru̲pə́y rā́kṛe, xò yawá ru̲pə́y ye astā́wzi pə lā́re ke pə́ṭa kṛà."

(8) sáxt saṛí či̲ dā́ xabə́ra wā́wreda, pə mə́nḍa də mu̲lā́ kara

rā́ǥay aw ru̱péy ye le mu̱lā́ na wéǥu̱ṣtè.

(9) mu̱lā̀ nasru̱dín wèrta wéwayel: "mā̀ ta xwdā́y ru̱péy rā́kṛe,

xo léka či̱ yawá ru̱péy ye tā́ péṭa kṛà;

(10) dzá, dā́ ba ṣé yì či̱ nè té tsè wéwāye aw nè zé."

(11) sáxt saṛáy lā́ṛ aw le qāzí na ye ámer rā́woṛ.

(12) mu̱lā̀ nasru̱dín wèrta wéwayel: "no xár aw čapén de rā́ka

či̱ dérsara lā́ṛ sem."

(13) či̱ mākamé ta wlā́ṛel, qāzí mu̱lā́ ta pe ǥu̱sá šu.

(14) mu̱lā́ qāzí ta wéwayel: "qāzí sāhí̱ba, té mé xapà kéẓa,

(15) de dé saṛí dā́ xúy da. zé ḍāréẓem či̱ òs ba wéwāyi či̱

dā́ xár aw čapén hám de mā́ di."

(16) sáxt saṛí či̱ dā́ xabéra wā́wreda, bexí lewanáy su aw pe

čapéne ye xapéṛe wélagawele či̱ le mu̱lā́ ye wébāsi.

(17) qāzí yaw ḍér tú̱nd saṛáy we. sáxt saṛí ta ye wéwayel:

(18) "lā́s de le mu̱lā́ lére ka aw tú̱nd dzà,

(19) ka byā́ de pe čā́ dāwá wékṛa, sáxta sazā́ ba dárkem."

GLOSSARY

(1) nā́dāra adj. V 'moneyless, poor'

(2) xwā, pl. xwā́we, xwāgā́ne f 3, f 5 'side'

saxt, fem. sáxta adj. I 'miserly, difficult'

sādá adj. V 'simple, simple-minded, naive'

(3) bām, pl. bāmúna m 1 'roof'

wéxot 3d sing.masc.past II of xéžem, past xat- verb II (intrans.) 'to climb, rise'

pe zóra adv. 'loudly, strongly' (zor m 'power')

duˁā́wo obl.pl. of duˁā́, pl. duˁā́we, duˁāgā́ne f 3, f 5 'prayer'

brid m '(sudden and quick) start, attack'

(4) sel num. 'hundred'

ru̱péy dir.pl. of ru̱péy f 4 'rupee'

káma dir.sing.fem. of kam adj. I 'less, little'

yi 3d sing.pres. II of aux. yem; dialectal for wi

(5) moẕí, pl. moẕyā́n m 2 'miser; crook'

wā́wreda 3d sing.fem.past II of áwrem, past awred- verb II (trans.) 'to hear'

nèhnawí num. '99'

du̱smā́l (also desmā́l), pl. du̱smālúna m 1 'handkerchief'

wétaṛele 3d pl.fem.past II of taṛém verb I 'to tie'

werwā́čawele 3d pl.fem.past II of wèračawém verb I (trans.) 'to throw (to him, to her, to them)' (prefix wer-)

(6) wéšmerele 3d pl.fem.past II of šmerém verb I 'to count'

le . . . sara prep.-adv. phrase 'from'

(7) astā́wzi obl.sing. of astā́wzay, pl. astā́wzi m 4 'messenger'

lā́re obl.sing. of lā́r, pl. lā́re f 1 'way, road'

péṭa kṛà 3d sing.fem.past II of peṭawém verb IV-A (trans.) 'to hide, steal' (peṭ adj. I 'hidden,secret')

(8) pə mə́nḍa adv. 'running, in a run' (mə́nḍa f 1 'run')

kára adv. 'to the house'

wə́ǵuṣte 3d pl.fem.past II of ǵwā́ṛəm, past ǵuṣt-
verb II (trans.) 'to demand, ask for'

(9) lə́ka či̱ conj. 'it seems that'

(10) nə́ . . . nə́ conj. 'neither . . . nor'

(11) qāẓ̈í, pl. qāẓ̈yā́n m 2 'judge'

rā́woṛ 3d sing.masc.past II of rāwṛə́m verb I
'to bring'

(12) xar, pl. xrə m 5 'donkey, ass'

čap̌én, pl. čapéne f 1 '(Afghan) overcoat'

də́rsara adv. 'with you' (prefix də́r- or dar-)

(13) maẖkamé obl.sing. of maẖkamá, pl. maẖkamé f 2 'court'

ǵ̱usá, pl. ǵ̱usé f 2 'fury, anger, grief'

(14) mə neg.particle 'not'

xapá adj. V 'angry, annoyed, sad'

xapà kéẓəm verb IV 'to become angry'

(15) xuy, pl. xuyúna m 1 'habit, custom'

ḍāréẓəm, past ḍāred- verb II (intrans.) 'to be
afraid, to fear'

(16) bexí adv. 'absolutely, entirely, completely'

lewanáy, fem. lewanə́y adj. III 'crazy, mad'

xapə́ṛe dir.pl. of xapə́r f 1 'grasp (of fingers),
claw'

wə́lagawəle 3d pl.fem.past II of lagawə́m verb I (trans.)

'to attach, put on, grab'

(17) tu̠nd, fem. tú̠nda adj. I 'sharp, quick, quick-tempered'

(18) lére kawém verb IV (trans.) 'to remove, take away'

(19) daʕwā́, pl. daʕwā́we, daʕwāgā́ne f 3, f 5 'accusation'

sazā́, pl. sazā́we, sazāgā́ne f 3, f 5 'punishment'

dárkem 1st sing.pres. II of darkawém verb IV (trans.)

'to give (to you)' (prefix dar- or der-)

NOTES

This text, like texts 4, 5, was written by A. Ahad Yari. His dialect shows some very common features (see below).

A grammatical analysis of this text was included in the Pashto translation of GP: de paṣtó gṛāmár (Kabul, College of Literature of Kabul University, 1961), translated by Mohammad Rahim Elham, pp. 210 ff.

Mulā Nasru̠din, written nas̤r aldin, is the hero of many popular Afghan stories.

(3) dwā́wo for duʕā́wo

(4) ne contracted from ne (na) 'not' and the pron.part. ye (GP § 78.2)

(8) kara or kór ta (GP § 55.4d)

(10) yi for wi (as in 4)

(11) lāṛ for wlāṛ past II of dzem verb IV

qāzí for qāz̤i

(12) lā́ṛ sem for wlā́ṛ šem pres. II of dzem; but wlā́ṛel (13)

(13) mākamé for mahkame

(15) de mā dialectal for zmā. de is the author's form for the prep. də.

da 'is' here for day. In some dialects da is used for masc. and fem.

(16) su also səm (12 above) for šu, šəm in many Afghan dialects, also in Kandahar (GP § 30.2)

(19) dāwá, pl. dāwé colloquial for daʕwā́ (dāwā́)

TRANSLATION

Mulla Nasrudin

(1) The story goes that one day Mulla Nasrudin was without money.

(2) Next to his house a miserly man was living who was even more simple-minded than the Mulla.

(3) Mulla climbed to the roof and loudly he (suddenly) began to pray:

(4) "O god, give me a hundred rupees. If one of them is missing, I don't take them"

(5) When the miser heard this talk, he tied 99 rupees into a handkerchief and threw them to Mulla's roof.

(6) Mulla counted the money and said to himself:

(7) "God, you certainly gave me a hundred rupees, but the messenger stole one rupee on the way."

(8) When the miser heard this statement, he came running to Mulla's house and demanded the rupees from Mulla.

(9) Mulla Nasrudin said to him: "God gave me the rupees, but it seems that you stole one of them.

(10) Go, it will be good, if neither you say anything nor I."

(11) The miser went and brought an order from the judge.

(12) Mulla Nasrudin told him: "Then give me (your) donkey and 'chapan', so that I go with you."

(13) When they went to the court, the judge became angry at Mulla.

(14) Mulla said to the judge: "Mr. Judge, don't get annoyed.

(15) It's a habit of this man. I fear that he will say now that this donkey and 'chapan' are also his ("mine")."

(16) When the miser heard this talk, he got altogether wild and laid his hands on the chapan in order to take it off Mulla.

(17) The judge was a very quick-tempered man. He said to the miser:

(18) "Take your hand away from Mulla and go quickly.

(19) If you made an accusation against someone again, I will give you a severe punishment."

EXERCISES

I. QUESTIONS ON TEXT:

Write answers in Pashto to the following questions:

١٠ سخت سړی چېری اوسېده ؟

٢٠ ملا کومه دعا وکړه ؟

٣٠ موږي ناداره سړی و ؟

٤٠ روپۍ شنګه د ملا و کور ته راغلې ؟

٥٠ یوه روپۍ ولې کمه وه ؟

٦٠ سخت سړي له چا نه امر راووړ ؟

۰۷ قاضي ولي په غصه شو ؟

۰۸ موذي ولي لېونی شو ؟

۰۹ چېن د چا وه ؟

۰۱۰ سخت سړي روپۍ ببرته واخيستلې ؟

II. GRAMMAR:

(1) Identify in texts 6 and 7 the verbal forms grammatically and investigate their syntactical and semantic significance: e.g., osedé (7.2) 'was living', wéxot 'climbed (7.3), ba xwrém 'will be eating' (6.8), etc.

(2) Study in texts 1 to 7 the use of past I, past II, and the perfect tenses, and decide which English tense forms correspond to the Pashto forms (GP §§ 92, 96).

(3) Describe the formation of past II (from past I?) in the following forms: rānénawot (2.6), rágay (2.3), ksénāst (3.5), wéke (7.3), wáčawele (7.5), ráwoṛ (7.11).

(4) Review the classes of the Pashto verb (GP §§ 83-88):

What is the suffix of the intransitive IV-A verb?

What is the 3d sing.masc.past ending?

(5) How is the imperative formed? (GP § 91)

(6) Write Pashto sentences using the Pashto forms in parentheses and Pashto equivalents for the English forms:

(a)	mulā́	bā́m ta	wéxot.
	(halekā́n, čérga 'hen')		(wlāṛ)
	(čərg, čergā́n, čérge,		(was climbing,
	ṭelefuní)		climbs, has climbed)

(b) m̲u̲lā́ paysé wə́šmerəle.

(māmurín, m̲u̲dír, spinẓíray) (wə́sātəle, rā́kṛe, dárkṛe)

(was counting, counts, has been counting, will be counting, will count)

(c) Ahmáda, paysé rā́ka!

(raís s̤ā̲h̲i̲b, kučnyā́n, spinẓíray, haləkā́n) (wə́šmera, wə́rkṛa, wə́sāta)

(don't give me, give them, don't count)

(d) saṛáy de m̲u̲lā́ kara rā́ǵay.

(saṛí, bəzə́rg, moz̲í, paṣtāné) (rawā́n šu, nénạwot)

(was coming, had come, will be coming, will come)

UNIT 8

موجوده نثر

نثر د ادب یوه مهمه برخه او یو ضروري شی دی. یوه ژبه هغه وخت ترقی کولای شي چه نثر یې وسعت ومومي او د نثر لمن یې له هر ډول مضامینو څخه ډکه شي. د پښتو نثر په دې موجوده عصر کښې لکه چه ګورو د ترقۍ پر لاره قدم ایښی دی. هر ډول مضامین او نثرونه لکه تاریخی، تعلیمی، ادبی، اصلاحي، اجتماعي، فکاهي، سیاسي، علمي او داسې نور پکښې داخل شوي دي. ګرامري، لغوي او د ډرامو نثرونه هم پدې وخت کښې ورو ورو په ډېرېدو دي.

لنډه دا چه د زمانې د غوښتنې سره سم د پښتو په موجوده نثر کښې پوره تحول او بدلون راغلی دی، او هر ډول کتابونه پکښې که څه هم لږ دي، لیکل شوي او لیکل کېږي.

د موجوده نثر سبک نزدې د منشي احمد جان روان کړی سبک دی. ساده او روان، په محاوره برابر، په پښتو لغاتو ښایسته، په خوږو او لنډو جملو ښکللی د دې وخت د نثر سبک ګڼل کېږي. هو! لکه چه په هر وخت کښې ځینې کمزوري او خراب لیکونه وي، په دې وخت کښې هم البته چه دغسې لیکونه شته، مګر هغو ته اعتبار نه ورکول کېږي.

TRANSCRIPTION

mawjudá náser

(1) náser de adáb yawà mu̱hi̱ma bárxa aw yàw zarurí šáy day.

(2) yawà žéba háǥa wáxt taraqí kawélāy šì či̱ náser ye wasʿát wémumi aw de náser lamén ye le hár ḍáwl mazāmíno tsexa ḍáka ši.

(3) de paṣtò náser pe dé mawjudá áser kṣe léka či̱ góru de taraqéy per lāro qadám íṣay dày.

(4) hár ḍàwl mazāmín aw nasrúna léka tārixí, tālimí, adabí, i̱slāhí, i̱jti̱māí, fakāhí, si̱yāsí, i̱lmí aw dáse nór pèkṣe dāxi̱l šéwi di.

(5) grāmarí, lu̱ǥawí aw de ḍrāmó nasrúna hám pe dé wáxt kṣe wró wró pe ḍeredó di.

(6) lánḍa dá či̱ de zamāné de ǥuṣténe sara sám de paṣtó pe mawjudá náser kṣe purá tahawél aw badlún rāǥélay day,

(7) aw hàr ḍáwl ki̱tābúna pèkṣe, ka tsé hàm léẓ di, likèl šéwi aw likèl kéẓi.

(8) de mawjudá náser sábk nezdé de Mu̱nšì Ahmád Ján rawán kéṛay sábk day.

(9) sādá aw rawán, pe mehāwerá barābár, pe paṣtó lu̱ǥáto ṣāystá, pe xwaẓó aw lánḍo ju̱mló ṣkelélay, de dé wáxt de náser sábk gaṇèl kéẓi.

(10) hó! léka či̱ pe hár wáxt kṣe dzíne kamzóri aw xaráb likúna wì, pe dé wáxt kṣe hám albatá či̱ daǥáse likúna

štá, mágar hagó ta etibā́r né warkawə̂l kézi.

GLOSSARY

mawjudá adj. V 'modern'

nā́sər, pl. nasrúna m 1 'prose, prose-writing'

(1) adáb, Ar.pl. adabiā́t 'literature' (m)

zarurí adj. V 'necessary'

šay, pl. šayā́n, ši m 2, m 3 'thing'

(2) žə́ba, pl. žə́be f 1 'language, tongue'

taraqí, pl. taraqə́y f 4 'progress'

wasʕát, pl. wasʕatúna m 1 'broadening, expansion'

wə́mumi 3d sing.pres. II of múməm, past mund- (mind-) verb II (trans.) 'to find'

lamə́n, pl. lamə́ne f 1 'hem, edge, area'

mazāmíno obl.pl. of mazmún, Ar.pl. mazāmín 'article, subject' (also m 1)

ḍáka ši 3d sing.fem.pres. II of ḍakézəm verb IV-A (intrans.) 'to become full, rich' (ḍak adj.I 'full')

(3) paṣtó f 'Pashto'

ʕásər, pl. ʕasrúna m 1 'age, era'

lə́ka či conj. 'as'

qadám, pl. qadamúna m 1 'step'

íṣay day 3d sing.masc.perf. of (i)ẓdə́m verb IV (trans.) 'to place, put'

(4) lə́ka conj. 'like, as'

tārixí adj. V 'historical'

taʕlimí adj. V 'educational'

adabí adj. V 'literary'

i̱slāẖí adj. V 'correcting, improving, moral'

i̱jti̱māʕí adj. V 'sociological, social'

fakāhí adj. V 'comical, satirical'

si̱yāsí adj. V 'political'

ʕi̱lmí adj. V 'scientific'

pə́kṣ̱è adv. 'in it, there'

dāxì̱l šə́wi di 3d pl.masc.perf. of dāxi̱léẓəm verb IV-A (intrans.) 'to get included, to enter'

(5) grāmarí adj. V 'grammatical'

lu̱ǥawí adj. V 'lexical'

ḍrāmó obl.pl. of ḍrāmá, pl. ḍrāmé f 2 'drama, play'

wró wró adv. 'slowly, gradually'

ḍeredó obl. of ḍeredə́l verb.subst. of ḍeréẓəm verb IV-A (intrans.) 'to increase' (ḍer adj.I 'much')

(6) lanḍ, fem. lánḍa adj. I 'short, brief'

zamāná, pl. zamāné f 2 'time'

ǥu̱ṣtə́na, pl. ǥu̱ṣtə́ne f 1 'demand'

sam, fem. sáma adj. I 'even, equal, direct, straight'

purá adj. V 'complete'

taẖawə́l, pl. taẖawəlúna m 1 'change, reform'

badlún, pl. badlumúna m 1 'change'

(7) ka tsə́ hàm conj. 'although, even though'

ləẓ adj. I 'little, small (in number, quantity)'

(8) sabk, pl. sabkúna m 1 'style'

rawā̀n kəṛay dir.sing.masc.perf.part. of rawānawə́m verb IV-A (trans.) 'to make clear, improve'

(9) rawā́n, fem. rawā́na adj. I 'easy flowing'

mah̲āwará (məh̲āwərá), pl. mah̲āwaré f 2 'conversation'

barābár, fem. barābára adj. I 'resembling, equal, patterned alike'

lug̸̲ā́to obl. pl. of lug̸̲ā́t, pl. lug̸̲atúna, Ar. lug̸̲ā́t m 1 'word'

ṣāystá adj. V 'pretty, attractive'

ṣkəlélay, fem. ṣkəléle adj. IV 'beautified'

xwaẓó obl.pl. of xoẓ, fem. xwaẓá adj. II 'sweet, attractive'

j̲umló obl.pl. of j̲umlá, pl. j̲umlé f 2 'sentence'

gaṇə̀l kéẓi 3d sing.pres.I passive of gaṇém verb I 'to consider'

(10) ho part. 'yes'

kamzóri dir.pl.masc. of kamzóray, fem. kamzóre adj. IV 'weak' ("with little power")

xarā́b, fem. xarā́ba adj. I 'bad'

likúna dir.pl. of lik m 1 'writing; letter'

albatá adv. 'of course'

dag̸áse dem.pron. 'such'

i̲ʿti̲bā́r, pl. i̲ʿti̲bārúna m 1 'value, esteem'

šta 3d pres. '(there) are; is' (also sta)

NOTES

This selection is taken from de paṣtó de adáb tāríx ("A History of Pashto Literature") by Sadiqullah Rishteen (ṣadiq alláh ri̲ṣtín) (Kabul, 1954), p. 143f. Rishteen, a native of Ghaziābād in the province of Ningrahār, is the author of many books and articles on the Pashto language. He was the president of the Pashto Academy in Kabul, is now Pashto adviser to the Afghan Ministry of Education and teaches Pashto at Kabul University.

(1) zarurí for z̈aruri

(2) Note the Arabic spellings in this text: naser, wasʿat, maz̈āmin, ʿaser (3), taʿlimi (4), i̲slāhi, i̲jti̲māʿi, ʿi̲lmi, tahawel (6), mahāwara (9), i̲ʿti̲bār (10).

wémumi use of present II, see GP § 90.5a

(3) íṣay perf.part., see GP § 93.4a, 4b

(4) adjectives in í see GP § 76.2a

(6) ǵu̲ṣténa f 1 from ǵwā́ṛem, past ǵu̲ṣt-, for word formation see GP § 67.5a

(7) likèl šéwi 3d pl.masc.perf.passive of likém without aux. di, probably due to the influence of Persian, see GP § 96.3.

(8) Munši Ahmad Jān, a native of the Peshawar region, is the author of many books on Pashto.

(10) kamzóray, for word formation see GP § 76.1

eti̲bā́r for i̲ʿti̲bār

TRANSLATION

Modern Prose

(1) Prose (writing) is an important part and a thing necessary in literature.

(2) A language can make progress at that time when its prose may have found a wider scope and the area of its prose writing may be enriched from all kinds of subjects.

(3) The prose of Pashto in this modern era, as we see, has taken steps forward on the roads of progress.

(4) All types of subjects and prose, such as historical, educational, literary, moral, sociological, comical, political, scientific (ones) and others like that have been included in it.

(5) Grammatical, lexical (prose),and the prose of dramas are also at this time slowly on the increase.

(6) To put it briefly: in accordance with the demands of the time in modern Pashto prose a complete reform and change has come,

(7) and all kinds of books, even though they are small (in number),have been written in it and are being written.

(8) The style of modern prose is close to the style improved by Munshi Ahmad Jan.

(9) Simple and clear, patterned like conversational speech, pretty with Pashto vocabulary, beautified with nice and short sentences: (this) is considered the style of the prose of this time.

(10) Yes, as in each time there will be some weak and bad writings, also at this time there is, of course, such writing but it is not valued.

EXERCISES

I. QUESTIONS ON TEXT:

Write answers in Pashto to the following ten sentences:

۱. نثر د کوم شي مهمه برخه ده ؟

۲. یوه ژبه کله ترقي کولی شي ؟

۳. کوم ډول مضامین او نثرونه لیکل کېږي ؟

٤. د ډرامو نثرونه هم په پښتو کښې داخل شوي دي ؟

٥. مدققین کوم قسم نثرونه لیکي ؟

٦. په پښتو کښې ډېر کتابونه اوس ترجمه شوي دي او ترجمه کېږي ؟

۷. په ادب کښې د منشي احمد جان نثر اهمیت لري ؟

۸. د موجوده نثر سبك باید څنګه وي ؟

۹. د پښتو د نثر بدلون ضروري و که نه ؟

۱۰. و کمزورو او خرابو لیکونو ته اعتبار ورکول کېږي که نه ؟

II. GRAMMAR:

A. Study and explain the occurrence of present II (perfective present) forms in texts 1-8 (GP § 90).

B. Describe the formation of the following present II forms (from present I ?): wi (5.1), xlāṣ kṛi (6.18), wə́darezu (6.18), yi (7.10), dárkəm (7.19), wémumi (8.2), ḍáka ši (8.2). Where do present I (imperfective present) forms contrast with present II forms? (GP § 89)

C. Write Pashto sentences with present II forms using the appropriate Pashto forms in parentheses and the Pashto equivalents of the English forms:

1. də dé də pā́ra rāǵəlay dày či ṭelefún jóṛ kṛì.
   (kitā́b wṛā́nde kawə́m, maqālé tàqdimawə́m, mewé xwrə̀m)

2. spinẓíray ba mewá wə́xwri. (áxləm, warkawə́m, rāwṛə́m)
   (day, zə, paṣtún, kučnyā́n, muẓ) (will be eating, will take, will be taking, will give them, will be bringing)

3. náṣər tsə́nga wə́liku?
   (kitā́b, kitābúna) (rawānéẓəm, rawānawə́m, wā́yəm, tarjumá kawə́m)

4. pə ǵám aw ṣādí kṣe hāẓír wi.
   (ṣār, dā́ jamʕiyát, xarā́b likúna) (melé kéẓi, héts imtiyā́z nə́ larə̀m, iʕtibā́r nə́šta)

D. Rewrite text 4 using present II forms indicating a usual and likely occurrence: e.g., də nawróz pə wrádz melá wə́si, etc.

UNIT 9

پالوده

په کندهار کښې د پالودې وخت د اول مني يعني د ميزان څخه شروع کېږي او تر جوزا پورې دوام کوي . نو پالوده تقريباً په کال کې اته مياشتې موجوده وي يو سړی چه کوزده وکړي ، د خپلې نجل کور ته د دود په ډول يو څو مجمې پالوده ورلېږي . پالوده تر لسو مجمو کمه نه وي او ډېرې يې تر پنځوسو مجمو بلکه زياتو پورې هم رسېږی . د پالودې مجمې که لږې وي د يوه سړي پر سر ، او که ډېرې وي ، د څلورو يا پينځو تنو پر سر څو څو مجمې د نجلۍ کور ته په خورا ښايسته او ښکلي وضعيت ورو ړل کېږي . مثلاً پنځوس مجمې د پينځو تنو پر سر يو پر بل سربېره پرتې وي . د هر سړي د مجمو پر سر يوه مجمه د مروارېو (جالې) پرته وي . دا جاله چه په مجمه کښې په مخروطي شکل پرته او په قسم قسم رنگونو گلداره او رنگ شوې او د هر ډول گلانو بوټي پرې د رول شوي وي وړله کېږي . دا ښايسته دوې درې مجمې په مخ کښې ، نورې پسې روانې وي ؛ پداسې حال کښې چه د زوم د کور يو لا رښوونی (ځری) ورسره وي . د نجل کور ته چه پالوده ورو ړي ، د پالودې مزدوران ، مجمې پر سر ، ولاړ وي ، او تر هغو يې نه بړدي څو کومه هديه او تحفه ورنکړه شي . بالاخره چه يو څه ورکړي ، نو پالوده کښېږدي . د نجلۍ کورنۍ پالوده په کور او کلي او لرې او نژدې خپلوانو و وېشي ، او په سبا روځ پالوده والا په خالي مجمو پسې سړی راولېږي او مجمې يوسي . د نجل د کور د خوا د زوم د کور سړي ته چه د پالودې سره راغلی وي يوه خولۍ يا پگړۍ د تحفې په توگه يا يې په هغه گړۍ ورکړي او يا يې کور ته ورواستوي

TRANSCRIPTION

pāludá

(1) pə kandahā́r kṣe də pāludé wáxt də awál mə́ni yā́ne də mizā́n tsəxa šu̱rò kéẓi aw tər jawzā́ pòre dawā́m kawì.

(2) no pāludá taqribán pə kā́l ke atə́ myā́šte mawjúda wì.

(3) yàw saṛáy či̱ kozdá wə́kṛi, də xpə́le njə́l kór ta də dód pə ḍáwl yàw tsó majmé pāludá wərleẓí.

(4) pāludá tər láso majmó káme né wi aw ḍére ye tər pi̱ndzóso majmó, bálke zyā́to pòre hám raséẓi.

(5) də pāludé majmé ka léẓe wi də yawə́ saṛí pər sár, aw ka ḍére wi, də tsalóró yā pindzó tàno pər sár tsó tsó majmé də njələ́y kór ta pə xwarā́ ṣāystá aw ṣkéḷi wazi̱yát warwṛə̀l kéẓi.

(6) masalán pi̱ndzós majmé də pindzó tàno pər sár yáw pər bə́l sarbə́ra praté wi.

(7) də hár saṛí də majmó pər sár yawá majmá də mirwārə́yo (jālé) pratá wi.

(8) dā́ jālá či̱ pə majmá kṣe pə maxrotí šákəl pratá aw pə qí̱səm qí̱səm rangúno guldā́ra aw ràng šə́we aw də hár ḍáwl gu̱lā́no búṭi prè darawə̀l šə́wi wi, wṛə̀la kéẓi.

(9) dā́ ṣāystá dwé dré majmé pə máx kṣe, nóre pəsè rawā́ne wì:

(10) pə dā́se hā́l kṣe či̱ də zúm də kór yaw lā́rṣowénay (dzéray) wə̀rṣará wi.

(11) də njə́l kór ta či̱ pāludá wárwṛi, də pāludé mazdurā́n, majmé pər sár, walā́ṛ wì,

(12) aw tər háǥo ye nə́ ẓdì tsò kúma hadyá aw tofá warnə́kṛa šì.

(13) bə́lāxi̱rà` či̱ yàw tsə́ wárkṛi, nò pāludá kṣə́ẓdi.

(14) də njələ́y koranə́y pāludá pə kór aw kə́li aw lə́re aw nəždé xpəlwā́no wə́weši,

(15) aw pə sabā́ rwádz pāludàwālā́ pə xālí majmó pəsè saṛáy rāwə́leẓi aw majmé yósi.

(16) də njə́l də kór də xwā́ də zúm də kòr saṛí ta či̱ də pāludé sara rāǥə́lay wi, yawà xwalə́y yā pagṛə́y də tofé p̣ə tóga yā́ ye pə haǥə́ gaṛə́y wàrkṛi aw yā́ ye kór ta wərastawí.

GLOSSARY

pāludá, pl. pāludé f 2 "paluda"

(1) awál, fem. awála adj. I 'first'

mə́ni obl.sing. of mə́nay, pl. mə́ni m 4 'autumn'

yáʿne adv. 'that is, i.e.'

Mizā́n m "Mizān"

tər . . . póre prep.-adv.phrase 'until, up to'

Jawzā́ f "Jawzā"

dawā́m m 'duration'

dawā́m kawə́m verb IV 'to last'

(2) taqribán adv. 'approximately'

atə́ num. 'eight'

myā́šte dir.pl. of myāšt f 1 'month'

mawjúda dir.sing.fem. of mawjúd adj. I 'present, extant'

(3) kozdá, pl. kozdé f 2 'engagement'

kozdá kawə́m verb IV 'to get engaged'

njəl, pl. njə́le f 1 'girl, fiancée'

yàw tsó indef.pron. 'some'

majmé dir.pl. of majmá f 2 'tray, dish, platter'

wərleẓí 3d sing.pres. I of wərleẓə́m verb I (trans.) 'to send to them' (wər- prefix)

(4) láso obl. of las num. 'ten'

pi̱ndzóso obl. of pi̱ndzós num. 'fifty' also pandzós

bálke adv.,conj. 'even, but'

zyā́to, obl.pl. of zyāt, fem. zyā́ta adj. I 'more, increased' (4.14)

raséẓi̤ 3d sing.pres. I of raséẓəm, past rased- verb II (intrans.) 'to reach, arrive'

(5) sar, pl. sarúna m 1 'head, top'

tsalóro obl. of tsalór num. 'four'

tsó tsó indef. pron. 'some'

njələ́y, pl. njúne f 6 'girl'

ṣkə́li obl.sing.masc. of ṣkə́lay, fem. ṣkə́le adj.IV 'pretty, attractive' waz̤ʿi̱yát, pl. waz̤ʿi̱yatúna m 1 'arrangement, situation'

warwṛ̀əl kéẓi see Notes and (11) below

(6) mas̱alán adv. 'for instance'

sarbéra adv. 'upon, on top'

praté dir.pl.fem. of prot, fem. pratá adj. II 'placed, lying'

(7) mirwāréyo obl. of mirwārí m 3 pl. 'noodles, mirwāri'

jālé obl.sing. of jālá, pl. jālé f 2 'noodles'

(8) maxrot̲í adj. V 'conical, cone-shaped'

šákəl, pl. šaklúna m 1 'shape, form'

qí̱səm, pl. qi̱smúna m 1 'kind, type'

rangúno obl.pl. of rang, pl. rangúna m 1 'color; manner, way'

gu̱ldā́ra adj. V 'colored' (also gu̱ldā́r adj. I)

ràng šə́we (wi) 3d sing.fem.perf. II of ràng kéẓəm verb IV 'to become colored'

gu̱lā́no obl.pl. of gu̱l, pl. gu̱lā́n m 2 'flower'

búṭi dir.pl. of búṭay m 4 'plant'

darawə̀l šə́wi wi 3d pl.perf.II passive of darawə́m verb I (trans.) 'to place, put; stop'

wṛə́la kéẓi 3d sing.fem.pres. I passive of wṛəm, pres. II yŏs-, past I wṛ-, past II yŏwṛ- verb IV (trans.) 'to carry (off)'

(9) max (also məx), pl. maxúna m 1 'front; face'

pəsé adv. 'behind, after'

(10) zum, pl. zumā́n m 2 'bridegroom'

lārṣowə́nay, pl. lārṣowə́ni m 4 'guide'

dzə́ray, pl. dzə́ri m 4 'guide'

wə́rsara adv. 'with them' (prefix wər and sara)

(11) wárwṛi 3d pl.pres. II of warwṛə́m verb I (trans.) 'to carry to them'

mazdurā́n dir.pl. of mazdúr m 2 'servant'

walā́ṛ dir.pl.masc. of walā́ṛ , fem. walā́ṛa adj. I 'standing'

ẓdi see i̲ẓdí (1.11)

(12) tso conj. 'until'

hadyá, pl. hadyé f 2 'gift'

tuẖfá, pl. tuẖfé f 2 'gift'

(13) bí̲lāxi̲rà adv. 'finally'

yàw tsə́ indef.pron. 'something'

(14) xə́lwā́no obl.pl. of xpəl, pl. xpəlwā́n m 2 'relative'

koranə́y f 4 'family'

wə́weši 3d pl.pres. II of wə́šəm verb I (trans.) 'to distribute'

(15) sabā́ adv. 'tomorrow'

pāludàwālā́ m 'paluda salesman'

xālí adj. V 'empty'

rāwə́leẓi 3d sing.pres. II of rāleẓə́m verb I 'to send to us' (prefix rā-) (3 above)

yósi 3d sing.pres. II of wṛəm verb IV (8 above)

(16) xwaléy, pl. xwaléy, xwạli(g)ā́ne f 4, f 5 'hat'

pagṛéy, pl. pagṛéy, pagṛi(g)ā́ne f 4, f 5 'turban'

pe tóga adv. 'in the manner, as'

yā́ . . . yā́ conj. 'either . . . or'

gaṛéy f '(point of) time'

werástawí 3d pl.pres. I of werastawém verb I (trans.) 'to send to (them)' (prefix wer-)

NOTES

This text is from paṣtaní dodúna ("Afghan Customs") by the Literature Branch of the paṣtó ṭoléna (Kabul: 1957), and was written by Abdul Khāliq Wāsaei.

pāluda is an Afghan dish consisting of milk rice, sirup and a kind of noodles called mirwārí or jālá (from Persian) (7 below).

(1) Mizān is from September 24 to October 24: Jawzā from May 22 to June 21.

(2) wi 3d sing.pres. II of aux. In this text many present II forms occur beside occasional present I forms like werleẓí (3), wṛéla kéẓi (8), ẓdi (12), werastawí (16), to indicate customary but merely probably events (GP § 90.2). Examples are: wi (4) (6) (7) (9) (10) (11), wárwṛi (11), warnékṛa ši (12), wárkṛi, kṣéẓdi (13), wéweši (14), rāwéleẓi, yósi (15), wárkṛi (16). Perfect II forms occur in the same meaning (GP § 96.4a):

darawèl šéwi wi (8), rāǵélay wi (16)

(5) warwṛèl kéẓi 3d pl.fem.pres. I passive here for warwṛéla kéẓi of warwṛém verb I 'to bring to them'

(10) lārṣowénay in the sense of lārṣowúnkay 'showing the way' (GP § 93.2a)

(12) warnékṛa ši 3d sing.fem.pres. II passive of warkawém verb IV 'to give to them'. As to position of the negation né see GP § 102.1c.

tofá for tuh̲fa

(13) kṣéẓdi pres. II of ẓdem verb IV

bélāxi̱rà (bí̱lāxi̱rà) is written bālāxi̱ra

(14) nežde obl.pl.masc. adj. V variant of nezdé

(15) rwadz variant of wradz f 1 'day'

TRANSLATION

(1) In Kandahar the time for paluda starts the beginning of fall ("first fall"), i.e., in Mizan, and lasts until Jawza.

(2) Thus about eight months in the year paluda will be available.

(3) Somebody who gets engaged customarily sends to the house of his girl some trays of paluda.

(4) (Of) paluda there will be no less than ten trays and more than that up to fifty trays but it goes even beyond that.

(5) The trays of paluda, if they should be small in number, on the head of one man, and, if they should be many, on the heads of four or five persons -- a certain number of trays is being carried to the house of the girl in a very pretty and attractive arrangement.

(6) E.g., fifty trays may be placed on the heads of five people, one on top of the other.

(7) One tray of mirwari (noodles) will be placed on top of the trays of each man.

(8) These noodles, which are placed on the tray in conical shape and flowery and colored by various kinds of colors and upon which plants of every kind of flowers will have been put, are being carried.

(9) These pretty two (or) three trays will be in front, the others will follow behind,

(10) in such a way that a guide from the family of the bride-groom will be with them.

(11) When they have taken the paluda to the house of the girl, the paluda servants, the trays on their heads, will be standing,

(12) and they do not put them (down) until some gift and present will be given to them.

(13) Finally when they will give them something, then they will put down the paluda.

(14) The family of the girl will distribute the paluda in the house and the village and (among) far and near relatives.

(15) And the next day the paluda salesman will send a man after the empty trays, and he will carry the trays away.

(16) From the girl's house to the man from the groom's house, who will have come with the paluda, they will give a hat or turban as a present either at that time or they send it to his house.

EXERCISES

I. QUESTIONS ON TEXT:

Write answers in Pashto to the following ten questions:

١. په کندهار کې د پالودې وخت کله وي ؟

٢. څو مجمې پالوده د نجل کور ته ورلېږلې کېږي ؟

٣. د پالودې مجمې د څو تنو پر سر وروړلې کېږي ؟

٤. مرواري کوم شکل ، رنگ او وضعیت لري ؟

٥. له مزدورانو سره د زوم د کور له خوا څوك حاضر وي ؟

٦. د پالودې مزدوران تر څه وخته مجمې پر سر ولاړ وي ؟

٧. دا ټوله پالوده د نجلۍ په کور کښې خوړله کېږي ؟

٨. خالي مجمې څوك وړي ؟

٩. د نجلۍ د کور له خوا څه شی لارښوونکي ته ورکول کېږي ؟

١٠. د پالودې لېږل د چا دود دی ؟

II. GRAMMAR:

A. Find examples of the passive phrases in texts 8 and 9 and identify them grammatically (GP § 97).

B. Rewrite the following active Pashto sentences by changing them into passive constructions;

e.g., m̲ulā́ paysé wə́šmerəle (7.6): paysé də m̲ulā́ lə xwā̀ wə́šmerəle šwé.

1. sáxt saṛí dā́ xabə́ra wā́wreda (7.8).

2. yaw bə́l kitā́b mi tarjumà kə́ṛəy dəy (1.9).

3. t̲āləbā́no pu̲ṣtə́na wə́kṛa (2.6).

4. šéx ye wə́west (2.12)
5. pəxwā̃nó xálko wə́ne karə́le wə̃ (6.11).
6. spinẓíri i̱nˤā́m wā́xist (6.13).
7. wə́ne zə́r mewá wə́niwəla (6.13).

UNIT 10

ا ــ کاریزکن د نهېدلي کاریز له خټو لاندې
دوه ساعته وروسته ژوندی راوایستل شو.

کوهدامن : بابه خان کاریزکن چه د کوهدامن د کره باغ بازار تــه نژدې کاریز د یوې برخې د نهېدلو په اثر تر ختـو او خاورو لانـدې شوی و ، له دوو ساعتو نه وروسته ژوندی له خاورو څخه راوایستل شو. هغه کاریزکن د کره باغ د کلای بي بي اوسېدونکی دی. د کره باغ حاکـم پخپله د هغه د نجات په عملیاتو کښې گـډون درلود ، تر دې چه هغه نهېدلې خاورې یوې خوا ته شوې ، او بابه د بې هوشۍ پـه حال کښې ژوندی ورڅخه راوایستل شو. او له یو ساعت تداوۍ نـه وروسته بېرته روغ رمټ شو او خپل کور ته لاړ.

ب ــ د قندهـار حکامو او مامورینو تـه د
دولت د پروگرامو په باب د توضیحاتو ورکول

وړمه ورځ د قندهار د ولایت د نائب الحکومه تر ریاست لانـدې د دارالحکومګۍ په سالون کښې یو مجلس شوی و ، چه په هغه کښې د قندهار د مرکز مامورینو د کاتب تر درجې پورې ، لویو حاکمانو ، محلي حاکمانـو ، علاقداارانو ، او د حکومتو او علاقداریو مامورینو گـډون کړی و. پدغـه مجلس کښې نائب الحکومه د دولت د پروگرامو او د هغو په تطبیقولـو کښې د مامورینو د وظیفو په باب وینا وکړه او د هغوی د زیاتـې همکارۍ هیله یې وکړه.

TRANSCRIPTION

(a) kā̀rezkán də naṛedə́li kāréz lə xáṭo lā̀nde dwá
sāáta wrústa žwandáy rāwə́estəl šù.

Kodāman: (1) Bā̀ba Xā́n kā̀rezkán či̲ də Kodāmán də Karabā́ǥ bā́zār ta nəždé kā̆réz də yawe bárxe də naṛedə́lo pə asár tər xáṭo aw xā́wro lā́nde šə́way wə, lə dwó sāáto na wrústa žwandáy lə xā́wro tsə̀xa rāwə́estəl šu.

(2) haǥá kārezkán də Karabā́ǥ də Kalā́y Bibí osedúnkay dáy.

(3) də Karabā́ǥ hākí̲m pəxpə́la də haǥá də ni̲jā́t pə amali̲yā́to kṣə gaḍún dərlód,

(4) tər də́ či̲ haǥá naṛedə́le xā́wre yawé xwā́ ta šwè, aw Bābá´ də behušə́y pə hā́l kṣə žwandáy wə́rtsəxa rawə́estəl šu.

(5) aw lə yáw sāát tadāwə́y na wrústa bə́rta róǥ ramáy šu aw xpə́l kór ta lā́ṛ.

(b) də Kandahā́r hu̲kā́mo aw māmuríno ta də dawlát də
progrāmó pə bā́b də tawzihā́to warkawə́l.

(1) wə́ṛma wrádz də Kandahā́r də wi̲lāyát də nāyə̀bəlhu̲kumá tər ri̲yāsát lā́nde də dā̀ru̲lhu̲kumagə́y pə sālún kṣə yaw majlí̲s šə́way wə,

(2) či̲ pə haǥə́ kṣə də Kandahā́r də markáz māmuríno də kātí̲b tər darajé pòre, lóyo hāki̲mā́no, màhalí hāki̲māno, aḷāqadārā́no, aw də hu̲kumató aw alāqadārə́yo māmuríno gaḍún kə̀ṛay wə.

(3) pə daǥá majlí̲s kṣə nāyə̀bəlhu̲kumá də dawlát də progrāmó

aw de hagó pe tatbiqawélo kse de māmuríno de wazifó pe bā́b waynā́ wékṛa aw de hagúy de zyā́te hamkāréy híla ye wékṛa.

GLOSSARY

(a) kā̀rezkán, pl. kā̀rezkanā́n m 2 'canal digger'

kā̀réz, pl. kāṛezúna m 1 'canal'

naṛedéli obl.sing.masc.perf.part. of naṛéẓem, past naṛed- verb II (intrans.) 'to fall down, collapse'

le . . . lā́nde prep.-adv.phrase 'from below'

xáṭo obl.pl. of xáṭa, pl. xáṭe f 1 'mud'

rāwéestel šu 3d sing.masc.past II passive of rābā́sem verb III 'to pull out'

(1) bāzā́r, pl. bāzārúna m 1 'bazaar'

de . . . pe asár prep.-adv.phrase 'because of'

xā́wro obl.pl. of xā́wra, pl. xā́wre f 1 'dust, earth'

lā̀nde šéway we 3d sing.past perf. of lā̀nde kéẓem verb IV 'to get below, underneath'

le . . . na prep. 'from'

(3) h̲ākí̲m, pl. h̲āki̲mā́n m 2 '(local) governor', Ar.pl. h̲u̲kā́m

pexpéla adv. 'by oneself, personally' (prep. pe and xpel adj. I)

ni̲jā́t m 'rescue'

ʿamali̲yā́to obl. of ʿamali̲yā́t Ar.pl. m 'operations'

gaḍún m 'participation'

(4) behušéy obl.sing. of behuší f 4 'unconsciousness'

wértsexa adv. 'from it'

(5) tadāwéy obl.sing. of tadāwí f 4 'medical treatment, cure'

róğ ramáy, fem. róğa raméy adj. 'completely recovered' (roğ, fem. róğa adj. I 'healthy, sound')

bérta adv. 'again' (1.11: bírte)

(b) ḫukā́mo obl.pl. (10a.3 above)

dawlát, pl. dawlatúna m 1 '(central) government, power'

progrāmó obl.pl. of progrā́m, pl. progrāmúna m 1 'program'

de . . . pe bā́b prep.-adv.phrase 'concerning, about'

tawẕiḫā́to obl. of tawẕiḫā́t Ar. pl. m 'explanations, descriptions'

(1) wéṛma wrádz f 'day before yesterday'

wi̱lāyáṭ, pl. wi̱lāyatúna m 1 'province'

nāyèbelḫu̱kumá (nāyi̱bu̱lḫu̱kumá), pl. nāyèbelḫù̱kumagā́n m 2 'governor (of a province)'

ri̱yāsát, pl. ri̱yāsatúna m 1 'chairmanship'

ter . . . lā́nde prep.-adv.phrase 'under'

dā̀ru̱lḫu̱kumagéy obl.sing. of dā̀ru̱lḫu̱kumagí, pl. dā̀ru̱lḫu̱kumagéy f 4 '(governor's) administration building' sālún, pl. sālunúna m 1 'reception room'

majlí̲s (majlés), pl. majli̲súna m 1 'meeting, gathering'

(2) kātí̲b, pl. kāti̲bā́n m 2 'secretary, clerk'

darajé obl.sing. of darajá, pl. darajé f 2 'rank, degree'

lóyo h̲āki̲mā́no obl.pl. of lóy h̲ākí̲m, pl. lóy h̲āki̲mā́n m 2 'district governor' (adj. loy 'big')

mah̲alí h̲āki̲mā́no obl.pl. of mah̲alí h̲ākí̲m m 2 'local governor' (mah̲alí adj.V 'local')

ʿalāqadārā́no obl.pl. of ʿalāqadā́r, pl. ʿalāqadārā́n m 2 'rural administrator'

h̲u̲kumató obl.pl. of h̲u̲kumát, pl. h̲u̲kumatúna m 1 'government, governmental district'

ʿalāqadāréyo obl.pl. of ʿalāqadārí, pl. ʿalāqadāréy f 4 'rural district'

gaḍún kawém verb IV 'to participate'

(3) tat̲biqawélo obl. of tat̲biqawél verb.subst. m pl. 'carrying out, applying, application' (from tat̲biqawém verb IV-A 'to apply')

waz̄ifó obl.pl. of waz̄ifá, pl. waz̄ifé f 2 'duty, task, assignment'

waynā́, pl. waynā́we, waynāgā́ne f 3, f 5 'speech'

hamkāréy obl.sing. of hamkārí, pl. hamkāréy f 4 'cooperation'

híla, pl. híle f 1 'hope'

NOTES

Text 10a is from the Kabul daily Iṣlāḥ, issue of October 3, 1960, p. 6. Text 10b is from the Kabul daily Hēwād, issue of July 10, 1958, p. 4.

The underground canal (kāréz) is important for irrigation in Afghanistan.

naṛedéli attributive use of perf.part., see GP § 93.4c (also 4 below)

sāʕáta plural, see GP § 63.1a, 1b

(1) Kohdāman is a fertile area directly north of the city of Kabul. Qarabagh, here spelled karabāġ, is a village on the main road from Kabul to Charikar.

naṛedélo, also warkawél (10b), taṯbiqawélo (10b.3) are forms of verbal substantives, which are masc.pl. forms (GP § 93.3)

xáṭo, xā́wro: mass nouns usually occur in the plural (GP § 63.3a)

(2) Kalā́y Bibí is a Persian place name. qalā́, pl. qalā́we, qalāgā́ne f 3, f 5 'fort, fortress, village' Bibí is a woman's name.

osedúnkay, fem. osedúnke adj. IV is the verbal adjective of ósəm (osézəm) verb II, here used as a substantive (GP § 93.2a).

(5) lāṛ for wlāṛ

(b) Kandahār is often still spelled Qandahār (but see text 9), but the q is always pronounced as /k/ in this name.

(3) pə daǥá here written together (GP § 42.5b) daǥá, haǥó, haǥúy, also haǥə́ (2), haǥá (10a.2, 3, 4 above). Note the final stresses on dem.pron. forms, which indicate references to previously mentioned nouns. dáǥa would be anticipatory or emphatic (GP § 80.3,4).

TRANSLATION

Text 10a

Canal-digger was pulled out alive two hours afterwards from below the mud of a fallen canal

Kohdaman: (1) The canal-digger Bāba Xān, who had become [buried] under mud and earth because of the collapsing of one part of a canal close to the bazaar of Kohdaman's Karabagh, was pulled out alive from the earth after two hours.

(2) That canal-digger is a resident of "Bibi's Fort".

(3) The (local) governor of Karabagh participated himself in the rescue operations,

(4) until the fallen earth was brought ("became") to one side and Baba was pulled from it in a state of unconsciousness.

(5) After one hour's medical treatment he became again completely recovered and went to his house.

Text 10b

The giving of explanations to Kandahar's governors and officials about the programs of the (national) government

(1) The day before yesterday under the chairmanship of the governor of the province of Kandahar a meeting was held in the reception-room of the governor's administration building,

(2) in which the officials of the capital of Kandahar (down) to the rank of clerk, district governors, local governors, rural administratρrs, and the officials of the governmental and rural districts participated.

(3) At this meeting the governor (of the province) made a speech about the programs of the government and the duties of the officials in carrying them out and expressed the hope of their increased cooperation.

EXERCISES

I. QUESTIONS ON TEXT:

Answer the following questions in Pashto:

١. کاریزکن څنګه تر خاورو لاندې شوی و ؟

٢. بابه خان چېرې اوسېده ؟

٣. بابه خان څونه وخت وروسته راوابستل شو ؟

٤. د کره باغ حاکم د بابه خان د راابستلو په وخت کښې څه وکړه ؟

٥. بابه خان د راابستلو په وخت کې په کوم حال و ؟

٦. آیا بابه خان د راابستلو نه وروسته سمدستي کور ته ولاړ ؟

٧. د مامورینو مجلس په کوم ځای کې و ؟

٨. په مجلس کښې چا ګډون کړی و ؟

٩. د کندهار د مرکز کاتبانو هم په دې مجلس کې برخه اخیستې وه ؟

١٠. چا ویناوې وکړې ؟

II. GRAMMAR:

A. Explain formation and use of the nominal forms derived from verbs (GP § 93) and the potential phrases (GP § 95) that have occurred in the texts:

ḍeredó (8.5), ṣodélọ (4.5), wahélo (4.7) ṭākéli (4.2),

karéne (6.3), g̸uṣténe (8.6), kawéla̅y ši (8.2).

B. Write the nominal forms of the verb and the optative (GP § 94) of the following verbs:

nísəm, dzəm, ṭākém, rāwṛém, áxləm, joṛawém,

raséẓəm.

Examples: taṛém

verbal adjective: taṛúnkay, fem. taṛúnke

verbal substantive: taṛél, obl. taṛélo

passive participle I: taṛél, fem. taṛéla

passive participle II: wétaṛəl, fem. wétaṛəla

perfect participle: taṛélay, fem. taṛéle

optative: taṛ(él)ā̄y

UNIT 11

يوازې پښتو

دا لوست په يوازې پښتو ليکم، چه د بلې ژبې يو توری پکښې نشته.

هوکې! د ژبې ښه والی هم دغه دی چه هره ژبه ښايي دومره ارته وي چه د ژبې څښتن هر راز د زړه وينا په خپله ژبه ويلای شي. که څه هم ژبې يو د بله و مرستې ته سره اړې دي او يوازې کومه ژبه بشپړه نه ليدله کېږي، بيا هم ځينې ژبې له خپله ځانه دونه ويناوې او توري لري چه څښتن يې مړنی وي، نو په لږ زيار د پردو له اړی څخه وزي.

د عربو ژبه هغه ژبه ده چه د نړۍ د ژونديو او لويو ژبو څخه بلله کېږي. خو سره له دغه هم ځينې پردي توري پکښې سته چه د دغې ژبې پوهانو راښوولي دي. دغسې هم د اوسنۍ ژوندۍ نړۍ لويې ژبې لکه انګرېزي او فرانسوي يا نورې ژبې پردي، لاتيني يا يوناني توري پخپل منځ کښې لري.

پاړسو هم يوه خوږه ژبه ده چه دا زر کاله راهيسې د مېړنيو مشرانو تر سيوری لاندې يې روزنه کېږي. خو سره له دې دونه روزنې هم و يوازې پاړسو ليکلو ته بيچ نه ليدل کېږی، او ډېره به درنه وي چه يوازې پاړسو وليکله شي. هرو مرو به و عربي ژبې ته اړ شو او که نه يوه ليکه يا دوې درې ليکې به په ډېر زيار وليکلې شي. له ښه مرغه زموږ پښتو ژبه ډېره ارته ده. موږ که لږ څه زيار وکاږو، نو په خپله ژبه به هرڅه په يوازې پښتو وليکو، که څه هم موږ اړ نه يو چه هرو مرو به يوازې پښتو ليکو. د نړۍ ټولې ژبې يوه

د بلې په مرسته بشپړه کېږي، خو بيا هم دا د ژبې ښه والی دی چې
يوه ژبه دومره ارته وي او دومره توري ولري چې د بلې ژبې له اړې
څخه ووزي. دا څرګنده ده چې زموږ پښتو ژبه د هر څه د پاره بېل
بېل توري لري او د لوېو غرو په لمنو کښې د سپينو پښتنو په زړو کښې
ښخ دي. که څوک پلټنه پسې وکړي، ډېرې ويناوې او ډېر توري به
ومومي چې اوس نشته يا موږ ته څرګند نه دي.

TRANSCRIPTION

yawā́ze paṣtó

(1) dā́ lwást pə yawā́ze paṣtó likə́m či̲ də bə́le žə́be yáw tóraỳ pə̀ke ˀnə́sta.

(2) hóke! də žə́be ṣəwā́lay ham dáǵa dáy čī hára žə́ba ṣā́yi dómra árta wi, či̲ də žə́be tsəṣtán hár rā́z də zṛə́ waynā́ pə xpə́la žə́ba wayə́lāy ši.

(3) ka tsə́ hám žə́be yáw də bə́la wə mrā́ste ta sarà áṛe di aw yawā́ze kùma žə́ba bə̀̆speṛ́a nə́ lidə̀la ké̦zi, byā́ hám dzi̲ńe žə́be lə xpə́la dzā́na dóna waynā́we aw tóri larí či̲ tsəṣtán ye maṛanáy wi,

(4) nə̀ pə lə́ẓ zyā́r də pradó lə aṛə́y tsəxa wúzi.

(5) də arábo žə́ba háǵa žə́ba da či̲ də naṛ́ə́y lə žwandə́yo aw lwáṛo žə́bo tsə̀xa balə̀la ké̦zi.

(6) xo sarā́ lə dáǵə hám dzí̲ne pradí tóri pəkè stā́ či̲ də də́ǵe žə́be pohā́no rāṣowə́li di.

(7) daǵáse ham də osanə́y žwandə́y naṛə́y lwáṛe žə́be lə̀ka

angrezí aw frānsawí yā nóre žébe pradí, lāṭịní´yā yunāní, tóri pə xpə́l mándz ke larí.

(8) pāṛsó hám yawà xwaẓá žə́ba da či dá zə́r kā́la rāhíse də meṛanə́yo məšərāno tər syóri lānde ye rozə́na kéẓi.

(9) xo sará lə dé dóna rozə́ne hám wə yawā́ze pāṛsó likə́lo ta bíč nə́ lidə̀l kéẓi,

(10) aw ḍéra ba draná wi či yawā́ze pāṛsó wə́likəla ši.

(11) harú marú ba wə arabí žə́be ta áṛ šù aw ka ná, yawá líka yā dwé dré líke ba pə ḍér zyā́r wə́likə̀le ši.

(12) lə ṣə̀ mə́rǵa zmíẓ paṣtó žə́ba ḍéra árta da.

(13) míẓ ka lə́ẓ tsə̀ zyā́r wə́kāẓu, nò pə xpə̀la žə́ba ba hártsə·pə yawā́ze paṣtó wə́liku,

(14) ka tsé hám míẓ àṛ nə̀ yu či harú marú ba yawā́ze paṣtó likú.

(15) də naṛə́y ṭóle žə́be yawá də bə́le pə mrásta bə́šperaṛa kéẓi.

(16) xo byā́ hám dā́ də žə́be ṣəwā́lay dày či yawá žə́ba dóna árta wi aw dómra tóri wə́lari či də bə́le žə́be lə aṛə́y tsəxa wə́wuzi.

(17) dā́ tsargánda da či zmíẓ paṣtó žə́ba də hártsə də pāra bél bél tóri larí aw də lóyo ǵró pə laménə ke də spíno paṣtanó pə zṛó ke ṣáx di.

(18) ka tsók palaṭə̀na pəsə̀ wə́kṛi, ḍére waynā́we aw ḍér tóri ba wə́mumi či ós nə́šta yā míẓ ta tsargánd nə́ di.

GLOSSARY

yawā́ze adj. V 'only'

paṣtó, pl. paṣtówe, paṣtogā́ne f 3, f 5 'Pashto'

(1) lwast, pl. lwastúna m 1 'lesson' (lwə́ləm, past lwast- verb II 'to read')

tóray, pl. tóri m 4 'letter, sound, word'

(2) hókè interj. 'yes, indeed'

ṣəwā́lay m 4 '(high) quality'

ṣā́yi adv. 'of necessity'

art (árat), fem. árta adj. I 'wide, rich'

tsəṣtán (tsaṣtán), pl. tsəṣtanā́n m 2 'owner, master'

rāz m 'kind, type'

zṛə, pl. zṛúna m 1 'heart'

(3) ka tsə́ hám conj. 'although'

mrásta (mrə́sta), pl. mráste f 1 'aid, help'

aṛ, fem. áṛa adj. I 'in need of, dependent on'

bə́špəṛ, fem. bə́špəṛa adj. I 'complete'

wínəm, past lid- verb III (trans.) 'to see'

byā́ hám conj., adv. 'even so'

dóna dem.pron. 'so much, so many'

maṛanáy, fem. maṛanə́y adj. III 'powerful'

(4) zyār m 'effort'

pradáy, fem. pradə́y adj. III 'foreign'

aṛí, pl. aṛə́y f 4 'dependence'

(5) ʕaráb m 'Arab'

naṛə́y f 4 'world'

lwaṛ, fem. lwáṛa adj. I 'superior, high, great'

bóləm, past bal- verb II (trans.) 'to call'

(6) poh, pl. pohā́n m 2 'scholar'

rāṣéyəm, past rāṣow- (rāṣod-) verb III (trans.) 'to show' (prefix rā-)

(7) osanáy, fem. osanéy adj. III 'present, current' (os adv. 'now')

angrezī́ f 'English' (also adj. V)

frānsawī́ (farānsawī́) f 'French' (also adj. V)

lāṭinī́ adj. V; f 'Latin'

yunānī́ adj. V; f 'Greek'

mandz, pl. mandzúna m 1 'middle, center'

(8) pāṛsó f 'Persian'

xoẓ, fem. xwaẓá adj. II 'sweet, attractive'

rāhī́se part. 'since, hither'

meṛanáy, fem. meṛanéy adj. III 'powerful, able, courageous'

méšər, pl. meš(ə)rā́n m 2 'leader'

syóray, pl. syóri m 4 'shadow'

rozéna, pl. rozéne f 1 'education, cultivation'

(9) bič m '(envisaged) solution, possibility'

(10) drund, fem. draná adj. II 'heavy, difficult'

(11) harú marú adv. 'certainly, definitely'

ʕarabī́ adj. V; f 'Arabic'

líka, pl. líke f 1 'line'

(12) merǵ m 'fortune'

(13) kā́ẓem verb I (trans.) 'to pull out'

zyā̀r kā́ẓem 'to exert one's effort'

hártse indef. pron. 'everything'

(17) tsargánd, fem. tsargánda adj. I 'clear, evident, known'

bel, fem. béla adj. I 'separate'

ǵar, pl. ǵrúna m 1, m 5 'mountain'

spin, fem. spína adj. I 'white'

ṣax, fem. ṣáxa adj. I .'buried'

(18) palaṭéna, pl. palaṭéne f 1 'investigation, research, search'

néšta '(there) is not; are not' (neg. né and šta)

NOTES

This selection, like unit 1, was taken from <u>de paṣtó kelí</u> ("The Key to Pashto"), Vol. II, part 3, 51st lesson (Kabul: 1940), pp. 211-213.

(1) tóray is used here as a Pashto form instead of luǵát (12.1) or lafẓ̄ (12.9)

nésta for néṣta in Kandahar, Logar and elsewhere (GP § 30.2), also sta (6 below), but néšta (18 below), ši (2, 10, 11).

(2) árta wi, present II after ṣā́yi (GP § 90.5b)

wayélāy ši potential phrase (GP § 95)

(3) yáw de béla masc. sing., here for yawá de béle (15 below)

waynáwe plural form (f 3) usual in Kandahar

(4) pradó i.e., žébo

(8) pāṛsó here for fārsí

(10) wə́likəla ši present II of passive phrase

(11) wə́likəle ši as above; present I occurs: likə̀la kéẓi (3 above), balə̀la kéẓi (5), lidə̀l kéẓi (9) (GP § 97)

(12) mə́rǵa obl.case II (GP § 65.1b)

TRANSLATION

Only Pashto

(1) This lesson I write in Pashto only, so that there is not a single word of another language in it.

(2) Yes indeed! The quality of a language is also this that every language ought to be that rich that the speaker of the language can say everything that he desires to express ("every kind of talk of his heart"), in his own language.

(3) Although languages are dependent on each other for help and any language by itself is not seen as complete, yet some languages have by themselves so many expressions and words that their speaker may be powerful,

(4) then with little effort they move out of the dependence on foreign (ones).

(5) The language of the Arabs is that language which is considered one of the living and superior languages of the world.

(6) Yet in spite of that there are some foreign words in it which the scholars of this language have shown to us.

(7) In the same way also the important languages of the present living world like English and French or other languages have right in their midst foreign, Latin or Greek,words.

(8) Persian is also one attractive language which has been cultivated for these (last) thousand years under the care of able leaders.

(9) Yet in spite of this much cultivation the potential of writing pure ("only") Persian is not seen,

(10) and it will be very hard to have pure Persian written.

(11) Inevitably we will depend on the Arabic language and if not: one or two, three lines will be written with a great effort.

(12) Fortunately our Pashto language is very rich.

(13) If we make (just) some little effort, we will write everything in our language in pure Pashto,

(14) although we are not required that we must write only Pashto.

(15) All the languages of the world become complete through each other's help.

(16) But still that is the quality of a language that one language be that rich and that it contain that many words that it may escape from the dependence on another language.

(17) It is obvious that our Pashto language has separate words for everything and that they are buried at the edges of huge mountains in the hearts of pure Pashtoons.

(18) If someone would search after them, he will find many expressions and many words, that don't exist now or are not known to us.

پښتو څنگه ولیکو ؟

ځینې وایي پښتو باید سوچه کړو، پردي لغات ترینه وباسو او یو ټکی فارسي یا عربي پکښې پرې نږدو.

دا نظریه په ډېر افراط بناء ده او دا کار کېدونکی نه دی. په دنیا کښې داسې ژبه نشته چه پردي لغات پکښې نه وي او نیلې، ریښې یې له نورو ژبو سره تړلې نه وي. جهان اوس لکه یو کور داسې دی او د ملتونو فرهنگي او اجتماعي تعلقات ورځ په ورځ زیاتېږي. اوس د هرچا غږ د بل غوږ ته رسېږي او نا آشنا آوازونه یو له بله آشنا کېږي.

هره ژبه له بلې نه څه اخلي او څه ورکوي.

د اولسونو د گډ ژوند سیاست په ژبو باندې هم تاثیر لري او پردي لغتونه خپلېږي. هغه وخت چه هېوادونه یو له بله ډېر لرې و او اولسونه به یو د بل په ژبه ښه نه پوهېدل، بیا هم په ژبو کښې دخیل کلمات موجود و او د لغاتو په نړۍ کښې معرب، مفرس، مفغن الفاظ پیدا شوي و. نو اوس دا څنگه کېدای شي چه په پښتو ژبه کښې دې پردي لغات نه وي. هغه نوې معناگانې او نوي مفهومونه چه په جهان کښې اوس را پیدا کېږي، طبعاً په پښتو کښې نوم نلري، او دا نشي کېدای چه ټولو ته د نوو اختراعاتو په شمول په پښتو ژبه کښې نوي نومونه پیدا کړو. که څوک په دې فکر کښې وي چه مونږ دې له نورو ژبو نه څه نه اخلو او یوازې پښتو لغتونه دې استعمالوو، د دې معنا دا ده چه خپله ژبه دې محدوده وساتو او خپل فرهنگ دې په ډېر ابتدایي حال پرېږدو.

TRANSCRIPTION

paṣtó tsə́nga wə́likù?

(1) dzí̲ne wā́yi paṣtó bā́yad sučá kṛù, pradí lu̲ǥā́t tréna
wə́bāsù, aw yàw ṭə́kay fārsí yā arabí pəkè prenə́ẓdu.

(2) dā́ nazaryá pə ḍér i̲frā́t bi̲nā́ da aw dā́ kā́r kedúnkay nə́
dày.

(3) pə dunyā́ ke dā́se žə́ba nə́šta či̲ pradí lu̲ǥā́t pəkṣè nə́ wi
aw níle, riṣé ye lə nóro žə́bo sara taṛə́le nə́ wi.

(4) jahā́n ós lə̀ka yàw kór dā́se dày, aw də mi̲latúno farhangí
aw i̲jti̲māí tā̀lu̲qā́t wrádz pə wrádz zyātéẓi.

(5) ós də hárčā̀ ǥáẓ də bə́l ǥwáẓ ta raséẓi aw nāāšnā́
āwāzúna yáw le bə́la āšnā̀ kéẓi.

(6) hára žə́ba lə bə́le na tsə́ áxli aw tsə́ warkawí.

(7) də u̲ləsúno də gáḍ žwánd si̲yāsát pə žə́bo bā̀nde hám
tā̀sír larí aw pradí luǥatúna xpəléẓi.

(8) háǥa wáxt či̲ hewādúna yáw lə bə́la ḍér lére wə, aw
u̲ləsúna ba yáw də bə́l pə žə́ba ṣə́ nə́ pu̲hedə́l, byā́
hám pə žə́bo ke daxíl kali̲mā́t mawjúd wə,

(9) aw də lu̲ǥā́to pə naṛə́y ke mu̲aráb, mu̲farás, mu̲faǥán
alfā́z paydā̀ šə́wi wə.

(10) no ós dā́ tsə́nga kedā́y ši či̲ pə paṣtó žə́ba ke de pradí
lu̲ǥā́t nə́ wi.

(11) háǥa nə́we mā́nāgāne aw nə́wi mafhumúna či̲ pə jahā́n ke
ós rāpaydā̀ kéẓi, tabán pə paṣtó ke núm nə́larì,

(12) aw dā́ nə́ši kedā́y či̱ ṭólo ta de néwo i̱xti̱rā́āto pə šu̱múl pə paṣtó žə́ba ke néwi numúna paydā́ kṛù.

(13) ka tsók pə dé fí̱kər ke wì či̱ múnẓ de lə nóro žə́bo na tsé nə̀ àxlu, aw yawā́ze paṣtó lu̱ǵatúna de i̱stemālawú, də dé mānā́ dā́ da či̱ xpə́la žə́ba de mahḍúda wésātu aw xpə́l farháng de pə ḍér i̱bti̱dāyí hā́l préẓdu.

GLOSSARY

(1) bā́yad adv. 'of necessity' ("ought to", "must")
sučá adj. V 'pure'
sučà kawə́m verb IV 'to purify'
lu̱ǵát, pl. lu̱ǵatúna, Ar.pl. luǵā́t m 1 'word'
ṭə́kay, pl. ṭə́ki m 4 'point, dot, word'
fārsí f 'Persian (language)' also adj. V

(2) nažaryá (nažari̱yá), pl. nažaryé f 2 'opinion'
i̱frā́t m 'exaggeration'
bi̱nā́ adj. V 'based' (also bi̱nā́ f 5 'base')

(3) níla, pl. níle f 1 'root'
riṣá, pl. riṣé f 2 'root'

(4) jahā́n m 1 'world'
mi̱lát, pl. mi̱latúna m 1 'nation' (also mi̱llát)
farhangí adj. V 'cultural'
taʿalú̱q, Ar.pl. taʿalu̱qā́t m 'relation'
zyātéẓəm verb IV-A (intrans.) 'to increase'
(zyāt adj. I)

(5) g̸aẓ m 1 'sound, voice' variant of ẓag̸ (1.4)

g̸waẓ, pl. g̸waẓúna m 1 'ear'

nāāšnā́ adj. V 'unfamiliar'

āwā́z, pl. āwāzúna m 1 'voice, sound'

āšnā́ adj. V 'familiar'

(7) gaḍ, fem. gáḍạ adj. I 'mixed, joined, integrated'

žwand m 'life'

si̲yāsát, pl. si̲yāsatúna m 1 'policy'

tās̲ír, pl. tās̲irúna, Ar. tās̲irā́t m 1 'influence'

xpəléẓəm verb IV-A (intrans.) 'to become one's own, to be adopted' (xpəl adj. I)

(8) hewā́d, pl. hewādúna 'country' (also hi̲wā́d)

pu̲héẓəm, past pu̲hed- verb II (intrans.) 'to understand'

daxíl, fem. daxíla adj. I 'borrowed'

kali̲má, pl. kali̲mé f 2, Ar. kali̲mā́t m 'word'

(9) mu̲`aráb, fem. mu̲`arába adj. I 'made into Arabic, Arabicized'

mu̲farás, fem. mu̲farása adj. I 'made into Persian, Persianized'

mu̲fag̸án, fem. mu̲fag̸ána adj. I 'made into Pashto (Afghan), Afghanized'

lafẕ, pl. lafẕúna, Ar. alfā́ẕ m 1 'word'

paydā́ adj. V 'found, created'

paydā̀ kéẓəm Verb IV (intrans.) 'to be found, born, created'

(11) maʕnā́, pl. maʕnāgā́ne f 5 'meaning'

mafhúm, pl. mafhumúna m 1 'meaning'

rāpaydā́ adj. V 'created, found' (prefix rā-)

ṯabʕán adv. 'naturally'

(12) i̱xti̱rā́ʕ, pl. i̱xti̱rāʕgā́ne, Ar. i̱xti̱rāʕā́t f 5 'invention'

šu̱múl m 'inclusion, adoption'

paydā́ kawém verb IV (trans.) 'to create, give birth to, find' (see 9 above)

(13) i̱sti̱ʕmālawém verb IV-A 'to use, make use of' (i̱sti̱ʕmā́l m 1 'use')

mahdúd, fem. mahdúda adj. I 'limited'

farháng, pl. farhangúna m 1 'lexicon, vocabulary; knowledge'

i̱bti̱dāyí adj. V 'elementary, primitive'

NOTES

This selection was taken from Gul Pacha Olfat's i̱mlā́ aw i̱nšā́ ("A Few Notes on the Orthography and Composition of the Pashto Language"), (Kabul: 1959), p. 60. The author is president of the Paṣto ṭoléna in Kabul and a prominent Pashto poet and writer.

(1) tréna consists of tre (tər and ye) and the part. na.

prenéẓdu present II (perfective present) after bā́yad with the negation nə́ between prefix and verbal stem.

(2) kedúnkay, fem. kedúnke is the verbal adj. from kéẓəm (GP § 93.2a).

(3) taṛə́le wi perfect II phrase (GP § 96.4a)

(4) tā̀luqā́t for taʕaluqā́t

(7) gaḍ occurred in the adv. phrase pə gáḍa (5.6)

(8) ba . . . puhedə́l. The modal part. ba with a past I (imperfective past) form stresses duration and repetition (GP § 92.4a).

(10) kedā́y ši (also 12 below) potential phrase of kéẓəm

(11) mānāgā́ne for maʕnāgā́ne (GP § 7.3)

(13) istemā̀lawú for istiʕmālawu (GP § 8.3); mānā́ (or manā́) for maʕnā

de . . . áxlu, de . . . istiʕmā̀lawú, de . . . wə́sātu, de . . . préẓdu (prédu), also de . . . wi (10 above): the "imperative" particle de (Kandahar di) occurs before present I (imperfect present) and present II (perfective present) forms (GP §§ 89.4, 90.3c)

TRANSLATION

How Are We to Write Pashto?

(1) Some say we should make Pashto pure, take foreign words out from it, and not leave one word of Persian or Arabic in it.

(2) This opinion is based on great exaggeration and this job cannot be done.

(3) In the world there is no such language where there would not be foreign words in it and where roots, stems would not be linked by them with other languages.

(4) The world is now thus like one house, and the cultural and social relations of the nations increase day by day.

(5) Now everybody's voice reaches the ear of the other, and unfamiliar sounds become mutually familiar.

(6) Each language takes something from the other and gives something.

(7) The peoples' policy of an integrated life has influence also on languages, and foreign words are adopted.

(8) At that time when countries were very far from one another and peoples did not (usually) understand each other's languages well, even then loan words were present in the languages,

(9) and in the lexical world Arabicized, Persianized, Afghanized words had been created.

(10) How can this happen then now, that there should not be any foreign words in the Pashto language.

(11) Those new meanings and new denotations which are now created in the world, naturally do not have a name in Pashto.

(12) And this cannot be done that in the adoption of new inventions we create new names in the Pashto language for all (of them).

(13) If somebody should be of this opinion that we should not take anything from other languages and should use only Pashto words, then the meaning of this is that we should keep our language limited and leave our own lexicon in a very primitive state.

UNIT 13

د کوم ځای دی ؟

يو کور يې دلته دی ، بل په کابل کښې ، بل په يو بل ځای کښې . څه ځمکه په کوهدامن کښې لري ، څه په بغلان کښې ، څه په يو بل ځای کښې . نغدې روپۍ يې په رشوتونو دلته پيدا کړې ، مگر گټه ورباندې نور بانکونه کوي ، په يو بل ځای کښې .

ته وايه چه دی د کوم ځای دی ؟

مينه يې له دې خلکو سره نشته ، او د نورو ملکونو خلک ورته ډېر گران دي . د دې ځای ژبه يې نزده ، او په پرديو ژبو افتخار کوي .

د دې وطن له شعر او موسيقي نه خوند نه اخلي او د خارجي موزيک په صفت مهربري نه .

مونږ ته په نخوت او نفرت گوري او د پرديو مستخدمينو په مقابل کښې ډېره تواضع کوي .

ته وايه چه دی د کوم ځای دی ؟

دی د هيڅ ځای نه دی ، ځکه چه هر ځای د ده دی او سړی ورته هرځايي ويلی شي .

هو ! دا هغه مرغه دی چه څلور فصلونه په څلورو مملکتونو کښې تېروي او وطن نه لري .

وطن نه پېژني ، د يوه وطن په هوا کښې نه الوزي او د وطن سړې او تودې نه شي تېرولی .

دا هغه عياش دی چه بې له عيش و راحت نه نور څه نه پېژني او له وطن سره هيڅ مينه او علاقه نلري .

مونږ هغه کسان د دې وطن بللی شو چه د وطن په کانو او
بوټو سر ورکوي او په سختو ورځو کښې د وطن په کاریږي ، که څه هم
پوله او پټې نلري ، او په زړو کوڅو او جونګړو کښې اوسي .
هو! زما په عقیده دا وطن د هغه چا نه دی چه د ډېرو
ځمکو قبالې یې اخیستې دي ، بلکه د هغه چا دی چه د وطن مینه
یې په زړه کښې ده او له وطن سره علاقه لري .

TRANSCRIPTION

də kúm dzā́y dày?

(1) yáw kór ye də́lta dày, bə́l pə Kābú̱l ke, bə́l pə yàw bə́l dzā́y ke.

(2) tsə́ dzmə́ka pə Koḍāmán ke larí, tsə́ pə Bag̸lā́n ke, tsə́ pə yàw bə́l dzā́y ke.

(3) nág̸de ru̱pə́y ye pə ri̱šwatúno də́lta paydā́ kṛè, mágar gáṭa wə̀rbā́nde nór bānkúna kawí, pə yàw bə́l dzā́y ke.

(4) tə́ wə́wāya či̱ dáy də kúm dzā́y day?

(5) mína ye lə dé xálko sara nə́šta, aw də nóro mu̱lkúno xálk wə́rta ḍér grā́n di.

(6) də dé dzā́y žə́ba ye nə́zda aw pə pradə́yo žə́bo i̱fti̱xā́r kawì.

(7) də dé watə́n lə šér aw mosiqí na xwánd nə́ àxli aw də xāri̱jí mozík pə si̱fát maṛə́ẓi nà.

(8) múnẓ ta pə naxwát aw nafrát góri aw də pradə́yo mu̱staxdi̱míno pə mu̱qābí̱l ke ḍéra tawāzó kawì.

(9) tə́ wə́wā̀ya či̱ dáy də kúm dzā́y dày?

(10) dáy də héts dzā́y né day, dzə́ka či̱ hár dzā́y də dé day aw
saṛáy wə̀rta hardzāyí wayə́lay ši.

(11) hó! dā́ háǥa mərǥə́ day či̱ tsalór faslúna pə tsalóro
mamlakatúno ke tèrawí aw watán né larí.

(12) watán né pə́žanì, də yawə́ watə́n pə hawā́ ke né álwuzì
aw də watə́n saṛé aw tawdé nə́ ši terawə́lày.

(13) dā́ háǥa ayā́š day či̱ bé lə áyš u rāhát na nór tsè né
pə́žani aw lə watə́n sara héts mína aw alāqá nə́larì.

(14) múnẓ háǥa kasā́n də dé watə́n balə́lay šu či̱ də watə́n pə
kāṇó aw búṭo sár warkawí aw pə sáxto wrádzo ke
də watə́n pəkāréẓi,

(15) ka tsé hám púla aw paṭáy nə́larì, aw pə zaṛó koḍə́lo aw
jongéṛo ke ósi.

(16) hó! zmā́ pə aqidá dā́ watán də háǥə čā̀ né day či̱ də
ḍéro dzmə́ko qabālé ye axíste dì, bálke də háǥə čā̀
day či̱ də watə́n mína ye pə zṛé ke da aw lə watə́n
sara alāqá larí.

GLOSSARY

(1) Kābu̱l also Kābə́l 'Kabul' (province and capital of
Afghanistan)

(3) naǥd, fem. náǥda adj. I 'in cash'

ri̱šwát, pl. ri̱šwatúna m 1 'bribe'

gáṭa, pl. gáṭe f 1 'profit'

bānk, pl. bānkúna m 1 'bank'

(5) mína, pl. míne f 1 'love'

xalk for xalq (3.13)

mu̲lk, pl. mu̲lkúna m 1 'country'

grān, fem. grā́na adj. I 'dear'

(6) zda adj. V 'learned, acquired'

i̲fti̲xā́r m 1, Ar. pl. i̲fti̲xārā́t 'pride'

(7) wat̲án, pl. wat̲anúna m 1 'country, native land' (obl. wat̲ə́n)

ši̲ʿr, pl. ši̲ʿrúna m 1 'poetry'

mosiqí f 4 'music'

mozík m 'music'

xāri̲jí adj. V 'foreign'

s̤i̲fát, pl. s̤i̲fatúna m 1 'praise'

maṛéẓəm verb IV-A (intrans.) 'to become full, to get enough' (moṛ, fem. maṛá adj. II 'full, satisfied')

(8) naxwát m 'arrogance'

nafrát m 1 'hatred, hate'

mu̲staxdí̲m, Ar. pl. mustaxdi̲mín m 'employee'

pə mu̲qābí̲l kṣe adv. 'in front of'

tawāz̤úʿ f 5 '(polite) humbleness'

(10) dzə́ka či̲ conj. 'because'

hardzạ̄yí, pl. hardzāyā́n m 2 "a man from everywhere"

(11) fás̤əl, pl. fas̤lúna m 1 'season'

mamlakát, pl. mamlakatúna m 1 'country'

terawə́m verb IV-A (trans.) 'to spend' (ter adj. I 'passed, gone by, spent')

(12) hawā́, pl. hawāgā́ne f 5 'air, climate'

álwuzəm, past alwat- verb II (intrans.) 'to fly'

saṛé aw tawdé f pl. 'troubles, hardships'

(13) ʕayā́š m 'man of luxury, playboy'

ʕayš, pl. ʕayšúna m 1 'luxury'

bé le . . . na prep. phrase 'without'

rāhát, pl. rāhatúna m 1 'comfort'

ʕalāqá, pl. ʕalāqé f 2 'interest, fondness'

(14) kas, pl. kasā́n m 2 'person'

kā́ṇay, pl. kā́ṇi m 4 'rock, stone'

pəkāréẓəm verb IV-A (intrans.) 'to become needed, useful' (pə kār adv.)

(15) púla, pl. púle f 1 'piece of land'

paṭáy, pl. paṭí m 3 'land'

zoṛ, fem. zaṛá adj. II 'old'

koḍə́l(a), pl. koḍə́le f 1 'hut'

jongə́ṛa, pl. jongə́ṛe f 1 'shack'

(16) ʕaqidá, pl. ʕaqidé f 2 'opinion'

qabālá, pl. qabālé f 2 'deed (of ownership)'

NOTES

This selection is from paṣtó naṣrúna ("Pashto Prose"), edited by Muhammad Din Žwāk (Kabul: 1956), p. 62f., and is taken from Gul Pacha Olfat's likpóha ("Stylistics").

(2) Kohdāman see Notes on text 10a. Baghlan (Baǥlān) is a Pashto-speaking town in the province of Qataghan.

(6) də dé dzā́y žə́ba refers to Pashto.

nə́dza like nə́šta (5). The negation nə́ is often written as a part of the following word: also nə́lari (13, 15 below), but nə́ larí (11 below).

(7) waṯə́n is the obl.sing. of waṯán (also 12, 13, 14, 16) (GP § 55.2).

šer for ši̱ʕr

(8) tawāzó for tawāẕuʕ

(10) wayə́lay ši potential phrase; in Kandahar, elsewhere often in writing to avoid confusion with the perf. part.: wayə́lāy (GP § 95). Note also nə́ ši terawə́lày (12 below), balə́lay šu (14)

(12) saṛé aw tawdé "cold and hot" from soṛ, fem. saṛá adj. II 'cold' and tod, fem. tawdá adj. II 'hot'

(13) ayā́š for ʕayāš, ayš for ʕayš, alāqá for ʕalāqa

ʕáyš u rāẖát phrase with the Persian conj.

(14) sár warkawí "give (their) heads"

(16) aqidá for ʕaqida

qabālé is often colloquially qawālé (kawālé)

axíste short form of perf.part. (GP § 93.4b)

TRANSLATION

Where is he from?

(1) One house of his is here, one in Kabul, one somewhere else.

(2) He has some land in Kohdaman, some in Baghlan, some somewhere else.

(3) He obtained cash here through bribes, but other banks in another place make a profit from it.

(4) You tell (me): Where is he at home? ("Of which place is he?")

(5) His love is not for these people (here), and the people of other countries are very dear to him.

(6) He does not know the language of this place and takes pride in foreign languages.

(7) He has no taste for the poetry and music of this country and does not tire of the praise of foreign music.

(8) He looks at us with arrogance and hatred and is very humble in front of foreign employees.

(9) You tell (me): where is he at home?

(10) His home is nowhere, because every place is his and one can call him a 'man of everywhere'.

(11) Yes (indeed)! This is that bird who spends four seasons in four countries and has no (native) country.

(12) He does not know a native country; he does not fly in the air of one country and cannot endure the hardships of the country.

(13) This is that man of luxury who does not know anything else except luxury and comfort and who has no love for, or interest in his (native) country.

(14) We can call those persons (part) of this country who sacrifice their lives for the rocks and bushes of the country and who become useful to the country in difficult days,

(15) even if they own no piece of land and live in old huts and shacks.

(16) Yes (indeed)! In my opinion this country is not the (home) of that one who has acquired the deeds of much land but of that one in whose heart is love for his country and who is (sincerely) interested in his country.

ا ــ سپورټونه

د نوي ښار په کلوپ کښې له غرمې نه وروسته له څلورو بجو څخه تر پينځو بجو پورې د آزادی پهلوانۍ کورس پرانيستلی او د ګډون کوونکو ورتګ آزاد دی.

ب ــ د ژوندون په ښکلی او د لوستلو وړ مجله کښې اشتراک وکړئ.

که غواړئ چه د هېواد په ډېره ښکلی مجله کښې اشتراک وکړئ، که مو خوښه وی چه له ډېرو مهمو پېښو څخه خبر شئ،

که مو زړه غواړی چه د سينما او سپورټ د قهرمانانو ښه عکسونه لاس ته درشي، د ژوندون په مجله کښې اشتراک وکړئ. د ژوندون مجله د پايتخت د سترو ترجمانانو او لوړو ليکوالو محصول ده. دغه مجله د ښځو له پاره د ژوند مشاوره، د ذوق د څښتنانو له پاره د هنر مجموعه، او د هغه چا له پاره چه يوازې دی، ښه رفيقه ده.

ج ــ د خاورو تېل او سره مرچ په کار دی

يو څه وطنی سره مرچ، يو من په څلوېښت افغانۍ، او څو دانې مهتاب چاپ د خاورو د تېلو ډک پيپونه، يو پيپ په يو سلو پينځه افغانۍ، پېرودل کېږي.

څوک يې که د داوطلبۍ خيال لري، د يو زر درې سوه نه دېرش کال د عقرب د لسمی ورځی چه د داوطلبۍ وروستۍ ورځ ده، د سهار په لسو بجو دی د ستر درستيز پېرودونکي ته ورشي. شرطونه يې په آزاده توګه کتلای شی.

TRANSCRIPTION

(a) sporṭúna

də néwi ṣā́r pə ku̲lúp ke lə ǥarmé na wrústa lə tsalóro bajó
tsexà tər pindzó bajó póre də āzā́de pālawānéy kórs
prānistélay aw də gaḍún kawúnko wərtág āzā́d day.

(b) də žwandún pə ṣkéle aw də lwastélo wā́ṛ mu̲jalá kṣe
i̲šti̲rā́k wékṛəy

(1) ka ǥwā́ṛəy či̲ də hewā́d pə ḍéra ṣkéle mu̲jalá kṣe i̲šti̲rā́k
wékṛəy, ka mo xwā́ṣa wì či̲ lə ḍéro mu̲hayéjo péṣo
tsəxa xabár šəy,

(2) ka mo zṛé ǥwā́ṛi či̲ də sinəmā́ aw spórṭ də qārāmānā́no
ṣé aksúna lā́s ta dárši, də žwandún pə mu̲jalá kṣe
i̲šti̲rā́k wékṛəy.

(3) də žwandún mu̲jalá də pā̀ytáxt də stéro tàrju̲mānā́no aw
lwā́ṛo likwā́lo māsúl da.

(4) dáǥa mu̲jalá də ṣédzo lə pā́ra də žwánd mu̲šāwí̲ra, də záwq
də tsəṣtanā́no lə pā́ra də hu̲nár majmoá, aw də háǥə
čā́ lə pā́ra či̲ yawā́ze day, ṣá rafíqa dà.

(c) də xā́wro tél aw sré mréč pə kā́r di.

(1) yaw tsé watani sṛé mréč, yáw mán pə tsalwéṣt afǥānéy,
aw tsó dāné mā̀tāb-čā́p də xā́wro də télo ḍák pipúna,
yáw píp pə yáw sélo pindzé afǥānéy, perodèl kéẓi.

(2) tsók ye ka də dā̀watalabéy xyā́l larí, də yáw zèr dré
sawa néderš kā́l də aqráb də laséme wrádze či̲ də

dā̀watalabə́y wrustə́y wrádz da, də sahā́r pə láso
bajó de də stə́r drastíz perodúnki ta wáṛ̌i.

(3) šartúna ye pə āzā́da tóga katə́lāy ši.

GLOSSARY

(a)

sporṭ m 1 'sport'

kulúp m 1 'club'

ǵarmá f 2 'noon'

bajá f 2 'o'clock'

pahlawānī́ (pālawānī́) f 4 'wrestling'

kors m 1 'course'

prānī́zəm, past prānist- verb II (trans.) 'to open'

wərtág m 1 'going (there), admission'

(b)

žwandún m 1 'life'

ṣkə́lay (ṣkúlay) adj. IV 'pretty, attractive'

lwə́ləm, past lwast- verb II (trans.) 'to read'

mujalá (majalá) f 2 'magazine'

waṛ adj. I 'worth, worthy of, fit for'

ištirā́k m 1 'subscription'

(1) xwaṣ adj. I 'agreeable, liked, pleasing'

muhayə́j adj. I 'exciting'

pə́ṣa f 1 'event'

xab(a)réẓem verb IV-A (intrans.) 'to become informed'
(xabár adj. I see 6.6)

(2) sinemā́ f 3, f 5, 'film, movies'

qahramā́n m 2 'star, hero'

ʕaks m 1 'picture'

dərdzə́m verb IV (intrans.) 'to go to you' (prefix dər- or dar-)

lā́s ta dərdzə́m 'to become available to you, to be obtained by you'

(3) pāytáxt m 1 'capital'

stər adj. I 'great'

tarjṵmā́n m 2 'interpreter, translator'

likwā́l m 'writer'

maḫṣ̈úl m 1 'result'

(4) ṣ̌ə́dza f 1 'woman'

mṵšāwí̱ra f 1 '(female) adviser'

ẕawq m 1 'interest'

hṵnár m 1 'art'

majmoʕá f 2 'collection'

rafíqa f 1 '(female) friend'

(c)

tel m pl. 'oil' (also tel m 1)

də xā́wro tél 'kerosene'

sur, fem. sra adj. II 'red'

mreč m pl. 'pepper'

pe kā́r adv. 'needed, in need of'

(1) waṯaní adj. V 'domestic, native'

man, pl. mnúna m 1 (Afghan weight)

tsalwéṣt num. 'forty'

dānā́ f 2 'piece'

ḍak adj. I 'full'

pip m 1 '(big) can'

perém, past perod- verb II (trans.) 'to buy'

(2) dā̀waṯalabí f 4 'competitive bidding, competition'

ʿaqráb m Aqrab (Afghan month)

xyā́l m 1 'thought, thinking'

sahā́r m 1 'morning'

lasém adj. I 'tenth' (las '10')

(3) šarṯ m 1 'condition'

NOTES

The selections in this unit illustrate everyday prose in announcements and advertisements in Afghanistan's newspapers. 14(a), (b), and (c) are all from the Kabul daily Iṣlāḥ and contained in the issues of October 17, 4, and 13, 1960, respectively.

The glossary gives from unit 14 on only the classification of the words (m 1, f 2, adj. III, etc.), no longer any predictable forms.

(a) gaḍún kawúnkay 'participant', verbal adj. (GP § 93.2a)

prānistə́lay . . . day perfect (phrase) I (GP § 96.2,3)

(b)

(2) aksúna for ʕaksuna

mo pron.part. 2d pl. 'of you (people)'

qāramānā́no for qahramānāno

(3) māsul for maḥṣul

majmoá for majmoʕa

(c) tel, mrə́č are plural forms (GP § 63.3a)

(1) mā̀tāb-čā́p for mahtābčāp adj. I 'moon [Persian]-printed', 'marked with a moon' indicating the trade mark of the brand of kerosene

pèrodə̀l kéẓi pres. I passive (GP § 97)

(2) Aqrab 10, 1339 equals November 1, 1960

wrustə́y for wrustanə́y

stə́r drastíz "quarter-master general", the title of a high official in the Ministry of Defense

perodúnkay 'buyer' verbal adj.

de . . . wárši present II with "imperative" particle de (GP § 90.3c)

yáw zə̀r dré sawa (səwa) nə́ derš usually pronounced with conjunction aw(o) added: zéro . . . sawao.

(3) katə́lāy ši potential phrase (GP § 95)

TRANSLATION

(a) Sports.

In the club of the new city from 4:00 p.m. to 5:00 p.m. a course in free (style) wrestling has begun and admission for participants is free.

(b) Subscribe to "Zhwandun" (Life), the pretty magazine good for reading.

(1) If you want to subscribe to the country's most attractive magazine, if you wish to be informed of many exciting events,

(2) If your heart wants to come by good pictures of the heroes of movies and sport, subscribe to the magazine "Zhwandun".

(3) The magazine "Zhwandun" is the product of great translators and able writers of the capital.

(4) This magazine is for women an adviser on living, for people of taste a collection of the arts, and for anyone who is alone a nice companion.

(c) Kerosene and red pepper is wanted.

(1) Some domestic red pepper, one "man" for 40 afghanis, and some "moon"-brand cans full of kerosene oil, one can for 150 afghanis, are being bought.

(2) Someone, if he has competitive bidding for this in mind, is to come on the 10th day of Aqrab of the year 1339, which is the last day of the competition, at 10:00 a.m. to the buyer for the quarter-master general.

(3) He can freely look at the conditions for this.

ا ــ د شیخ متی د اساسی ښوونځی د
ودانۍ د بنسټ تیږه کېښودل شوه

قندهار: پرون د قلات د لوی حکومت د شیخ متی د اساسی ښوونځــــی د ودانۍ د بنسټ تیږه د حکومت د کفیل له خوا کېښودل شوه .

په دی وخت کښی مامورین ، مخــــور او یو شمیر د زده کوونکــــو اولیــــاء حاضــــر و .

ب ــ د ملی شوری د کمیسونو پوښتنــو
تــــه یی ځوابونــــه ورکــــړل

کابل: د ملی شوری د خارجه چارو د کمیسیون په غونډه نن سهــــار په لس نیمو بجو د تجارت د وزارت تجارتی لوی مدیر ډاکتــــر محمد اکبر عمــــر نوموړی کمیسیون ته حاضر ، او د افغانستان د شاهی حکومت او د پولنــــد د جمهوریت د حکومت تر منځ د مالو د تبادلی ، تادیاتو ، او د اقتصادی ، علمی او تخنیکی همکاریو د موافقه لیکو په باب یی د کمیسیون د خولی پوښتنو تــــه په خوله ځوابونه ورکړل .

همدغه راز له غرمی نه وروسته په دوو بجو د علــــی آباد د روغتیا د مؤسسو رئیس دکتور کرام الدین د ملی شوری د مالی او بودجی د چارو د کمیسیون په غونډه نوموړی کمیسیون ته حاضر ، او د خپل نه دبرش ــ شلوېښت مالــــی کال د بودجی په باره کښی یی د کمیسیون پوښتنو ته په خوله ځوابونه ورکــــړل او لیکل شوی پوښتنی یی د ځواب لیکلو له پاره له ځان سره واخیستلی .

ج — د هوا حالات

هغه يو جوی اختلال چه پرون د ارال د بحيري په جنوب شرق کي و ، د جنوب شرق خوا ته روان دی . نن به د هېواد غربی ، شمال – غربی ، او شمالی برخی په وريځ او د دوړو او خاورو په جګړو متأثری کېږی . د افغانستان په مرکزی او شرقی سيمو کښې به يو څه وريځی پيدا شی .

د هېواد په نورو برخو کښې به په هوا کښې کوم مهم تغير پېښ نشی .

TRANSCRIPTION

(a) de Šex Matí de asā́sí ṣowendzí de wadānéy de bensét̩ tíẓa kéṣodel šwa

(1) Qandahā́r: parún de Qalā́t de lóy hu̱kumát de Šèx Matí de asā́sí ṣowendzí de wadānéy de bensét̩ tíẓa de hu̱kumát de kafíl le xwā́ kéṣodel šwa.

(2) pe dé wáxt ke māmurín, mexawér, aw yáw šmér de zdakawúnko awli̱yā́ hāzi̱r we.

(b) de mi̱lí šorā́ de kemisyunó puṣténo ta yè dzawābúna wárkṛel.

(1) Kābu̱l: de mi̱lí šorā́ de xāri̱já čā́ro de kemisyún pe ǵuṣténa, nén sahā́r pe làs nímo bajó de ti̱jārát de wezārát tijāratí lóy mu̱dír Ḍākṭár Mahmàd Akbár Omár numwéṛi kemisyún ta hāzi̱r,

(2) aw de afǥāni̱stā́n de šāhí hu̱kumát aw de polí̱nd de jamhuri̱yát de hu̱kumát ter mándz de māló de tabādalé, tā̀di̱yā́to, aw de ì̱qti̱sādí, i̱lmí, aw tàxnikí hamkāréyo de mawā̀fi̱qalíko pe bā́b ye de kemisyún de xwlé puṣténo ta pe xwlé dzawābúna wárkṛel.

(3) hamdáǥa rā́z le ǥarmé na wrústa pe dwó bajó de Alyābā́d de roǥtyā́ de mu̱asi̱só raís Du̱ktúr Kì̱ramudín de mi̱lí šorā́ de mālí aw bùdi̱jé de čā́ro de kemisyún pe ǥuṣténa numwéṛi kemisyún ta hāzí̱r,

(4) aw de xpél néderš tsalwéṣt mālí kā́l de budi̱jé pe bā́ra ke yè de kemisyún puṣténo ta pe xwlé dzawābúna wárkṛel,

(5) aw likèl šéwe pu̱ṣténe ye de dzawā̀b likélo le pā́ra le dzā́n sara wā́xistelè.

(c) de hawā́ hālā́t

(1) háǥa yàw jawí i̱xti̱lā́l či̱ parún de Arā́l de bahiré pe jenúbi̱ šárq ke we, de jenúbi̱ šárq xwā́ ta rawā́n day.

(2) nén ba de hewā́d ǥarbí, šamā̀l ǥarbí, aw šamālí bárxe pe weryádz aw de dúṛo aw xā́wro pe jegedó mu̱taasí̱re kṛí.

(3) de afǥāni̱stā́n pe markazí aw šarqí símo ke ba yáw tsé weryádze paydā́ ši.

(4) de hewā́d pe nóro bárxo ke ba pe hawā́ ke kù̱m mu̱hí̱m taǥír péṣ nési.

GLOSSARY

(a)

asāsí adj. V 'fundamental, basic' (asā́s m see 16.20)

ṣowəndzáy m 3 'school'

wadāní f 4 'building'

bənsə́ṭ m 1 'foundation, base, basis'

tíẓa f 1 'stone'

(1) parún adv. 'yesterday'

kafíl m 2 'provisional appointee'

(2) məxawár adj. I 'prominent' also m 5

šmer m 1 'number'

zdà kawúnkay adj. IV 'learner, learning, pupil'

(zdà kawə́m verb IV 'to learn') here m 4

walí, Ar.pl. awliyā́ m 'guardian'

ḫāẓír adj. I 'present' (also ḫāẓə́r, 5.12)

(b)

milí adj. V 'national'

šorā́ f 3, f 5 'council'

kəmisyún m 1 'commission, committee'

dzawā́b (also jawā́b) m 1 'answer'

(1) xārijá adj. V 'foreign'

čā́ra f 1 'affair'

nən adv. 'today'

nim adj. I 'half'

ti̱jārát (also tu̱jārát) m 'commerce, trade'

wəzārát m 1 'ministry'

ti̱jāratí (also tu̱jāratí) adj. V 'commercial'

lóy mu̱dír m 2 'director-general' (official rank)

ḍākṭár m 2 'doctor'

numwə́ṛay adj. IV 'mentioned'

(2) šāhí adj. V 'royal'

polí̱nd m 'Poland'

jamhuri̱yát (jamhuryát) m 1 'republic'

māl m 1 'goods, ware'

tabādalá f 2 'exchange, trade'

tādi̱yá (tādyá), Ar.pl. tādi̱yā́t f 2 'payment'

i̱qti̱ṣādí adj. V 'economic'

taxnikí adj. V 'technical'

mawā̀fi̱qa-lík m 1 'written agreement'

xwlə f 2 'mouth'

pə xwlə́ adv. 'oral'

(3) roǥtyā́ f 'health'

mu̱asi̱sá f 2 'institution, installation', colloquial: mosi̱sá

du̱ktúr (also daktúr) m 2 'doctor'

bu̱di̱já (bodi̱já) f 2 'budget'

mālí adj. V 'financial, fiscal'

(4) pə bārá kṣe adv. 'concerning, about'

(c)

hawá f 3 'air, weather, climate'

(1) jawí adj. V 'atmospheric'

ixtilál m 1 'disorder'

bahirá f 2 'sea'

jənúb m 'South'

šarq m 'East'

(2) ġarbí adj. V 'western'

šamàl-ġarbí adj. V 'northwestern'

šamālí adj. V 'northern'

wəryádz f 1 'cloud' (also wredz)

dúṛa f 1 'dust squall'

jəgéẓəm verb IV-A (intrans.) 'to rise' (jəg adj. I 'high')

mutaasirawə́m verb IV-A (trans.) 'to touch, affect, influence' (mutaasír adj. I 'influenced')

(3) markazí adj. V 'central'

šarqí adj. V 'eastern'

síma f 1 'area'

(4) taġír m 1 'change'

NOTES

The selections in this unit continue the samples of everyday Pashto prose as found in the daily Islāh; they are taken from the issues of October 12, 1960 (a, b) and October 4, 1960 (c).

(a) Šex Mati was a religious man who lived some 700 years ago and, according to the péṭa xazāna (see text 23), wrote in Pashto. His shrine is in Qalāt in the province of Kandahār.

kṣéṣodəl šwà 3d sing.fem. past II passive of ẓdəm, here for kṣéṣodəla šwà

(1) lóy h̲ukumát is a governmental district larger than a local district (mah̲alí h̲ukumát), which in turn is larger than a rural sub-district (ʿalāqadārí) (see text 10b).

asāsí ṣowəndzáy is a regular, government-supported primary school. The word ṣowəndzáy ("place of pointing out") was created for maktáb.

də kafíl lə xwā́ The actor in a sentence with a passive phrase as verb can only be expressed by a particle phrase (GP § 97.3)

(2) məxawə́r m pl. of məxawár (GP §§ 69.4, 55.2)

hāzír for h̲āz̤i̲r

(b) mi̲lí šorā́. The National Council is, with the 'House of Nobles', the Afghan parliament. It has 171 members who are elected for three-year terms.

šorā́ is usually written šorı

(1) xāri̲já for xāri̲jí (13.7)

Omár for ʿumar

ḍākṭár from English doctor; du̲ktúr (daktúr) (3 below) from French docteur, German Doktor

numwéṛay from num m 1 'name' and wéṛay perf.part of wṛəm (GP § 93.4)

(2) polí̲nd pronounced also polénd, poláynd and polí̲nḍ, etc.

(3) ʕAliābā́d is the location of the medical center of the University of Kabul.

Ki̲ramudín is written kịrām aldin

(5) likə̀l šéwe 'written; having been written' is a passive perfect participle phrase

(c)

(1) jənúbi̲ šárq written jənub šarq, is a Persian phrase.

(2) šamā̀l-ǥarbí is derived from the Persian phrase šamā́li ǥárb

mu̲taasí̲re agrees with dir.pl.fem. bárxe (GP § 103.3b)

(4) péṣ ši like mu̲taasí̲re kṛi (2) and paydā́ ši (3) are present II forms after ba indicating future events (GP §§ 89.3, 90.3d)

TRANSLATION

(a) The foundation stone was laid for the Shekh Mati primary school building.

(1) Kandahar: Yesterday the foundation stone for the Shekh Mati primary school building of the district of Kalat was laid by the acting district governor.

(2) At that time officials, prominent people, and a number of guardians of the students were present.

(b) They gave answers to the questions of the Commissions of the National Council.

(1) Kabul: At the request of the foreign affairs commission of the National Council today in the morning at half-past ten, Dr. Muhammad Akbar Omar, the director-general of commerce of the Ministry of Commerce, appeared before the mentioned commission,

(2) and he gave orally answers to the oral questions of the commission concerning the agreements on exchange of goods, payments, and economic, scientific, and technical cooperation between the royal government of Afghanistan and the government of the republic of Poland.

(3) The same way at two o'clock in the afternoon the president of the medical center ("health institution") of Aliabad, Dr. Kiramudin, appeared at the request of the commission for financial and budget affairs of the National Council,

(4) and he orally gave answers to the questions of the commission concerning the budget of his fiscal year 39-40.

(5) And he took written questions with him in order to write answers.

(c) Weather Conditions

(1) That atmospheric disturbance which was yesterday in the southeast of the Aral Sea is moving towards the south-east.

(2) It will affect today the western, northwestern, and northern parts of the country through clouds and the raising of dust squalls and dust.

(3) In the central and eastern parts of Afghanistan some clouds will develop.

(4) In other parts of the country no important change in the weather will occur.

UNIT 16

افغانستان

افغانستان یو غرنی مملکت دی چه تقریباً دوه سوه اویا زره مربع میله وسعت، او تر دوولسو ملیونو زیات نفوس لري. مشهور ښارونه یې کابل، کندهار، هرات، مزارشریف، قطغن، ننگرهار، او پکتیا نومیږي. د افغانستان ډېره مهمه او لمړۍ ژبه پښتو ده چه ډېر خلک خبرې په کوی او د دې هیواد ملی ژبه بلله کیږي. تر پښتو وروسته فارسی ژبه ډېر عمومیت لري، چه له ایرانی فارسي څخه لږ توپیر لري. که څه هم په افغانستان کښې یو شمېر هندوان، سکان، او یهودیان ژوند کوي، مگر د مسلمانانو شمېر تر نه‌نوي فیصده زیات دی.

د افغانستان حکومت شاهي دی، قوانین یې ټول پر اسلامي مقرراتو باندې چه "شرع" ورته وایی بنا شوی دی. مقننه قوه په پاچا، د ملی شورا مجلس، او د اعیان په مجلس پورې اړه لری. د ملی شورا غړی چه شمېر یې یو سل او یو اویا کسه دی، راساً د خلکو له خوا د رأیو په اکثریت د افغانستان د ټولو ولایاتو او علاقو څخه د درو کالو له پاره انتخابیږي. د اعیان د مجلس غړی چه شمېر یې شپېتو تنو ته رسیږي، د پاچا له خوا ټاکل کیږي. د اعیان د مجلس غړی باید د ډېرې تجربې او پوهې خاوندان وی، او د خپل هیواد له پاره یې پخوا تر دې وظیفې ډېر مهم مهم او د ستایلو وړ کارونه او خدمتونه کړی وی.

د اجرائیې قوه و کابینې ته ورسپارله شوې ده. کابینه د وزیرانو و هیئت ته وایی چه د دوی مشر صدراعظم بلل کیږي. ټول وزیران د خپلو اجراآتو په باره کښې و ملی شورا ته راساً مسئولیت لري. ملی شورا

هر وخت د دوی د اجراآتو مراقبت کوی او د لزوم په وخت کښی کولای شی
چه د دوی د اجراآتو په باره کښی له دوی څخه لازمه پوښتنی وکړي .

د پاره د دې چه د مملکت د ډیرو مهمو مسئلو په فیصله کولو او
د هغوی په باره کښی د تصمیم نیولو په برخه کښی د ټول ملت اراده په
ښه ډول سره څرګنده، او شامله وي، نو په داسی مهمو مواقعو کښی د مملکت
بارسوخ او ډېر مهم اشخاص و مرکز ته رابلل کیږی، چه د دغو مهمو مسئلو په
باره کښی خپل نظریات ښکاره کړی او لازم تصمیمونه ونیسی. د دغو مهمو اشخاصو
جرګه د لویی جرګې په نامه سره یادیږي .

افغانستان یو بیطرفه مملکت دی چه د نړۍ د ټولو مملکتو سره
دوستانه روابط لري، او په دې عقیده دی چه د نړۍ ټولی خړپړتیاوی
او جنجالی مسئلې د صلحی له لاری، د حق بینۍ پر اساس په خبرو اترو
سره حل کېدلای شي .

TRANSCRIPTION

afǥānistā́n

(1) afǥānistā́n yaw ǥaranáy mùmlakát dəy či taqrī́bandwá sàwa awyā́ zə̀rə murabā̀ mílə wasát, àw tər dwóləsu milyúnu zyā́t nufús lərì.

(2) maš̌húr ṣārúnə ye Kābə́l, Kandahā́r, Hirā́t, Mazā́ri šarìf, Qataǥán, Nangrahā́r, aw Paktyā́ numī́ẓi.

(3) də afǥānistā́n ḍérə muhímə aw lùmṛə́y žə́ba pəṣtó də či ḍə́r xálək̗ xəbə́ri pə kəwí aw də dé hiwā́d milí žə́bə bəlèlə kī̄ẓi.

(4) tər peṣtó wrústə fārsí žə́bə ḍér umūmiyát lərì, či
lə irānə́y fārsí tsəxə lə́ẓ tawpír lərí.

(5) kə tsə́ hám pə afg̸ānistā́n kṣi yàw šmér hindwā́n, sikā́n,
aw yahudyā́n žwə́nd kəwì, mágar də musulmānā́nu šmér
tər nə́nəwì fisáda zyā́t də̀y.

(6) də afg̸ā́nistān hùkūmát šāhí də̀y, qawānín ye ṭól pər islāmí
muqararā́tu bā́ndi či šárʕa wə̀rtə wā́yi binā̀ šə́wi di.

(7) muqaniná quwá pə pāčā́, də milí šorā́ majlə́s, aw də
ayā́n pə majlə́s pū̀ri áṛa lərì.

(8) də milí šorā́ g̸ə́ṛi či šmér yè yáw sə́l aw yáw àwyā́ kásə
dəy, rāsán də xálku lə xwā́ də rā́yu pə aksariyát də
afg̸ānistā́n də ṭū́lu wilāyā́tu aw alāqó tsəxə də dró
kā́lu lə pā́rə intixābī́ẓi.

(9) də ayā́n də majlə́s g̸ə́ṛi či šmér ye špetó tanó tə rəsī́ẓi
də pāčā́ lə xwā́ ṭākə̀l kī́ẓi.

(10) də ayā́n də majlə́s g̸ə́ṛi bā́yad də ḍī́ri tajribé aw pū́hi
xāwandā́n wi, aw də xpə́l hiwā́d lə pā́rə ye pəxwā́ tər
dé wazifé ḍér muhím muhím aw də stāyə́lu wáṛ kārúnə
aw xidmatúnə kə́ṛi wi.

(11) də ijrāiyé quwá wə kābiné tə wə̀rspārə̀lə šéwe də.

(12) kābiná də wəzirā́nu wə hayát tə wā́yi či də dúy mə́šər
sàdri āzám bələ̀l kī́ẓi.

(13) ṭól wəzirā́n də xpə́lu ijrā́ātu pə bārá kṣi wə milí
šorā́ tə rāsán masūliyát lərì.

(14) milí šorā́ hár wáxt də dúy də ijrā́ātu murāqibát kəwí aw

de lazúm pe wáxt kṣi kewélā̀y ši či de dúy de ijrāā́tu pe bārá kṣi le dúy tsexe lāzimá puṣténi wékṛi.

(15) de pā́re de dé či de mumlakát de ḍī́ru muhímu masaló pe faysalá kewélu aw de hağúy pe bārá kṣi de tasmìm niwélu pe bárxe kṣi de ṭól milát irādá pe ṣé ḍáwl sère tsargánde aw šāmíle wi,

(16) no pe dā́si muhímu mawāqíu kṣi de mumlakát bārasúx aw ḍér muhím ašxā́s we markáz te rā̀belèl kī́ẓi,

(17) či de déğu muhímu masaló pe bārá kṣi xpél nazariyā́t ṣkārá kṛì aw lāzím tasmimúne wénisi.

(18) de déğu muhímu ašxā́su jergá de lū́yi jergé pe nāmé sere yādī́ẓi.

(19) afğānistā́n yaw betaráfe mumlakát dey či de neṛéy de ṭū́lu mumlakató sere dostāná rawābít lerì,

(20) aw pe dé aqidá dey či de neṛéy ṭū́li xeṛpeṛtyā́wi aw janjālí masalé de súlhi le lā́ri, de haqbinéy per asā́s pe xebéru etéru sere hàl kedélāy ši.

GLOSSARY

Afğānistā́n m 'Afghanistan' (East. Afğāni̲stā́n)

(1) ğaranáy adj. III 'mountainous'

mumlakát variant of mamlakát

awyā́ num. 'seventy'

murabáʕ f 3 'square' (East. mu̲rabáʕ)

mil m 1 'mile'

wasʕát m 1 'area, space'

dwóles num. 'twelve' (East. dwólas)

milyún m 1 'million'

nufús m 1 'population' (East. nufús)

(2) Nangrahā́r or Ningrahā́r (Afghan province)

numéẓem, past numed- verb II (intrans.) 'to be called'

ṣār m 1 'city, town, province'

(3) lumṛáy adj. III 'first' (East. lumṛáy)

(4) ʕumūmiyát m 1 'commonness, generality' (East. ʕumumiyát)

iranáy adj. III 'Iranian'

tawpír m 1 'difference' (topír 5.12)

(5) hindú m 2 'Hindoo'

sik m 2 'Sikh'

yahudáy or yahudí m 2 'jew'

žwènd (East. žwànd) kawə́m verb IV 'to live'

musulmā́n m 2 'muslim' (East. musulmā́n)

fis̤ád m 1 'percentage, percent'

(6) šāhí adj. V 'royal, monarchal'

per . . . bā́ndi (East. bā́nde) prep-adv.phrase 'upon'

islāmí adj. V 'islamic'

muqararā́t m pl. 'rules, principles' (East. muqararā́t)

šárʕa f "Sharʕa" (muslim law)

(7) muqaniná adj. V 'legislative' (East. muqaniná)

quwá f 2 'power'

pə . . . pū́ri (East. póre) prep.-adv. phrase 'upon, with'

áṛa f 1 'connection, dependence'

(8) ǥə́ṛəy m 4 'member, organ' (East. ǥə́ṛay)

rāsán adv. 'directly'

rā́ya f 1 'vote'

aks̱ariyát m 1 'majority'

intixābéẓəm verb IV-A (intrans.) 'to be elected, selected' (intixā́b, East. i̱nti̱xā́b m 1 'election')

(9) špeté num. 'sixty'

(10) tajribá f 2 'experience' (also tajru̱bá)

póhə f 1 'knowledge' (East. póha)

xāwánd m 2 'owner, possessor'

pəxwā́ tər adv.-prep.phrase 'before'

waz̄ifá f 2 'duty'

stā́yəm verb I (trans.) 'to praise'

xidmát m 1 'service' (East. xi̱dmát)

(11) ijrāiyá f 2 'executive, execution' (East. i̱jrāi̱yá, i̱jrāyá)

kābiná f 2 'cabinet'

wərspā́rəm verb I (trans.) 'to entrust (to them)' (prefix wər-)

(12) wəzír m 2 'minister' (East. wazír)

hayát m 1 'group, delegation'

s̤àdri aʿz̄ám m 2 'prime-minister'

(13) ijrāát m pl. 'actions'

masuliyát m 1 'responsibility'

(14) murāqibát m 1 'supervision, observation' (East. mu̱rāqi̱bát)

lazúm m 'necessity'

lāzimá adj. V 'necessary' (East. lāzi̱má)

(15) masalá f 2 'problem, matter'

taṣmím m 1 '(policy) decision'

pə bárxa kṣi adv. 'concerning'

irādá f 2 'intention, will' (East. i̱rādá)

šāmíl adj. I 'included'

(16) mawqíʕ, Ar.pl. mawāqíʕ f 'occasion, opportunity'

bārasúx adj. I 'influential'

šaxṣ, Ar.pl. ašxā́ṣ m 'individual'

(17) nazariyá f 2, Ar.pl. nazariyā́t m 'opinion'

lāzím adj. I 'necessary' (see 14 above)

(18) yādéẓəm verb IV-A (intrans.), 'to be called, remembered' (yād m 1 'memory')

(19) bèṯaráfə adj. V 'neutral' (East. bèṯaráfa)

dostāná adj. V 'friendly'

rābiṯá f 2, Ar.pl. rawābíṯ m 'relation' (East. rābi̱ṯá, pl. rawābí̱ṯ)

(20) xeṛpəṛtyā́ f 3 'controversy'

janjālí adj. V 'controversial'

ṣúlẖə f 1 'peace' (East. ṣúlẖa)

ẖaqbiní   f 4   'justice'

asā́s   m 1   'basis, foundation'

xəbə́ri ətə́ri   f pl.   'negotiations, discussion, talk'
  (East. xabə́re atə́re)

ẖal   m 1   'solution'

ẖàl kéẓi   verb IV   (intrans.)   'to be solved'

NOTES

This selection was written and transcribed by Mr. Noor Ahmad Shaker, who teaches Pashto at Kabul University. His Kandahar dialect is the one shown in unit 1 (see Notes of 1).

Compared to his speech the Eastern dialect has the following features:

(a) a for ə:

dir.pl.: zə́ra, míla (1), kása (8)

dir.pl. -úna: ṣārúna (2), kārúna, xi̲dmatúna (10), tas̤mimúna (17)

dir.fem. ́-a: ḍéra, mụhí̲ma, žə́ba, balə́la (3), da (3,11), šāmíla (15)

in particles: wrústa, tséxa (4), ka (5), wə́rta (6), ta (9), pā́ra, sara (15, 19, 20)

in weak-stressed syllables: larí (1), paṣtó, xabə́re, balə́la (3), balə́l (12), rā̀balə́l (16), beṯaráfa, naṛə́y (19), raséẓi (9), kawí, kawə́lāy (14)

(b) ay for əy

day (1, 5, 6, 8, 19, 20) ǵə́ṛay (8)

(c) weak-stressed e for i:

fem.obl.sing., dir.pl.: xabə́re (3), puṣtə́ne (14), ṭóle, lā́re, s̤úlh̲e (20)

other forms: kṣe or ke (5, etc.), hewā́d (3), bā́nde (6), dā́se (16), Herā́t (2)

(d) weak-stressed o for u:

obl.pl.: milyúno (1), mu̲su̲lmānā́no (5), ṭólo, rā́yo (8), wazirā́no (12), xpə́lo, i̲jrā́āto (13), mu̲hí̲mo (15), də́ǵo (17), ṭólo (19), xabə́ro atə́ro (20), etc.

(e) In Kandahar [ē] changes to [ī], [ō] to [ū] before i and u in the next syllable (GP §§ 8.2, 9.2): numéẓi (2), i̲nti̲xābéẓi (8), kéẓi (3, 9, 12, 16), yādéẓi (18), ç̣ére (10); póre (7), ṭólo (8, 19), póhe (10)

(f) The Eastern distinction between i̲ and i, u̲ and u is not found in Kandahar. Note ū in umūmiyát (4), hukūmát (6), masūliyát (13), lū́yi (18).

(5) fisáda obl. II case

(7) aʿyā́n majlə́s (or majlí̲s) "assembly of nobles"

(8) kā́lu (East. kā́lo) obl. of pl. kā́la (GP § 63.1b)

(9) tanó, here for tánu (East. táno)

(10) kə́ṛi wi perfect II phrase (GP § 96.4)

muhím muhím (East. mu̲hí̲m mu̲hí̲m) doubled phrase, see GP § 101.4a

(11) wərspārélə šə́we dà 3d sing.fem. perf.I of passive phrase

(12) sàdri āzám written ṣ̈adr ˁazam

(16) mawqíˁ is pronounced mawqé (GP § 8.3)

(18) nāmə́ obl.sing. of num (GP § 55.4c)

(20) ṣ̈ulḫa; informal: sóla f 1

TRANSLATION

Afghanistan

(1) Afghanistan is a mountainous country, which has an area of about 270,000 square miles and a population of more than twelve million.

(2) Its best-known provinces are called Kabul, Kandahar, Herat, Mazar-i-Sharif, Qataghan, Ningrahar, and Paktya.

(3) The most important and principal language of Afghanistan is Pashto which many people speak and which is called the national language of the country.

(4) Next to Pashto the Persian language, which has some difference from Iranian Persian, has a very wide spread.

(5) Although a number of Hindoos, Sikhs, and Jews live in Afghanistan, the number of muslims, however, exceeds 99 percent.

(6) Afghanistan's government is monarchal; its laws have all been based on Islamic principles, which are called "sharˁa".

(7) The legislative power is vested in the king, the National Council, and the Senate.

(8) The members of the National Council, whose number is 171 men, are elected directly by the people by the majority of the votes from all provinces and districts of Afghanistan for three years.

(9) The members of the senate, whose number reaches sixty, are selected by the king.

(10) The members of the senate must possess lots of experience and knowledge and must have done for their country, prior to this assignment, several important and praiseworthy jobs and services.

(11) The executive power has been given to the cabinet.

(12) "Cabinet" they call the group of ministers whose head is called prime-minister.

(13) All the ministers are directly responsible to the National Council concerning their executive actions.

(14) The National Council watches their actions all the time, and can at a necessary occasion ask them needed questions about their actions.

(15) In order that in deciding very important matters of the country and in adopting a policy concerning them, the intention of the entire nation be determined and included in a good manner,

(16) on such important occasions the country's influential and most important people are invited to the capital,

(17) to express their views on these important problems and to adopt the required (policy) decisions.

(18) The meeting of these important personalities goes by the name of "loya jirga" (big council).

(19) Afghanistan is a neutral country which has friendly relations with all the countries of the world.

(20) And it is of this opinion that all disagreements and controversial problems of the world can be solved peacefully on the basis of justice by negotiations.

UNIT 17

د افغانستان معارف

په افغانستان کښې تعلیم په لومړنیو ښوونځیو کښې، چه دوره یې شپږ کاله ده، اجباري دی. او تر هغه وروسته لوړ تعلیمات اختیاري دي، مګر حکومت ډېر کوښښ کوي چه متعلمین تشویق کړي چه و خپلو تعلیماتو ته دوام پسې ورکړي. وروسته تر لومړني ښوونځي درې کاله منځنی او بیا پسې درې کاله لوړ ښوونځی لوستل کیږي. هغه ښوونځی چه دوولس کاله تعلیم پکښې کیږي، لیسه بلله کیږي. وروسته تر لیسې څلور کاله د پوهنځي دوره ده. د پوهنځي د دورې له تمامولو څخه وروسته و متعلم ته لیسانس ورکول کیږي. په حکومتي مؤسسو کښې د لوړ ښوونځي برې لیک سل افغانۍ او لیسانس دوه سوه افغانۍ امتیاز لري، دغه رنګه ماسټري درې سوه او ډاکټري څلور سوه افغانۍ امتیاز لري.

په افغانستان کښې له لومړني ښوونځي څخه نیولې بیا د پوهنځي تر پایه پورې ټول تعلیم وړیا دی. برسېره پر دې ټول د تعلیم لوازم لکه قلم، پنسل، پنسل پاك، کاغذ، کتابچه، کتاب او داسې نور شیان د حکومت له خوا و شاګردانو ته وړیا ورکول کیږي. په افغانستان کښې ځینې متعلمین مسکینان دي، او ځینې متعلمین په وړو علاقو او کلو کښې ژوند کوي، هلته لوړ ښوونځي نشته، نو هرکله چه خپل لومړني تعلیمات پای ته ورسوي، د لوړو تعلیماتو له پاره و لویو ښارو ته راځي او هلته په لوړو مکاتبو کښې ځانونه داخلوي. و داسې زده‌کړیانو ته برسېره د تعلیم پر نورو لوازمو، لیلیه، دریشي تنخواه، حتی له کوره تر هغه ښاره پورې چه دوی تعلیم پکښې کوي، د لارې کرایه او سفرخرڅ هم د حکومت له خوا ورکول کیږي؛ او دغه مصارف بیا هیڅ

وخت له متعلم څخه نه اخیستل کیږی · نو د دې له امله د افغانستان
حکومت تر هرڅه زیات و معارف ته ډېره توجه لري او د مملکت د بودجې
یوه لویه برخه په همدې لاره کښې مصرفوی ·

د پاره د دې چه د معارف شاګردان په ښه ډول سره وروزل شی،
او د هیواد د خدمت له پاره ، څنګه چه ښایی، چمتو شی، نو د افغانستان
حکومت هر کال یو شمېر لایق متعلمین د لوړو تحصیلاتو د پاره د خارجی
هیوادو و مشهورو پوهنتونونو ته لیږی او د تحصیل په وخت کښې ټول مصارف
د حکومت له خوا څخه ورکول کیږي ·

TRANSCRIPTION

də afǥānistā́n maˁāríf

(1) pə afǥānistā́n kṣi tālím pə lumṛənéyu ṣowəndzéyu kṣi, či dawrá ye špáẓ kā́lə də, ijbārí dəy.

(2) aw tər haǥá wrústə lwéṛ tālimā́t ixtyārí di,

(3) mágar hukūmát ḍér koṣéṣ kəwí či mutā̀limín tašwíq kṛì či wə xpélu tālimā́tu tə dawā́m pəsi wárkṛi.

(4) wrústə tər lumṛəní ṣowəndzí dré kā́lə mandzanáy aw byā́ pəsi dré kā́lə lwéṛ ṣowəndzáy lwestə̀l kī́ẓi.

(5) háǥa ṣòwəndzáy či dwólәs kā́lə tālím pəkṣi kī́ẓi, ləsá bəlèlə kī́ẓi.

(6) wrústə tər ləsé tsəlór kā́lə də pohandzí̜ dawrá də.

(7) də pohandzí də dawré lə təmāməwélu tsəxə wrústə wə mutālím tə lisā́ns wə̀rkəwəl kī́ẓi.

(8) pə hukūmətí muasisū́ kṣi də lwə́ṛ ṣowəndzí baràylík səl
afǥā́nə́y àw lisā́ns dwá sàwa afǥā́nə́y imtiyā́z lərì;
daǥá rànge māsṭərí dré sáwa aw ḍā̀kṭarí tsəlór sáwa
afǥā́nə́y imtiyā́z lərì.

(9) pə afǥānistā́n kṣi lə lumṛəní ṣowəndzí tsəxə̀ niwə́le byā́
də pohandzí tər pā́ya pū̀ri ṭól tālím waṛyā́ dəy.

(10) barsérə pər dé, ṭól də tālím lawāzím, lə̀kə qalám, pinsíl,
pinsilpā́k, kāǥáz, kitābčá, kitā́b aw dā́si nór šayā́n də
hukūmát lə xwā́ wə šāgərdā́nu tə waṛyā́ wə̀rkəwə̀l kī́ẓi.

(11) pə afǥānistā́n kṣi dzíni mutālimín miskinā́n di, aw dzíni
mutālimín pə weṛó alāqó aw kélu kṣi žwénd kəwì,
háltə lwə́ṛ ṣowəndzí néstə,

(12) no hárkə̀lə či xpél lumṛəní tālimā́t pā́y tə wérəsəwì, də
lwéṛu tālimā́tu lə pā̀rə wə lū́yu ṣāró tə rādzí aw háltə
pə lwéṛu makātíbu kṣi dzānúnə dāxiləwí.

(13) wə dā́si zdàkṛyā́nu tə barsérə də tālím pər nū́ru lawāzímu,
layliyá, dərīší, tanxā̀, hátā́ lə kórə tər háǥa ṣārə
pū́ri či dúy tālím pəkṣi kəwí, də lā́ri kirāyá aw
safàrxárts hám də hukūmát lə xwā́ wərkəwə̀l kī́ẓi;

(14) aw dáǥa masāríf byā̀ híts wáxt lə mìtālím tsəxə né
axistə̀l kī́ẓi.

(15) no də dé lə amála də afǥānistā́n hukūmát tər hártsə
zyā́t wə maāríf tə ḍérə tawajó lərì.

(16) aw də mamlakát də būdijé yawà lóya bárxə pə hamdé
lā́ra kṣi masrafawí.

(17) de pā́re de dé či de maārī́f šāgerdā́n pe ṣé ḍáwl sere wérozel ši, aw de hiwā́d de xidmát le pā́re, tsénge či ṣā́yi, čamtú ši,

(18) no de afġānistā́n hukūmát hár kā́l yáw šmèr lāyéq mutā̀limī́n de lwéṛu tahsilā́tu de pā́re de xārijí hiwādó we mašhúru pohantunúnu te līẓí.

(19) aw de tahsī́l pe wáxt kṣi ṭól masārī́f de hukūmát le xwā́ tsexe wèrkewèl kī́ẓi.

GLOSSARY

maʿārī́f m pl. 'education' (East. maʿārī̲f)

(1) taʿlī́m, Ar.pl. taʿlimā́t m 'education, teaching, instruction'

lumṛenáy adj. III 'elementary' (East. lumṛanáy)

ijbārí adj. V 'compulsory' (East. i̲jbārí)

dawrá f 2 'period, time'

(2) ixtyārí adj. V 'optional' (East. i̲xtyārí)

(3) koṣéṣ m 1 'effort' (East. koší̲š)

mutaʿlī́m, Ar.pl. mutaʿlimī́n m 'student' (East. mu̲taʿlī̲m)

tašwiqawém verb IV-A (trans.) 'to encourage'

(4) mandzanáy adj. III 'intermediate, middle'

lwélem, past lwest- (East. lwast-) verb II (trans.) 'to read'

(5) lesá f 2 'high-school'

(6) pohandzáy m 3 'college'

(7) təmāməwə́m (East. tamāmawə́m) verb IV-A (trans.)
'to finish' (tamā́m adj. I 'finished')

lisā́ns m 1 'licenciate, bachelor's degree' (East. li̲sā́ns)

(8) h̲ukūmətí (East. h̲u̲kumatí) adj. V 'governmental'

baraylík, pl. barilikúna m 1 'diploma, certificate'

daǥá rángə (East. ránga) adv. 'this (mentioned) way'

māsṭərí f 4 'master's degree'

ḍākṭarí f 4 'doctor's degree'

(9) waṛyā́ adj. V 'gratis, free'

(10) barsérə (East. barséra) pər adv.-prep.phrase
'in addition'

lawāzím m pl. 'necessities, equipment' (East. lawāzí̲m)

qalám m 1, m 2 'pen'

pinsíl m 1, m 2 'pencil' (East. pi̲nsí̲l)

pinsilpā́k m 1 'eraser' (East. pi̲nsi̲lpā́k)

kāǥáz̲ m 1 'paper'

kitābčá f 2 'note-book' (East. ki̲tābčá)

šāgə́rd m 2 'student, apprentice'

(11) miskín m 2 'pauper' (also adj. I 'poor') (East. mi̲skín)

žwənd, East. žwand (16.5)

(12) hárkèla (hárkèlə) či conj. 'whenever' (East. či̱)

rəsəwə́m (East. rasawə́m) verb I (trans.) 'to send to, to make arrive'

maktáb m 1, Ar.pl. makātíb (East. makāti̱b)

dāxiləwə́m verb IV-A (trans.) 'to enter, register, enroll' (East. dāxi̱lawə́m)

(13) zdákṛəy, pl. zdakṛyā́n m 2 'student' (East. zdákṛay)

layliyá f 2 'dormitory, room and board'

dərīší f 4 'suit (of clothing)' (East. dərešī́)

tanxā́ f 3 'allowance, salary' written tanxwāh

ẖátā̀ adv. 'even' written ẖati

kirāyá f 2 'fare'

safár m 1 'trip, journey'

xarts m 1 'expense, price'

safàrxárts m 1 'travel expense(s)'

(14) mas̤ráf m 1, Ar.pl. mas̤āríf m 'expenses' (East. mas̤ārí̱f)

híts (East. héts) wáxt adv. 'never,(at) no time'

(15) də . . . lə amála prep.-adv.phrase 'because of'

tawajó f 3 'attention' written tawaju̱h

(16) mas̤rafawə́m verb IV-A (trans.) 'to spend' (mas̤ráf m,14 above)

hamdā́ dem.pron. 'this very, this same'

(17) rozə́m verb I (trans.) 'to train'

čamtú adj. V 'ready'

(18) lāyéq adj. I 'able'

tah̤s̤íl, Ar.pl. tah̤s̤ilā́t m 'education, training'

pohantún m 1 'university'

leẓém verb I (trans.) 'to send'

NOTES

Like the preceding unit 16 also this one was written and transcribed by Noor Ahmad Shaker of the University of Kabul, who speaks the Kandahar dialect.

The same differences between the Kandahar and the Eastern dialect as found in unit 16 (see its Notes) can also be observed here; e.g:

(a) East. /a/ for Kandahar /ə/: kawí (3) (13), kā́la (4), lwastə́l (4), dwólas (5), tsalór (6), hálta (12), ṣā́ra, kóra (obl. II, 13), bárxa (16), tsə́nga (17), etc.

(b) day (1), zdákṛay (13)

(c) East. /e/ for Kandahar /i/: pəse (3), dzíne (11), lā́re (13), héts (14), hewādó (18)

(d) East. /o/ for Kandahar /u/: taˁlimā́to (3), šāgərdā́no (10), etc.

(e) East. /o/ and /e/ for Kandahar [ū] and [ī]: lóyo (12), nóro (13), dəreší (13), póre (13), kéẓi (13, 14), leẓí (18), etc.

(1) tālím for taᵒlim; similarly yấni for yáᵒni (East. yáᵒne); mutālím for mutaᵒlim (7); maārif for maᵒārif (15) (GP § 7.3)

(8) muasisū́ kṣ̌i [o:] changes before i in kṣ̌i (GP § 42.4b)

(16) lā́ra here for lā́re (Kandahar lā́ri)

(17) wérozəl ši present II passive phrase

TRANSLATION

Education in Afghanistan

(1) In Afghanistan education in elementary schools, the duration of which is six years, is compulsory.

(2) And after this higher education is optional.

(3) But the government makes a great effort to encourage the students to continue their education.

(4) After the elementary school three years middle (school) and again after that three years high-school instruction is provided ("are being read").

(5) That school where twelve years of instruction is going on, is called "lesa".

(6) After high-school ("lesa") four years is the college period.

(7) After completing the period ("duration") of college, the bachelor's degree (licenciate) is given to the student.

(8) In government installations a high-school diploma carries with it a privileged bonus of 100 and a bachelor's degree a bonus of 200 afghanis. The same way a master's degree has a bonus of 300 and a doctor's degree a bonus of 400 afghanis.

(9) In Afghanistan from elementary school up to the end of college all education is free.

(10) In addition to that, all educational necessities like pen, pencil, eraser, paper, notebook, book, and other things like that are given free by the government to the students.

(11) In Afghanistan some students are paupers, and some students live in small districts and villages; there are no high-schools there,

(12) thus whenever they finish their elementary education, they come to big towns for more advanced education and enroll themselves in high-schools.

(13) To such students, aside from other educational necessities, dormitory, a suit, an allowance, even transportation fare and also travel costs from (their) home to that city where they study, is given by the government.

(14) And these expenses are never again collected from the student.

(15) Thus for this reason the government of Afghanistan pays more attention to education than to anything else.

(16) And it spends a large part of the budget of the country in this same way.

(17) In order that the students together be trained in a good manner and become ready for the service of the country as it should be,

(18) the government of Afghanistan sends each year a number of able students for higher education to well-known universities of foreign countries,

(19) and in the period of (their) studies all expenses are given to them by the government.

UNIT 18

د هیواد په شمالي ګوټ کښې د پټرولو
د تفحصاتو په هکله یو مصور راپورتاژ

ښاغلی سردار محمد داؤد صدراعظم چه د سنبلې په څورلسمه ورځ، د کانو او صنایعو له وزیر دکتور محمد یوسف او د تجارت له وزیر ښاغلي شېرزاد سره، د شمالي او لوېدیځو ولایتو د چارو د کتلو له پاره هغو خواوو ته تللی و، د مزارشریف د عرفاني، اقتصادي، صنعتي، او تعمیراتي بیلو بیلو شقوقو له کتلو څخه وروسته یې شبرغان ته تشریف یووړ. او په هغه ځای کښې یې د پټرولو د پلټنې چارې وکتلې.

ښاغلي صدراعظم په دې ځای کښې د خواجه ګوګردك په غره کښې د پټرولو د لومړی څا برمه‌کاري پرانیستله، او په یتیم طاق کښې یې د پټرولو د لومړي څا امتحاني تولیدات وکتل. له دې څا څخه په ورځ کښې ۲۰ ټنه پټرول ایستل کېږي.

ښاغلي صدراعظم په مزارشریف کښې په یوه وینا کښې وویل چه باید موږ په اوسنیو کامیابیو دومره خوشحال نه شو چه موږ له هغو درندو مسئولیتو او کارو څخه چه په مخ کښې مو دي غافل کړي.

د یتیم طاق له څا څخه چه ۴۰۰ متره ژوره ده، په ۲۴ ساعتو کښې ۲۰ ټنه پټرول ایستل کېږي.

پخوا له دې څخه د هغه په څو نورو ځایو کښې د استفادې وړ صنعتي ګیس تثبیت شوی، او د یتیم طاق د لومړي څا په ګیس لرونکو او تېل لرونکو خنډو کښې آزمویني رواني دي.

ښاغلي صدراعظم د هغه د چارو د پرمختګ او نتیجو په باب د هغه له انجنیرانو او کارګرو سره خبرې اترې وکړې، او دوی ته یې د ښو نتیجو مبارکي ورکړه، او د دوی زیات بریالیتوب یې وغوښت.

د شبرغان خلکو د هیواد د هر ډول خدمت له پاره د خپل چمتووالی
ډاډ ورکړ. ښاغلی صدراعظم په سرپل کښی د برمه کاری ښوونځی وکتوت . او
مزارشریف ته د بیرته تګ په لار کښی یی د مزارشریف د ملکی هوابازی ډګر
هم وکوت .

TRANSCRIPTION

de hewā́d pe šamālí góṭ ke de pi̱trólo de tafahu̱sā́to
pe hákela yaw mu̱sawár rāportā̀ž

(1) ṣāǵélay sardā́r Mu̱hammàd Dāwúd sádre āzám či̱ de su̱mbu̱lé pe tswarlaséma wrádz, de kānó aw sanāyé̥o le wazír du̱ktùr Mu̱hammád Yu̱sú̱f aw de ti̱jārát le wazír ṣāǵéli Šerzā́d sara, de šu̱mālí aw lwedídzo wi̱lāyató de čā́ro de katélo le pā́ra haǵó xwā́wo ta tlélay we,

(2) de Mazā́re šaríf de i̱rfāní, i̱qti̱sādí, sanatí, aw tāmi̱rātí bélo bélo šuqúqo le katélo tsexa wrústa ye Šebi̱rǵā́n ta tašríf yówoṛ.

(3) aw pe háǵe dzā́y ke yè de pi̱trólo de palaṭéne čā́re wékatèle.

(4) ṣāǵéli sàdre āʔám pe dé dzā́y ke de Xwā̀ja Gogi̱rdák pe ǵré ke de pi̱trólo de lu̱mṛéy tsā́ bàrmakārí prā́nistela,

(5) aw pe Yatimtā́q ke yè de pi̱trólo de lumṛí tsā́ i̱mti̱hāní tawlidā́t wékatel.

(6) le dé tsā́ tsexa pe wrádz ke šél ṭána pi̱tról estèl kéẓi.

(7) ṣāǥə́li sàdre āzám pə Mazā́re šaríf ke pə yawà waynā́ ke
wə́wayə̀l či bā́yad múẓ pə osanə́yo kāmyābə́yo dómra xušā́l
nə́ šu či̲ múẓ lə háǥo drandó masuli̲yató aw kāró tsəxa
či̲ pə mə́x ke mo dì, ǥāfi̲l kṛi.

(8) də Yatimtā́q lə tsā́ tsəxa či̲ tsalór sáwa mi̲tra žəwə́ra da,
pə tsalə́rišto sāató ke šə́l ṭána pi̲tról estə̀l kə́ẓi.

(9) pəxwā́ lə də́ tsəxa də haǥə́ pə tsó nóro dzāyó ke də
i̲sti̲fādə́ wáṛ sanatí gés tasbìt šə́way,

(10) aw də Yatimtā́q də lu̲mṛə́y tsā́ pə gés larúnko aw tél
larúnko xanḍó ke āzmoyə́ne rawā́ne di.

(11) ṣāǥə́li sàdre āzám də haǥá də čā́ro də pərmaxtág aw
natijó pə bā́b də haǥá lə i̲njini̲yarā́no aw kārgə́ro
sara xabə́re atə́re wə́kṛe,

(12) aw dúy ta yè də ṣó natijó mu̲barakí wárkṛa, aw də dúy
zyā́t baryālitób ye wə́ǥuṣt.

(13) də Šəbi̲rǥā́n xálko də hewā́d də hár ḍáwl xi̲dmát lə pā́ra
də xpə̀l čamtuwā́li ḍā́ḍ wárkəṛ.

(14) ṣāǥə́li sàdre āzám pə Sarepúl ke də barmakārə́y ṣowəndzáy
wə́kot.

(15) aw Mazā́re šaríf ta də bə́rta tág pə lā́r ke yè də Mazā́re
šaríf də mu̲lkí hawā̀bāzə́y ḍagár hám wə́kot.

GLOSSARY

goṭ m 1 'corner'

pi̲tról m pl. 'oil'

tafah̲ús̤, Ar.pl. tafah̲us̤ā́t m 'investigation, search'

də . . . pə hákəla prep.-adv.phrase 'concerning, about'

mu̲s̤awár adj. I 'illustrated'

rāportā́ž m 1 'report, reporting'

(1) s̤āǥə́lay m 4 'Mr.'

tswarlasə́m adj. I 'fourteenth' (tswárlas num. '14')

kān m 1 'mine'

s̤anˤát m 1, Ar.pl. s̤anāyə́ˤ 'industry'

lwedídz adj. I 'western'

(2) ˤi̲rfāní adj. V 'educational'

s̤anˤatí (su̲nˤatí) adj. V 'industrial'

taˤmirātí adj. V 'constructional, building'

šaq m 1, Ar.pl. šu̲qúq 'branch, section'

tašríf m 1, Ar.pl. tašrifā́t 'honor, distinguished presence'

(4) lu̲mṛáy adj. III 'first'

tsā f 5 'well' (also tsā(h) m 2)

barmakārí f 4 'drilling' (barmá f 2 'drill')

(5) i̲mti̲hāní adj. V 'exploratory, examining'

tawlíd, Ar.pl. tawlidā́t m 'production'

šəl num. 'twenty'

(6) ṭan m 1 'ton'

(7) kāmyābí f 4 'success'

ǥāfi̲lawə́m verb IV-A (trans.) 'to make unaware, neglectful' (ǥāfí̲l adj. I)

(8) mí̲tər m 1 'meter'

žəwə́r adj. I 'deep'

tsalérišt num. 'twenty-four'

(9) i̲sti̲fādá f 2 'use, utilization'

gés (also gays) m 1 'gas'

tas̲bitéẓəm verb IV-A (intrans.) 'to be proven, established'

(10) xanḍ m 1 'ditch'

āzmoyə́na f 1 'experiment'

(11) pərmə́xtàg (pərmáxtàg) m 1 'progress'

natijá f 2 'result'

i̲njini̲yár (i̲njinyár) m 2 'engineer'

kārgár (kārgə́r) m 2, m 5 'worker'

(12) mu̲barakí f 4 'congratulation'

baryālitób m 1 'success'

(13) čamtuwā́lay m 'readiness'

ḍāḍ m 1 'assurance'

(14) bérta tàg m 1 'return trip' (bérta adv. and tag m 1 'trip, journey')

mu̲lkí adj. V 'local, civil (not military)'

hawābāzí f 4 'flying, aviation'

ḍagár m 1 'field'

NOTES

This selection was taken from the daily Islāh, issue of October 12, 1960, p. 3. Sometimes medial e is written ی instead of ې here: hewā́d (headline, 13), bélo bélo (2) ges (9, 10), bérta (15).

(1) sumbulá (f 2) written sunbula, Afghan solar month lasting from August 24 to September 23. The 14th of sumbula is September 5.

tswarlasém, ordinal formed from cardinal num. (GP § 76.2c)

lwedídz adj. I 'western', created for ǵarbí; xatídz adj. I 'eastern' for šarqí (lwéẓem, past lwed- 'to fall, set'; xéžem, past xat- 'to climb, rise')

(2) bélo bélo doubled phrase, see 16.10

tašríf yówoṛ (3d sing.masc. past II of wṛem verb IV) "(he) took his distinguished presence away, (he) left", also tašríf rā́woṛ "(he) brought his distinguished presence, (he) came"

(4) ǵre obl.sing. of ǵar m 5, m 1 (GP § 55.3a)

(5) tsā here m 2

(6) estə̀l kéẓi pres. I passive of bā́səm, verb III (trans.)

(9) taṣbìt šə́way (day) perfect I phrase without aux. (GP § 96.3)

(11) kārgə́ro here obl.pl. of m 5 (GP § 55.2)

pər-máx-tàg new compound formation of pər máx (mə́x)

'ahead' and tag 'going, trip' (15 below: bérta-tàg 'return trip'). Compounds of free forms are rare in Pashto (GP § 67.1a), but note barmakā̄rí (4 above), ṣowəndzáy (14 below), hawā̄bā̄zí (15 below).

(14)(15) wə́kot 3d sing.masc. past II of gə́rəm verb III (trans.)

TRANSLATION

An illustrated report on the search for oil in the northern corner of the country

(1) Prince Muhammad Dawud, the prime minister, who on the 14th day of Sombola with the minister of mines and industries Dr. Muhammad Yusuf and with the minister of commerce Mr. Sherzad in order to inspect the affairs of the northern and western provinces had gone to these areas,

(2) left for Shiburghan after inspecting the different educational, economical, industrial, and constructional (government) sections of Mazar-i-Sharif.

(3) And there he inspected the oil research affairs.

(4) The prime minister opened in this place the drilling (operation) for the first oil well on the Khwaja Gogirdak mountain,

(5) and in Yatimtaq he inspected the exploratory production of the first oil well.

(6) From this well daily 20 tons of oil are obtained.

(7) The prime minister said in a speech in Mazar-i-Sharif that we should not become so satisfied with the present successes that they might make us unaware of those heavy responsibilities and tasks which are ahead of us.

(8) From the well of Yatimtaq, which is 400 meters deep, 20 tons of oil are extracted in 24 hours.

(9) Prior to this in some other places of it industrial gas fit for utilization has been established,

(10) and in the gas- and oil-containing fields of the first well of Yatimtaq experiments are going on.

(11) The prime minister discussed the progress and the results of its operations with its engineers and workers,

(12) and congratulated them on their good results and wished them (still) greater success.

(13) The people of Shiburghan gave assurance of their readiness for any kind of service to the country.

(14) The prime minister inspected in Saripul the school for (oil) drilling,

(15) and on the return trip to Mazar-i-Sharif he inspected also the civil aviation (air) field in Mazir-i-Sharif.

UNIT 19

د نړۍ سیاسي فعالیتونو ته یوه لنډه کتنه

ګرانو لوستونکو به په دې یو څو ورځو کښې په ورځپاڼو کښې په څو څو
واره دا خبر لوستی وي، چه د ملګرو ملتو د عمومي ټولنې سږنۍ پنځلسمه جرګه
به د ملګرو ملتو د موسسې په تاریخ کښې یوه بې‌ساری غونډې پېښه وي. او دا
ځکه چه د هرچا څخه مخکښې د شوروي اتحاد صدراعظم خروسچف د عمومي ټولنې
په کلیزو جرګو مرکو کښې د یو نوي رنګ او فوق العاده دلچسپۍ را پیدا کولو په
غرض دا فیصله وکړه چه هغه به پخپله په عمومي ټولنه کښې د شوروي اتحاد د
هیئت مشري کوي. او دې سره یې د نړۍ د نورو حکومتونو مشرانو ته هم
دا غږ وکړو چه هغوی دې هم په عمومي ټولنه کښې د خپلو هیئتونو مشري وکړي.
د نړۍ د سیاسي کتونکو په نبزد د خروسچف دا فیصله هسې د ټوکو ټکالو یوه
خبره نه ده. او هرچا ته معلومه ده چه د نړۍ د ډېرو هیوادو د سر
مشرانو د ملګرو ملتو د عمومي ټولنې په سږنیو کلیزو جرګو مرکو کښې د ګډون د پاره
نیویارک ته خپل ځانونه رسولي دي. په دې هیوادو کښې بیا په خصوصي ډول د
بېطرفه هیوادو د مشرانو د عمومي ټولنې په فعالیتونو کښې د برخې اخیستو د پاره
نیویارک ته رسېدل ډېر اهمیت لري.

TRANSCRIPTION

də naṛéy si̲yāsí faà̲li̲yatúno ta yawá lánḍa katə́na

(1) grā́no lwastúnko ba pə dé yàw tsó wrádzo ke pə wradzpā́ṇo ke pə tsó tsó wā́ra dā́ xabár lwástay wì,

(2) či̲ də məlgə́ro mi̲lató də u̲mumí ṭoléne saẓanéy pi̲ndzəlasə́ma

jərgá ba də məlgə́ro mi̱lató də mu̱asi̱sé pə tāríx ke yawà besā́ri ǥú̱nde péṣa wi.

(3) aw dā́ dzə́ka či̱ də hárčā̀ tsəxa mə́x ke də šorawí i̱ti̱hā́d sàdre āzám Xu̱rusčú̱f də u̱mumí ṭolə́ne pə kalízo jərgó marakó ke də yàw nə́wi ráng aw fàwqu̱lādá di̱lčaspə́y rā̀paydā̀ kawə́lo pə ǥaráz dā́ faysalá wə́kṛa

(4) či̱ haǥá ba pəxpə́la pə u̱mumí ṭolə́na ke də šorawí i̱ti̱hā́d də hayát məšərí kawì.

(5) aw dè sará sará ye də naṛə́y də nə́ro hu̱kumatúno məšərā́no ta hám dā́ ǥáẓ wə́kṛò či̱ haǥúy de hám pə u̱mumí ṭolə́na ke də xpə́lo hayatúno məšərí wə́kṛi.

(6) də naṛə́y də si̱yāsí katúnko pə nézd də Xu̱rusčú̱f dā́ faysalá hàse də ṭóko ṭakā́lo yawà xabə́ra nə́ da.

(7) aw hárčā̀ ta mālúma da či̱ də naṛə́y də ḍéro hewādó də sár məšərā́no də məlgə́ro mi̱lató də u̱mumí ṭolə́ne pə saẓanə́yo kalízo jərgó marakó ke də gaḍún də pā́ra Niw Yā́rk ta xpə̀l dzānúna rasawə́li dì.

(8) pə dé hewādó ke byā̀ pə xu̱susí ḍáwl də betaráfa hewādó də məšərā́no də u̱mumí ṭolə́ne pə faā̀li̱yatúno ke də bárxe axistó də pā́ra Niw Yā́rk ta rasedə́l ḍér ahmyát larì.

GLOSSARY

si̱yāsí (syāsí) adj. V 'political'

faˀā̀li̱yát (faˀā̀lyát) m 1 'activity, action'

katə́na f 1 'look, survey, review'

(1) wradzpā́ṇa f 1 'daily (newspaper)' (from wradz f 1 and pā́ṇa f 1 'leaf, sheet') (see Note on 18.11)

xabár m 1 'news'

(2) məlgə́ri mi̱latúna m pl. 'United Nations'

ʕu̱mumí adj. V 'general, common'

ṭolə́na f 1 'society, assembly'

saẓanáy adj. III 'this year's' (sàẓ kā́l adv. 'this year')

tāríx m 1 'history'

pi̱ndzəlasə́m adj. I 'fifteenth'

besā́ri adj. V 'unparalleled'

g̸ú̱nde part. 'like, as'

(3) dzə́ka či̱ conj. 'because'

mə́x kṣe adv. 'in front, ahead'

šorāwí i̱ti̱hā́d m 'Soviet Union' (i̱ti̱hā́d m 1 'unity, union')

kalíz adj. I 'annual' (kāl m)

jərgá maraká f 2 'conference, meeting'

fawqu̱lʕādá adj. V 'extraordinary' (written fawq u̱lʕāda)

di̱lčaspí f 4 'interest'

də . . . pə g̸aráz̤ prep.-adv.phrase 'for the sake of, because of'

(4) məšərí f 4 'chairmanship, leadership' (mə́šər m 2)

(5) g̸áẓ kawə́m verb IV see 1.4

(6) de . . . pe nézd prep.-adv.phrase 'in the opinion of, according to'

ṭóke ṭakā́le f pl. 'joke, joking'

háse adv. 'this way, thus' also dem.pron. 'such'

(8) xu̱ṣuṣí adj. V 'special'

NOTES

This selection was taken from the Kabul daily Iṣlāḥ, issue of October 3, 1960.

(1) lwastúnkay adj. IV 'reading, reader' (from lwélem, past lwast- 'to read'), katúnkay adj. IV 'on-looking, observer' (6 below) (from górem, past kat- 'to look at') are verbal adjectives used as nouns (GP § 93.2).

ba . . . lwástay wì perfect II with ba indicates uncertainty, a supposition (GP § 96.4c).

(3) šorawí adj. V 'Soviet' from šorā́ f 3 'council' (see 15b)

jergá maraká is a nominal phrase consisting of two substantives, similarly ṭóke ṭakā́le (6 below) (GP § 101.3).

(5) sará sará doubled phrase (GP § 101.4a)

de . . . wékṛi present II with particle de (GP § 90.3c)

wékṛo for wéke, wékeṛ, or in Kandahar wékey, is found in the Peshawar dialect and in some extreme Eastern and Southern dialects.

(7) saẓanə́yo. The paper has saẓanəy.

xpəl dzān and dzān (m 1) function like reflexive pronouns.

Here the reference is to the actor (məšərā́no) of the sentence (GP § 79.4).

(8) rasedə́l m pl.; axistó, obl. for axistə́lo, are verbal substantives (GP § 93.3).

TRANSLATION

A brief look at the political activites of the world

(1) The dear readers may have read in these few days over and over in the daily newspapers this news that

(2) this year's 15th meeting of the general assembly of the United Nations will be like a unique event in the history of the United Nations organization,

(3) and this is because Khrushchev, the prime minister of the Soviet Union, earlier than anybody, for the purpose of creating a new style and extraordinary interest in the annual meetings (and conferences) of the general assembly, made the decision

(4) to head personally the delegation of the Soviet Union to the general assembly.

(5) And together with this he called on the heads of other governments of the world that they also head their own delegations at this general assembly.

(6) In the opinion of the political observers of the world this decision of Khrushchev's is thus no joking matter.

(7) And it is known to everybody that top leaders of many countries of the world have gotten themselves to New York for participation in this year's annual meetings and conferences of the general assembly of the United Nations.

(8) But among these countries especially the arrival in New York of heads of neutral countries for the participation in the activities of the general assembly has great importance.

د قندهار د ښار نیول

گرگین ووژل شو، مگر د قندهار د ښار نیول او فتح کول لا څه آسانه کار نه و ځکه چه په ښار کی د گرجیانو ډېر عسکر پروت و او د کلا پر برجانو او دروازو یې توپونه ایښی وه. هغوی کولای شوه چه هم د میرویس سره مقابله وکړی او هم د ښار خلك د ټوپکو تر خولو لاندی کړی. لدې کبله نو باید داسی چاره سنجولې شوې وای چه نه د ښار خلك په قتل رسېدلی وای، او نه د ښار په نیولو کښی د میرویس آزادی غوښتونکی زلمیان د مقابلی سره مخامخ شوی وای. نو دا چاره یوه حربی خدعه وه چه میرویس کار ځینی واخیست، او هغه داوه چه پخپله ده د گرگین کالی واغوسته او د ده ملگرو د گرگین د ملگرو او ساتونکو کالی واغوستل او د هغوی په آسو سپاره شول. ترغونی ماښام په هغه دبدبه او بـرم لکه گرگین چه روانېدئ د ښار خوا ته روان شو. او نور یې درې زره پښتانه د ښار شا و خوا پټ کښېنول چه د ده اشارې ته معطل وی. چه د ښار دروازې ته راورسېدل، گرجی پیره دارانو د میرویس پر سوارلۍ د گرگین د سوارلۍ خیال وکړ، پرې یې ښودل چه ښار ته ننوزی. په مجردی چه ښار ته ننوتل، د دروازې او کلا پر محافظینو یې یرغل وکړ. په دې وخت کښی هغه درې زره پښتانه چه دباندی منتظر وه، هم ښار ته راداخل شول، او د گرجیو عسکر یې ټول تارومار کړل او ښار یې ونیو. او دستی میرویس اعلان وکړ او جارچی جار وواهه چه:

"د هغه چا مال او ځان په امان دی چه گرجی او پارسی عسکرو ته ساتی او ځای ورنکړی!"

TRANSCRIPTION

də Qandahā́r də ṣā́r niwə́l

(1) Gurgín wə́wəžəl šù, mágar də Qandahā́r də ṣā́r niwə́l aw fátha kəwə́l lā̀ tsə̀ āsā́na kā́r nə́ wu,

(2) dzə́ka či pə ṣā́r ki də gurjyā́nu ḍer askár prə́t wu aw də kalā́ pər brəjā́nu aw darwāzó ye topúnə íṣi wə.

(3) haǵúy kəwə́lāy šwə̀ či hám də Mir Wáys sərə muqābilá wə́kṛi aw hám də ṣā́r xálək də ṭopə́ku tər xwló lā́ndi kṛì.

(4) lə də́ kabála no bā́yad dā́si čārá sanjəwə́le šə́we wā̀y či nə́ də ṣā́r xálək pə qátəl rəsedə́li wā̀y,

(5) aw nə́ də ṣā́r pə niwə́lu kṣi də Mir Wáys āzādí ǵuṣtúnki zulmyā́n də muqābilə́ sərə maxāmàx šə́wi wā́y.

(6) no dā́ čārá yawá harbí xadʕá wə či Mir Wáys kā́r dzìni wā́xist,

(7) aw haǵá dā́ wə či pəxpə́lə də́ də Gurgín kālí wā́ǵustə,

(8) aw də də́ məlgə́ru də Gurgín də məlgə́ru aw sātúnku kālí wā́ǵustə̀l aw də haǵúy pə ā́su spārə́ šwə̀l.

(9) tarǵunáy māṣā́m pə háǵa dabdabá aw brám ləke Gurgín či rawānedə́y də ṣā́r xwā́ tə rawā́n šu.

(10) aw nór ye dré zə̀rə pəṣtānə́ də ṣā́r šā̀ wu xwā́ pə́ṭ kṣénəwə̀l či də də́ išārə́ mātál wi.

(11) či də ṣā́r darwāzé tə rā́wérəsedə̀l, gurjí payradā́rā́nu də Mir Wáys pər swārlə́y də Gurgín də swārlə́y xyā́l wə́kā,

(12) pré ye ṣodèl či ṣā́r tə nénəwzi. pə mujarádi či ṣār tə nénəwetèl, də darwāzé aw kalā́ pər muhāfizínu ye yarǵál wékəṛ.

(13) pə dè wáxt kṣi hága dré zére pəṣtāné či dəbā́ndi muntazír we, hám ṣā́r tə rā̀dāxíl šwèl,

(14) aw də gurjíyu askár ye ṭól tā̀rumā́r kṛèl aw ṣā́r ye wéniw.

(15) aw dəstí Mir Wáys elā́n wékəṛ aw jā́rčí jā́r wéwāhè či:

(16) də hága čā́ mā́l aw dzā́n pə amā́n dèy či gurjí aw pārsí askár wənésāti aw dzā́y warnékṛi.

GLOSSARY

(1) wážnəm, past waž- (Kandahar: wəž-) verb II (trans.) 'to kill'

fátha f 1 'conquest' written fath

āsā́na adj. V 'easy' (also āsā́n adj. I)

(2) gurjí m 2 'Georgian' (man from Gurjistān "Georgia") (East. gurjí)

ʿaskár m 'soldier'

kalā́ f 3 'fortress'

brəj m 2 'tower'

darwāzá f 2 'gate, door'

top m 1 'cannon, gun'

(3) hám . . . hám adv., conj. 'both . . . and also, as well as'

muqābilá f 2 'resistance, opposition' (East. muqābilá)

ṭopák m 5, m 1 'gun, rifle' (GP § 55.2)

lā́ndi (East. lā́nde) kawə́m verb IV (trans.) 'to put under'

(4) lə kabála adv. 'because (of)'

čārá f 2 'remedy, helpful scheme'

sanjawə́m (Kandahar: sanjəwə́m) verb I 'think up, imagine, devise'

qátəl m 1 'slaughter, murder'

(5) āzādí f 4 'freedom'

zulmáy (also zalmáy) m 2 'young man'

maxāmáx (məxāmə́x) adj. I 'confronted with'

(6) ḫarbí adj. V 'of war'

xadṛá f 2 'deceit, trick' less formal pronunciation xadá

dzíni (East. dzí̱ne see 5.4)

(7) kālí m pl. 'clothes'

áǥundəm, past aǥust- verb II (trans.) 'to put on (clothes)'

(8) ās m 1 'horse'

sparə́ẓəm verb IV-A 'to become mounted' (spor, fem. spará adj. II 'mounted, on horseback')

(9) māṣā́m m 1 'evening'

tarǥunáy māṣā́m m 'twilight' (tarǥunáy adj. III)

dabdabá f 2 'pomp, magnificence'

bram m 1 'splendor'

(10) šā̀ wu xwā́ adv. 'around' ("back and side", šā f 3 'back', xwā f 3)

pəṭ adj. I 'hidden, secret'

kṣenawə́m (Kandahar: kṣenəwə́m) verb I (trans.) 'to place, put, make sit'

išārá f 2 'signal' (East. i̲šārá)

maʕt̲ál adj. I 'waiting'

(11) rārasə́ẓəm (Kand. rārəsə́ẓəm) verb II (prefix rā-)

payradā́r m 2 'sentry'

swārlí f 4 'riders, riding party' (also swarlí)

xyā́l kawə́m verb IV 'to think' (see 14c.2)

(12) pə mujarádi či conj. 'immediately when' (East. mu̲jaráde či̲)

nənawə́zəm, past nənawat- verb II (intrans.) 'to enter' (see 2.6)

muh̲āfíz̄, Ar.pl. muh̲āfiz̄ín m 'guard' (East. mu̲h̲āfíz̄)

yarǵál m 1 '(sudden) attack'

(13) dəbā́ndi adv. 'outside' (East. dəbā́nde)

muntaz̄ír adj. I 'waiting' (East. mu̲ntaz̄i̲r)

rā̀dāxilə́ẓəm verb IV-A (intrans.) 'to enter, come inside' (East. rā̀dāxi̲lə́ẓəm) (prefix rā-, see 8.4)

(14) tārumārawə́m verb IV-A (trans.) 'to destroy, rout completely'

(15) dəstí adv. 'immediately'

iʕlā́n m 1 'announcement'

jārčí m 2 'news-crier'

jār m 1 'announcement'

jā́r wahə́m verb I 'to announce'

(16) māl m 1 'property'

dzān m 1 'life'

amā́n m 1 'protection'

NOTES

This selection is taken from Abdul Rauf Bēnawā's historical book Mir Ways niké ("Our Ancestor Mir Ways") (Kabul: paṣ̌to ṭoləna, 1946), p. 67f. Benawa, a native of Kandahar, is an important Pashto writer and the author of many books. He is the president of Radio Kabul now.

The transcription gives the pronunciation of Noor Ahmad Shaker of Kandahar and shows the same features of the Kandahar dialect as discussed in the Notes of units 16, 17: /ə/ for Eastern /a/ in zə́ra (13), topúna (2), pəxpə́la (7), wa (7), kaʷə́l (1), kawə́lāy (3), kṣ̌ə́nawəl (10), rāwə́rasedəl (11), lə́ka (9), sara (5), etc. /i/ for Eastern /e/: kṣ̌e, ke (2), dzíne (6), lā́nde (3), dəbā́nde (13), dā́se (4). /u/ for Eastern /o/: brəjā́no (2), ṭopə́ko (3), niwə́lo (5), məlgə́ro (8), ā́so (8), muh̲āfizíno (12), etc.

(1) Gurgin was the Persian governor of Kandahar, against whom the Pashtoon chief Mir Ways revolted in 1709.

(2) wu 3d sing.masc., wə 3d pl. masc. in Kandahar
Many Eastern dialects use wə also as 3d sing.masc.
íṣi wə past perf. phrase of (i)ẓdə́m verb IV (see 8.3)

(3) kawə́lāy šwə past of potential phrase; šwə́ here for šwəl (8 below)

(4) sanjawə́le šə́we wā̀y, perfect optative passive phrase
rasedə́li wā̀y, perfect optative phrase
maxāmàx šə́wi wā̀y (5 below), perfect optative phrase
The optative forms after bā́yad and with the negation nə́ emphasize lack of reality (GP § 94, 94.6). sanjawə́le instead of sanjawə́la (or sanjawə́l) is the sing.fem. form of the perfect participle used here to form the passive (GP § 93.4d).

(6) kā̀r áxləm 'to make use of'

(9) rawānedə́y, past I with typical Kandahar 3d sing.masc. ending -əy, contrasts in aspect with rawā́n šu past II.

(11) wə́kā for wə́keṛ literary and archaic

(12) nə́nəwetə̀l (East. nə́nawatə̀l) past II, nə̀nawatə́l past I; nə́nəwzi (East. nə́nawzi) present II, nə̀nəwə́zi (nə̀nawə́zi) present I (GP § 85.5a)
pré ye ṣodə̀l verbal phrase with past II of preẓdə́m Notice position of modal particle, see also wənə́sāti, warnə́kṛi (16 below); on word-order in

verbal phrases see GP § 102.

(14) wéniw literary for Kandahar wéniwey, East. wéniwe.

(15) elā́n for i̥lā́n

TRANSLATION

The Seizure of the City of Kandahar

(1) Gurgin was killed. But the seizure of the city and the conquest was still not any easy task,

(2) because many soldiers of the Georgians were located in the city, and they had placed cannons on the towers and gates of the fortress.

(3) They were in a position to oppose Mir Ways as well as to put the people of the city under the mouths of (their) guns.

(4) For this reason then such a (helpful) scheme ought to have been devised that neither the people of the city might be slaughtered

(5) nor in the seizure of the city Mir Ways' freedom-seeking young warriors might face opposition.

(6) Thus the plan was a trick of war which Mir Ways used.

(7) And it was this that he himself put on the clothes of Gurgin,

(8) and his friends put on the clothes of the friends and supporters of Gurgin and got on their horses.

(9) In the twilight of the evening he moved with this pomp and splendor like Gurgin, when he was on the move, in the direction of the city.

(10) And his other 3,000 Pashtoons he placed secretly around the city so that they might wait for his signal.

(11) When they reached the gate of the city, the Georgian sentries thought of the riders of Mir Ways as riders of Gurgin.

(12) They let them enter the city. Immediately after they entered the city, they made an attack on the guards of gate and fortress.

(13) At this time those 3,000 Pashtoons who were waiting outside also entered the city,

(14) and they routed all Georgian soldiers and took the city.

(15) And right away Mir Ways made an announcement and the news-crier spread the news that

(16) that person's possessions and life are spared who does not protect Georgian and Persian soldiers and does not give refuge to them.

لنډۍ

سبا به بیا کډی بار بېږی
د دښت گلان به ستا لمنی بویینه.

* * *

په ما دی څه کړی دی، خدایه،
چه نور دی گل کړه، زه غوټی ولاړه یمه.

* * *

خدای دی د رود د غاړی گل که
چه د اوبو په پلمه درشم بوی دی کمه.

* * *

ټوټی ټوټی په وینو راشې
چه پرهارونه دی گنډم، خوله درکومه.

* * *

جانان په جنگ کې تر شا راغی،
پر برنی ورکړې خوله پښېمانه یمه.

* * *

جانانه، هسی وخت به راشی
چه توپک واخلو لاس تر لاس سنگر ته ځونه.

* * *

یو وار دی لاس په لاس کی راکه،
دا لاس نیوی به دی تر ډېره یاد ومه.

* * *

که دیدن کېږی، گودر له راشه،
زه به منگی په لپه ورو ورو ډکومه.

✲ ✲ ✲

پر گودر سور سالو ښکاره شو،
ما وی دی تورو اوبو اور واخیست، مینه.

✲ ✲ ✲

ناري وهم، ږغ راته نه کېږي،
بیا به جهان راپسی گوري، نه به یمه.

✲ ✲ ✲

اشنا په ټوکو نه پوهېږی،
ما په خورو زلفو واهه، مرور شونه.

✲ ✲ ✲

TRANSCRIPTION

landẹ́y

(1) sabā̀ ba byā́ kā́ḍe bārẹ́ẓi,
də dā́ṣt g̲u̲lā́n ba stā̀ lamə́ne bù̄yawína.

✲ ✲ ✲

(2) pə mā́ de tsə̀ kə́ṛi di, xwdā́ya,
či̲ nór de gú̲l kṛə, zə́ ǥ̲u̲ṭə́y walā́ṛa yə́ma.

✲ ✲ ✲

(3) xwdā́y de də ród də ǥā́ṛe gú̲l ka
či̲ də obó pə palmā̀ dā́ršəm, búy de kə́ma.

✲ ✲ ✲

(4) ṭoṭé ṭoṭé pə wíno rā́še
či̲ parhārúna de ganḍə́m, xwlə́ darkawə́ma.

* * *

(5) jānā́n pə jáng ke tər šā̀ rā́ǥay,
pə̀r baranə́y warkə́ṛe xwlə́ pṣemā́na yə́ma.

* * *

(6) jānā́na, háse wáxt ba rā́ši
či̲ topā̀k wā́xlu, lā́s tər lā́s sangə́r ta dzúna.

* * *

(7) yáw wā́r de lā́s pə lā́s ke rā́ka,
dā́ lā̀s niwáy ba dè tər ḍéra yā̀dawə́ma.

* * *

(8) ka didā́n kṛé, gu̲də́r la rā́ša,
zə̀ ba mangáy pə lápa wró wró ḍā̀kawə́ma.

* * *

(9) pər gu̲də́r súr sālú ṣkārá šu,
mā̀ wé dé tóro obò ór wā́xist, mayə́na.

* * *

(10) nāré wahə́m, ẓáǥ rā̀ta nə́ kṛè,
byā́ ba jahā́n rā̀pəse góre, nə́ ba yə́ma.

* * *

(11) ašnā́ pə ṭóko nə́ pohéẓi,
mā̀ pə xwaró zú̲lfo wāhə́, marawár šū̀na.

* * *

GLOSSARY

(1) káḍạ f 1 'belongings, household goods'

bārẹ́zəm verb II (intrans.) 'to become packed, loaded' (bār m 1 'load')

daṣ̌t m 1 'desert'

buyawə́m verb IV-A (trans.) 'to smell' (buy m 1 'smell')

(2) g̱uṭə́y f 4 'bud'

(3) rod m 1 'river'

obə́ f pl. 'water'

palmā́ f 2 'pretense'

(4) ṭoṭé ṭoté f pl. 'pieces'

wíne f pl. 'blood'

parhā́r m 1 'wound'

ganḍə́m verb I 'to sew'

darkawə́m verb IV (trans.) 'to give to you' (prefix dar-, rākawə́m 1.4, warkawə́m 5.5)

(5) jānā́n m 2 'beloved'

jang m 1 'battle, war'

šā f 3 'back'

tər šā̀ rādzə́m 'to flee'

baranáy adj. III 'last night's'

pṣ̌emā́n (pəṣ̌emā́n) adj. I 'sorry, ashamed, repentant'

topak see ṭopák 20.3

(6) sangár (sangə́r) m 1 'barricade, trench, battle-
front'

(7) lā̀s-niwáy m 3 'hand-clasp, hand holding'

yā̀dawə́m verb IV-A (trans.) 'to remember' (yād m 1)

(8) didā́n m 1 'looking, seeing'

gudár (gudə́r) m 1 'ford, watering-place'

la part. 'to'

mangáy m 3 'jug, pitcher'

lápa f 1 'handful'

pə lápa adv. 'by the hollow of one's hand'

ḍakawə́m verb IV-A (trans.) 'to fill' (ḍak adj. I)

(9) sālú m 2 'head-covering, shawl'

ṣkārà ké̤zəm verb IV (intrans.) 'to appear, become
visible'

tor adj. I 'black'

or m 1 'fire'

ór áxləm verb II 'to catch fire'

mayén m 2 'beloved, darling'

(10) nārá f 2 'sound, shout'

nāré wahə́m verb I 'to call out'

rā́ta adv. 'to me' (prefix rā-)

rā́pəse adv. 'after me' (prefix rā-)

(11) aśnā́ m 2 'beloved, friend'

xor, fem. xwará adj. II 'dishevelled, scattered,
loose'

zṳ́lfe   f 1   pl.   'locks, tresses'
wahə́m   verb I   (trans.)   'to strike, beat'
marawár   adj.   I   'angry, offended, displeased'

NOTES

This selection was taken from lanḍə́y ("lunday (Anonymous Pushto Couplets)") by Abdul Rauf Benawa, ed. (Kabul: 1958) (pp. 5, 22, 28, 41, 42, 50, 74, 104, 106, 120, 129).

A lanḍəy is genuine Pashto folk poetry. The first line of each couplet has nine, the second line 13 syllables.

(1) buyawína like dzúna (6), šúna (11) poetic forms with final -na. yə́ma (2, 5, 10), kə́ma (3), darkawə́ma (4), yādawə́ma (7) are varieties of yəm, darkawə́m, yādawə́m that occur even colloquially.

(2) walā́ṛa identifies the speaker as a woman, also pṣemā́na (5).

(4) ṭoṭé ṭoṭé, expressive adverbial doubled phrase (GP § 101.4a), 'shattered to pieces, severely wounded'

rā́še 2d sing.pres. II of rādzə́m used in imperative meaning (GP § 90.3b)

(5) warkə́ṛe sing.fem.perfect participle of warkawə́m (GP § 93.4c)

(7) tər ḍéra (wáxta) 'for a long time' adv. phrase with obl. II form after the prep. tər

(8) kṛe poetic and dialectal for kawé (also 10 below); present I can express the wish of a person (GP § 89.2a)

(9) mayéna vocative of mayén m 2 (similarly jā́nā́na, 6 above)

wé for wayéle

(11) xor variant of xpor, fem. xpará adj. II

TRANSLATION

landəy

(1) Tomorrow again (their) belongings will be packed up,
The flowers of the desert will smell your skirts.

* * *

(2) What have you done to me, God!
That you made others bloom; I stand as a bud.

* * *

(3) May God make you a flower by the riverside,
That I may come to you, pretending (for) water, that I may smell you.

* * *

(4) (Severely) wounded, (smeared) with blood may you come to me
That I stitch your wounds, give you my lips.

* * *

(5) My beloved fled in battle;
I regret the kiss I gave him last night.

* * *

(6) My beloved, such a time will come
That we may grab the rifle, hand in hand we go to the battle-front.

* * *

(7) Put your hand once into mine;
This holding of your hand I'll remember for a long time.

* * *

(8) If you want to see me, come to the ford,
I will slowly be filling my jug with the hollow of my hands.

* * *

(9) At the ford a red shawl appeared;
I thought: these dark waters caught fire, my beloved.

* * *

(10) I call out (to you), you do not answer me;
Later you will be looking (all over) the world for me, I shall be no more.

* * *

(11) My beloved does not understand jokes;
I was striking him with my loose locks; he got angry.

* * *

UNIT 22

۱ ـ

توره چه تېرېږی خو ګذار لره کنه
زلفې چه ولول شی خو خپل یار لره کنه ؟
ولې راته وایې چه په ښکلیو نظر مکړه
سترګې چه پیدا دی خو دیدار لره کنه ؟
شبنم دې نمونځ روژه کا، زه به ډکې پیالې اخلم
هر سړی پیدا دی خپل خپل کار لره کنه ؟
تا وې چه زما د خولې بوسه لکه دارو ده
غواړم دا دارو د زړه پرهار لره کنه ؟
وینې مې د زړه خورې مګر نور څه لره ندی
زړه زما پیدا دی تا خونخوار لره کنه ؟
څه ژړا ، فریاد کړې د شهر د تورو زلفو
ته ورتلې پخپله دې تور مار لره کنه ؟
خود به ستا تر مخه د ګیا غندې څرګند شی
ګل د لاله راوړه خپل رخسار لره کنه ؟
می شته ، چنګ و نی شته ، د خپل یار سره ، خوشحاله
خپل بیاض په لاس کښې څه ګلزار لره کنه ؟

ب —

زه چه مست پـــه لب د یار یم، هیڅ حاجت د شراب نشته ·

اور د عشق مې زړه کباب کـړو ، هیڅ حاجت د کباب نشته ·

تمام تـــن مې وچ لرگـی شو ، رگ مې تار وریاندې پربووت ·

زیر و بم آواز تـــرې خبـږی ، هیڅ حاجت د رباب نشته ·

پـــر پرهار نمکپاشـــی کړی ، چه پرسش کـــوی له ما نـــه ·

حال مې خود ورته معلوم دی ، هیڅ حاجت د جواب نشته ·

لکـــه مرغ نیم بسمل یم ، تپش کـــړم په مزکـــه بانـــدې ·

ځان مې ورکړستا په عشق کې ، هیڅ حاجت د قصاب نشته ·

TRANSCRIPTION

(a)

(1) túra či̲ teréẓi xo gu̲zā́r lara kanà
zú̲lfe či̲ walwál ši xo xpèl yā́r lara kanà?

(2) wále rā̀ta wā́ye či̲ pe ṣkélyo nazár mé kṛà
stérge či̲ paydā́ di xo didā́r lara kanà?

(3) šéx de nmúndz, rožá kā, zé ba ḍáke pyālé áxlem
hár saṛáy paydā̧ day xpél xpél kā́r lara kanà?

(4) tā́ wè či̲ zemā́ de xwlé bosá léka dārú da
ǥwā́ṛem dā́ dārú de zṛe parhā́r lara kanà?

(5) wíne mè de zṛé xwré, mágar nór tsè lara né dì
zṛé zemā́ paydā́ dày tā́ xunxwā́r lara kanà?

(6) tse žaṛā́, faryā́d kṛè de šahéy de tóro zú̲lfo

tə́ wartlé pəxpéla dé tór mā́r lara kanà?

(7) xú̲d ba stā́ tər méxa də gi̲yā́ ǵùnde tsargánd šì
gú̲l də lālá, rā́wṛa xpəl ru̲xsā́r lara kanà?

(8) máy šta, čáng o náy šta, də xpə̀l yā́r sara, Xu̲šā́la,
xpél bayā́z pə lā́s ke dzá gu̲lzā́r lara kanà?

(b)

(1) zə či̲ mást pə láb də yā́r yə́m, héts hāját də šarā́b
nə́šta.
ór də í̲šq me zṛə́ kabā́b kṛò, héts hāját də kabā́b nə́šta.

(2) tamā́m tán me wə́č largáy šù, rág me tā́r wərbā́nde préwòt.
zìr o bám āwā́z trè xéži, héts hāját də ṛabā́b nə́šta.

(3) pər parhā́r namàkpāší kṛi, či̲ pu̲rsí̲š kawì lə mā́ na.
hā̀l me xú̲d wérta mālúm dày, héts hāját də jawā́b
nə́šta.

(4) lèka mú̲rǵ e ním bi̲smí̲l yèm, tapí̲š kṛèm pə mdzéka
bā̀nde.
dzā́n me wárkəṛ stā̀ pə í̲šq ke, héts hāját də qasā́b
nə́šta.

GLOSSARY

(a)

(1) túra f 1 'sword'
teréẓəm verb IV-A (intrans.) 'to become sharpened'
(terə́ adj. II 'sharp')

gu̲z̲ā́r m 1 'blow'

lara part. 'for, to'

kaná adv. 'or not?; certainly' (conj. ka and negation na, see Ex. 1, 2, 4, 8)

walwaléẓəm verb IV-A (intrans.) 'to become curled'

yār m 2 'beloved, darling, friend'

(2) wále adv. 'why'

nažár m 1 'seeing, look'

didā́r m 1 'seeing, look'

(3) nmundz variant of lmundz m 1 (see 5.8)

rožá f 2 'fasting'

rožá kawə́m verb IV 'to fast'

pyālá f 2 'cup'

(4) bosá f 2 'kiss'

dārú m 2 'medicine'

(5) xunxwā́r m 2 'murderer, beast of prey, cruel person' ("blood-eater")

(6) žaṛā́ f 3, f 5 'weeping, lament'

faryā́d m 1 'lamenting, complaining'

šahéy f 4 'beloved'

mār m 2 'snake'

(7) xu̲d adv. 'certainly'

gi̲yā́ f 3, f 5 'grass, weed'

də . . . ǵu̲nde prep.-adv.phrase 'like'

gú̲l də lālá m 2 'tulip'

tsargandéẓəm verb IV-A (intrans.) 'to become clear, appear' (tsargánd adj. I)

ru̱xsā́r m 1 'cheek'

(8) may m 'liquor'

čang m 1 '(small) harp'

nay m 1 'flute'

bayā́ẓ̂ m 1 '(poet's) note-book'

gu̱lzā́r m 1 'flower garden'

(b)

(1) mast adj. I 'intoxicated'

lab m (2) 'lip' (poetic)

ẖājá́t m 1 'necessity'

šarā́b m pl. 'liquor, wine'

ʕi̱šq m 1 'love'

kabābawə́m verb IV-A (trans.) 'to roast'

kabā́b m 1 'roast'

(2) tamā́m adj. I 'entire, whole'

tan m 'body'

wəč adj. I 'dry'

largáy m 3 'wood, stick'

rag m 1 'vein'

tār m 1 'thread, string'

prewə́zəm, past prewat- verb II (intrans.) 'to fall'

zir adj. I 'high-pitched'

bam (bəm) adj. I 'low-pitched'

rabā́b m 1 'rabab' (Afghan guitar-like instrument)

(3) namàkpāšī́ f 4 'spreading of salt' (Persian)

pu̲rsí̲š m 1 'question'

jawā́b variant of dzawāb (15b)

(4) mu̲rǥ m 2 'bird, fowl'

nìm bịsmí̲l adj. I 'half-butchered'

tapí̲š kawə́m verb IV 'to flutter'

q̤aṣā́b m 2 'butcher'

NOTES

The texts for this selection were taken from Abdul H̱ay H̱abibi's paṣtānə́ šu̲ʿarā́ ("Pashtoon Poets"), vol. I (Kabul: 1941), p. 165 and p. 284.

The first text (a) is a poem by the famous chief of the Khatak tribe and Pashto author Khushhal Khan Khatak (Xu̲šh̲āl Xān Xaṭak), who lived during the greater part of the seventeenth century. The second text (b) is attributed by Habibi to a descendant of Khushhal Khan called Xu̲šh̲āl Xān Šahid, who lived from about 1720 to about 1785.

(a) The first line of each couplet has 14 syllables, the second line 13 syllables. The poem in a slightly different form is also contained in C. E. Biddulph, AFGHAN POETRY OF THE SEVENTEENTH CENTURY (London: 1890), p. 50.

(a)

(2) kṛa poetic and dialectal for kawa (compare 21.8)

(3) kā poetic for kawí

xpə́l xpə́l indicates variety and wide distribution (GP § 101.4a)

(4) wé see 21.9

zəmā́ (also 5 below) is the form suggested by the metre; common in Eastern dialects beside zmā

(6) kṛe for kawé (see 2 above)

(7) gú̱l də lālá, used only in poetry, imitates the Persian gúl e lālá

(b) Each line in this poem has 16 syllables.

(1) pə láb də yā́r poetic for də yā́r pə láb, similarly ór də ʿísq poetic word-order for də ʿi̱sq óṛ. kṛo for kə, kəṛ; kəy (Kandahar), is a Peshawar or extreme Eastern form.

(2) rabā́b is still in common use in Afghanistan.

(3) kṛi for kawí (see 22a, 2 and 6 above), similarly kṛəm for kawə́m (4)

(4) mú̱rg̸ e ním bi̱smí̱l Persian phrase

mdzə́ka (see 5.3) is written mzəka مزکه by Habibi.

TRANSLATION

(a) Isn't it so?

(1) When the sword is sharpened -- for a blow, isn't it?
When the locks may become curled -- for one's beloved, aren't they?

(2) Why are you telling me: don't look at beauties?
The eyes that are created -- for seeing, aren't they?

(3) Let the pious one do his prayer, (his) fasting, I will be taking full cups,
Everybody is created for his own job, isn't he?

(4) You said that a kiss from your mouth is like medicine,
I want this medicine for the wound of my heart, don't I?

(5) You drink my heart's blood, but it is not for anything else.
My heart is created for you vampire, isn't it?

(6) Why do you cry, complain about the black locks of the beloved,
You were going to this black snake yourself, weren't you?

(7) Certainly against (your) face like grass will appear
the tulip; bring it to your cheek, won't you?

(8) There is wine, there is harp and flute, with your beloved, Khushhal,
Your notebook in your hand, go to the flower-garden, won't you?

(b)

(1) I who am intoxicated by the lips of my beloved:
there is no need for liquor;
Fire of love roasted my heart: there is no need of
a roast.

(2) My whole body became dry wood, my vein, a string,
fell on it;
A high and a low sound rises from it: there is no
need of a "rabāb".

(3) She pours salt on my wound when she asks me questions;
She knows my condition herself: there is no need of an answer.

(4) Like a half-butchered bird I am, I flutter on the ground;
I gave my life for your love: there is no need of a butcher.

UNIT 23

هسې وایي چه یو وقت خرښبون بابا او اسماعیل د سړبن او بیټنی نیکه په مخ کی ناست و. د دوی کور و د کسي پر غره. نو خرښبون د پلار او تره له خوا په تنگ او رخصت مأذون سو. اسماعیل نیکه داسې ناری وکړلې:

نارې

که یون دی یون دی مخکی ببلتون دی له کسي غره څخه ځی، خرښبون دی
که وروره، وروره! خرښبون وروره! ته چه ببلتون کړې زما ویر ته گوره
چه ځې مرغې له توری کرغې له همزولی پاته: ځې څه برغې له؟
د خدای د پاره خرښبون یاره چه هېر مو نکړې زموږ کهول واړه
زړه می رپېږی یار می ببلېږی ببلتون يې اور دی ځان په سوځېږی

نقل کا چه د اسماعیل بابا خرښبون هسې غبرگون وکاوه:

ځلوریځ د خرښبون بابا

ببلتانه ناره می وسوه په کور باندی نه پوهېږم چه به څه وی پېښ په وړاندی؟
له خپلوانو به ببلېږم په سرو سترگو دواړه سترگی می په وینو دی ژړاندی
اسماعیله! ستا نارو می زړگی سری کی ببلتانه خرښبون بیا له تا پردی کی
نه هېرېږی؛ که می بیا نه ستا یادی کی په چېږو د ویر به پرې سی د زړه مراندی
څمه څمه چه اورېد یون می دی و مخ ته د یانه څوری به اچوم و ترخ ته
ستاسی یاد به می وی بس د زړه و سخ ته که دا مځکه غرونه ټول سی لاندی باندی

TRANSCRIPTION

(1) hási wā́yi či yaw wáqt Xərəṣbún bābā̀ aw Ismāʕíl də
Səṛbán aw Beṭní nikə́ pə mə́x ki nā́st wə. də
dúy kór wù də Kisé pur ǥrə́.

(2) nò Xərəṣbún də plā́r aw trə́ lə xwā́ pə tág aw ruxsát
māzún su, Ismāʕíl nikə̀ dási nāré wə́kṛəlè:

nāré

(3) kə yún dəy yún dəy, — mə́xki beltún dəy.
lə Kisé ǥrə́ tsxə — dzí, Xərəṣbún dəy.

(4) kə wrórə wrórə! — Xərəṣbún wròrə!
tə či beltún kṛè, — zmā́ wír tə górə.

(5) či dżé Marǥé lə, — tóri karǥé lə,
hamzóli pā́tə: — dzé tsə̀ barǥé lə?

(6) də xwdā́y də pā́rə, — Xərəṣbún yā́ṛə,
či hér mu nékṛə, — zmúẓ kəhól wā́ṛə.

(7) zṛé mi rəpī́ẓi, — yā́r mi belī́ẓi,
beltún ye ór dəy, — dzā́n pə swədzī́ẓi

(8) náqəl kā́ či də Ismāʕíl bābā́ Xərəṣbún hási ǥbargún
wə́kāwə:

tsəlorídz də Xərəṣbún bābā́

(9) beltāné nārá mi wə́swə pə kór bā̀ndi,
nə puhéẓəm či bə tsé wi péṣ pə wṛā́ndi.

(10) lə xpə̀lwā́nu bə beléẓəm pə sró stə́rgu,
dwā́ṛə stə́rgi mi pə wínu di žəṛā́ndi.

(11) Ismā‘ílə! stā́ nāró mi zəṛgáy sráy kəy,
beltāné Xərəṣbún byā́ lə tā́ pradáy kəy.

(12) né heréẓə; kə mi byā́ né stā́ yādáy kəy,
pə čəṛó də wír bə prī́si də zṛé mrā́ndi.

(13) dzə́mə dzə́mə, či úẓd yún mi ḍə̀y wə máx tə,
də yāné tswárəy bə ā́čəwə̀m wə tráx tə.

(14) stā́si yā́d bə mì wi bás də zṛé wə sáx tə,
kə dā́ mdzə́kə ǵrúna ṭól si lā́ndi bā́ndi.

GLOSSARY

(1) bābā́ m 2 'father, dad'
niké m 2 'grandfather'
nāst adj. I 'sitting'
pur variant of pər

(2) plār m 1 'father'
trə m 1 'uncle'
ruxsát m 1 'excuse, permission to leave'
maẓunéẓəm verb IV-A (intrans.) 'to be permitted'
(māẓún adj. I 'permitted, granted')
nārá f 2 "nara" (type of poem) (see 21.10)

(3) yun m 1, obl. yāné 'trip, traveling'
beltún m 1, obl. beltāné 'departure, separation'
(GP § 55.4c)

(4) wror, pl. wrúṇa m 'brother'

wir m 'sorrow, grief'

(5) karǵá f 2 'barren land, desert' (obsolete)

ḥamzóləy adj. IV, also m 4 'of the same age, comrade, friend' (East. hamzólay)

barǵá f 2 'purpose, benefit' (obsolete)

(6) herawə́m verb IV-A (trans.) 'to forget'

kəhól (East. kahól) m 1 'family'

wā́ṛə indef.pron. 'all'

(7) rapéẓəm, past raped- verb II 'to shiver, shake, tremble' (Kand. rəpéẓəm)

beléẓəm verb IV-A (intrans.) 'to become separated' (bel adj.I)

swadzéẓəm, past swadzed- verb II (intrans.) 'to get burned' (Kand. swədzéẓəm)

(8) náqəl m 1 'tale'

náqəl kawə́m verb IV 'to tell'

ǵbargún m 1 'response, answer'

tsalorídz m 1 'quatrain' (obsolete) (Kand. tsəlorídz)

(9) pə wṛā́ndi (East. wṛā́nde) adv. 'ahead, in the future'

(10) žəṛā́nd adj. I (East. žaṛā́nd) 'weeping, crying'

dwā́ṛə adj. 'both' (East. dwā́ṛa)

(11) zəṛgáy m 3 'heart' (zṛə m 1 'heart')

suráy adj. III 'pierced, perforated'

suráy kawə́m verb IV 'to pierce'

(12) herẽ́ẓəm verb IV-A (intrans.) 'to be forgotten'

yādáy m 3 'remembrance, memory'

čāṛé f 2 'knife, dagger'

prekéẓəm verb IV (intrans.) 'to get cut'

mrā́ndə (East. mrā́nda) f 1 'fiber, tissue, string, rope (of tent)'

(13) tswárəy m 4 'provisions, food (for traveling)' (East. tswáray)

ačəwə́m (East. ačawə́m) verb I (trans.) 'to throw; pour'

trax m 1 'side of the body, armpit' (obsolete)

(14) yād m 1 'memory'

bas adv. 'enough'

sax m 1 'good fortune, happiness'

lā́ndi bā́ndi (East. lā́nde bā́nde) adv. 'upside down'

NOTES

This selection was taken from Muhammad Hotak's pə́ṭa xazāná ("Secret Treasury") in Abdul Ḫay Ḫabibi's annotated edition (Kabul: 1944), pp. 17, 19. The manuscript, written in 1924 by Muhammad ʕAbās Kāṣi and quite modern in its orthography, is in the library of the Department of Press in Kabul. It is stated that it is a copy of a manuscript written in 1886; and that the author, Hotak, wrote his Pashto literary history with its specimens in 1763 in Kandahar.

The text is given here in a Kandahar pronunciation as transcribed by Noor Ahmad Shaker. The same Kandahar features can be observed as in units 1, 16, 17, 20:

/ə/ /əy/ for Eastern /a/ /ay/:

wróra (vocative 4), yā́ra (6), góra (imp. 4), wə́swa (fem. 9),
dzə́ma (13), ka (4), tsxa (3), ta (13), žaṛā́nde (10),
čaṛó (12), ačawə́m (13), day (3), tswáray (13), etc.

/i/ for Eastern /e/:

háse (1), dā́se (2), mə́xke (3), bā́nde (9), wṛā́nde (9), stə́rge
(10), žaṛā́nde (10), me (7, 10, 11, 12, et.), mrā́nde
(12), stā́se (14), etc.

/u/ for Eastern /o/:

mo (6), wíno, xpəlwā́no, stə́rgo (10)

/ī/ for Eastern /e/:

rapéẓi, beléẓi, swadzéẓi (7), prési (12)

Other Kandahar features are s forms for š: su (2), wə́swa (9), si (14); the 3d sing.masc.past form in -əy: kəy (11, 12) (see 20.9)

(1) waqt archaic spelling for waxt

(3) This "nārá" has four lines with five syllables each, the third line has no rhyme.

tsxə for tsə́xə (East. tsə́xa)

(4) kṛe for kawé

(5) tóri pronounced tū́ri, hamzóli pronounced hamzū́li in Kandahar

(6) hér mo nékṛè verbal phrase, for word order of components see GP § 102.1

(7) Each "tsaloríd̲z" here has four lines and twelve syllables each. The rhyme scheme is aaba ccca ddda

(8) kā poetic for kawí

(11) sray for suráy

(12) pə čaṛó də wír for də wír pə čaṛó (Kandahar čəṛó)

TRANSLATION

(1) The story goes as follows: One time Old Karashbun and Ismail were seated in front of Saṛaban and Old Beṭnay. Their house was on Kisa mountain.

(2) Then Kharashbun was permitted by his father and uncle to go and leave. Old Ismail made this poem:

"Cries"

(3)	If there is a trip, there is a trip,	separation lies ahead.
	From Mount Kisa	he goes, it is Kharashbun.
(4)	O brother, brother!	brother Kharashbun!
	You who departs,	look at my sorrow.
(5)	That you go to Margha,	to a dingy barren land,
	Your friends remain:	for what purpose do you go?
(6)	For the sake of God,	dear Kharashbun,
	Do not forget us,	all our family.
(7)	My heart is trembling,	my dear friend is leaving,
	Separation from him is a fire,	(my) body burns in it.

(8) They say that Old Kharashbun replied to Old Ismail as follows:

Quatrains of Old Kharashbun

(9) A call for departure was made at my home,

I do not know what will happen in the future.

(10) I will part from my relatives with red eyes,

Both of my eyes are shedding tears of blood.

(11) Ismail, your "cries" pierced my heart,

Separation made Kharashbun again a stranger with you.

(12) You are not forgotten. If I did not remember you again,

By the knives of grief the strings of my heart will be cut.

(13) I am going, I am going, there is a long trip ahead of me,

My travel provisions I will be putting under my arm.

(14) The memory of you (all) will suffice for the happiness of my heart,

Even if this earth, these mountains all should be turned upside down.

UNIT 24

ګجرې

کلی بالکل دم وو. شېردل چه کور ته اورسېدلو نو د کور ټول بنديان اوده وو. د رښمينې خوا کې شيرينۍ هم اوده وه. او دی چه شيرينۍ ته د ښکلولو د پاره ورنژدې شو، نو هغې خوب کښې يوه سلګۍ اوويهله او د شېردل زړه ئې کړی مړی کړو.

شېردل چه خپل کټ لره راغی، نو سوچ ئې کولو چه د شيرينۍ د ګجرو د پاره څه بندوبست اوکړی. د هغه ذهن به په هره خبره نښتو او دوه دوه کېدو به: "که شيرينۍ له ګجرې نه راوړم، نو دا نول خو زه نه شم زغملی او که ښهر ته ځم، نو هغه هم نه کېږی". د هغه ذهن به بيا ونښتو: "يره يو خو بس خدائ ښه دی. که يو وزری نه وی، نو دا ويره خو به مې نه وه کنه چه که زه نه يم، نو خان به مې بال بچ د کوټو نه وباسی." او په دې سوچ سوچ کښې هغه اوده شو.

او چه ملا بانګ وئېلو، نو هغه بيا ويښ وو. هغه څادر په اوږه کړو، د دونکاچې نه ئې لور راواخستو او ښهر ته رااووتو. اصل کښې هغه شيرينۍ سره سترګې نه شوې برابرولی. او چه د نمرخاته نه لږ وروستو د هغه د ګوانډی زوی د هغه د پاره چائ راوړې او د هغه خوا کښې شيرينۍ ټولړی په سر نيولې، په سټرو سټرو قدمونو راروانه د ورايه ورښکاره شوه، نو د شېردل په ټول بدن کښې لکه چه ګرمه سيکه اوچورلېده. او چه هغه په بيړه ځان تر شيرينۍ اورسولو، نو دا ګرمه سيکه سترګو ته رارسېدلې وه.

TRANSCRIPTION

gajré

(1) kéle̱ bìlku̱l dám o. Šerdə́l če kór ta órasedəlo, nu
da kòr ṭól bandyā́n udə́ wu.

(2) da Rexmíne xwā́ ke Širinái hú̱m udá wa. aw dé̱ če
Širinái ta da xku̱lawú̱lo da pā́ra warnížde šo,

(3) nu haǥé xób ke yawá salgái ówahèla, aw da Šerdə́l zṛé
e kə́ṛi mə́ṛi kṛò.

(4) Šerdél če xpél káṭ lara rā́ǥe̱, nu sóč e kawélo če da
širinái da gajró da pā́ra sé bandubást ùkṛi.

(5) da haǥə́ zéhn ba pa hára xabə́ra nxató aw dwà ḍwà kedó
ba:

(6) "ka Širinái la gajré ná rā́wṛəm, nu dā̀ núl xu zə ná šəm
zǥamə́le, aw ka xā́r ta zə́m, nu haǥá u̱m ná kègi."

(7) da haǥé zéhn ba byā́ ónxato: "yára yáw xu̱ bás xu̱dé̱ xá
de. ka yawwazére ná wè, nu dā yára xu ba me ná
wa kaṇà,

(8) če ka zə̀ ná yəm, nu xā́n ba me bā́lbač da koṭó na óbāsi."

(9) aw pa dé sóč sóč ke haǥá udé šo.
aw če mu̱lā́ bā́ng wé̱lo, nu haǥá byā̀ wíx o.

(10) haǥə́ sādár pa ugá kṛo, da dunkāčé na e lór rawā́ǥi̱što,
aw bahár ta rāówato.

(11) ásəl ke haǥé Širinái sara stə́rge ná šwe barābarawú̱le.

(12) aw če da nwàr xātə́ na lèg rú̱sto da haǥə́ da gawānḍí zúy
da haǥə́ da pā́ra čāe rāwṛé,

(13) aw da haǵə́ xwā́ ke Širinái, ḍoḍái pa sár niwə́le, pa
stə́ṛo stə́ṛo qadamúno rārawā́na da wrā́ya wàṛxkārá šwa,

(14) nu da Šerdə́l pa ṭòl badán ke làka če gárma siká
óčùrleda.

(15) aw če haǵə́ pa bíṛa zā́ṇ tar Širinái óraṣawu̲lo, nu dā́
gárma siká stə́rgo ta rārasedə́le wa.

GLOSSARY

gajrá f 2 'bracelet, bangle'

(1) bílku̲l adv. 'completely' written bālku̲l

dam adj. I 'silent, quiet'

bandá m 2 'person, member of family; slave'

udə́ adj. II 'asleep' (East. bidə́, widə́)

(2) hu̲m for East. ham

ṣku̲lawə́m verb IV-A (trans.) 'to kiss'

warnižde adj. V 'near (her)' (prefix war-)

(3) xob m 1 'sleep'

salgə́y f 4 'sob'

salgə́y wahə́m verb I 'to sob'

kə́ṛi mə́ṛi adj. V 'disturbed, worried, upset'

kə́ṛi mə́ṛi kawə́m verb IV 'to disturb, worry'

e variant of ye

(4) kaṭ m 2 'charpoy, cot'

soč̣ m 1 'thinking'

sóč kawə́m verb IV 'to think'

bandubást m 1 'arrangement'

(5) ẕehn m 1 'mind'

nṣáləm, past nṣat- verb II (intrans.) 'to get entangled, stick, to get entrapped' (East. nṣə́ləm)

(6) nul m 1 'grief, sorrow'

zġamə́m verb I (trans.) 'to bear, endure'

(7) yára interj. (East. yā́ra)

yawwazə́re adj. IV 'alone, without a helper ("one-winged"), (East. yawwazáray) (wazár m 1 'wing')

wyára f 1 'fear' pronounced yára (East. wḗra)

(8) xān m 2 'landlord, chief of village'

bā́lbač m 'family, wife and children'

koṭá f 2 'room'

obā́səm verb I (trans.) 'to turn out, drive out'

(9) bāng m 1 'call (to prayers)'

wiṣ adj. I 'awake'

(10) uẓá f 2 'shoulder'

dunkā̌čá f 2 'platform'

lor m 1 'sickle'

bahár adv. 'outside'

rāwúzəm, past rāwat- verb II (intrans.) 'to come out' (prefix rā-)

(11) áṣ̤əl kṣe adv. 'in fact'

barābarawə́m verb IV-A (trans.) 'to make equal' (barābár adj. 'equal, straight')

(12) nmàr xāté m '(time of) sunrise' pronounced nwàr

xāté (nmar m 'sun' and xāté m 'rising')

wrústo variant of wrusta

gawānḍí m 2 'neighbor'

zoe, pl. zāmén m 'son' (East. zoy)

čáe f pl. 'tea' (East. čāy)

(13) stéṛe adj. IV 'tired' (East. stéṛay)

rārawā́n adj. I 'coming, moving (hither)' (prefix rā-)

da wrā́ya adv. 'from far, in the distance'

warṣkārà kéẓəm verb IV 'to appear, become visible to' (war- prefix)

(14) badán m 1 'body'

garm (Pesh. gárəm) adj. I 'hot'

siká f 2 'lead'

čurléẓəm (čúrləm), past čurled- verb II (intrans.) 'to turn around, revolve'

(15) bíṛạ f 1 'haste, hurry'

NOTES

This text was taken from a collection of short stories by Qalandar Momand entitled gajré (Peshawar: University Book Agency, 1958), pp. 7-9. The author, whose real name is Habibur-Rahman, is a well-known Pashto writer and editor residing in the Peshawar district. The text was transcribed by Mr. Khayal Bokhari, a native of the same region, himself

a Pashto writer and a staff member of the Pashto Academy
of the University of Peshawar.

Mr. Bokhari's Peshawar dialect shows the following
features:

[1] /s/ for East. /ts/; /z/ for East. /dz/: tsə (4),
     tsādár (10), dzem (6), dzān (15)

     /x/ for ṣ: Reṣmíne (2), ṣkuḷawélo (2), ṣār (6),
     wiṣ (9), etc.

     /g/ for ẓ (as in most Eastern dialects): kéẓi (6),
     uẓá (10), leẓ (12)

[2] /a/ frequently for East. /ə/: də (1, 2, etc.),
     pe (5), léka (14), ter (15)

[3] /ȩ/, a long lower mid-front vowel, for East. /áy/;
     /e/, a long mid-front vowel, often for East. /ay/;
     /ai/, with a lower high-front vowel as the second
     component, for East. /ey/, written ی :
     dáy (Pesh. dȩ́) 'he' (2), kélay (1), rāǵay (4),
     wayélo (9), xwdāy (7); day (Pesh. de, Kand. dey)
     'is' (7), zǵamélay (6), way (7), barābarawélay
     (11); Širinéy (2, 4, etc.), salgéy (3), ḍoḍéy (13)

[4] The most typical morpheme is -o for the 3d sing.mas.
     past forms: o 'was' (1), šo (2), kṛo (3), kawélo
     (4), kedó (5), etc.

     The prefix we- appears also as o (or ṵ): órasedelo
for wérasedə (1), rāówato for rāwéwātə (10), ṵ́kṛi for wékṛi

Other distinctions in individual word forms have been listed below.

(1) kéle̱ for East. kélay m 4; o for wə sing.masc.; wu for wə pl.masc.; da for də prep.; nu for no (frequent sentence connective)

(2) Reṣmina is Šerdi̱l's wife; Širinai is his young daughter who previously had asked him for bracelets. Her name is written Šerinəy in the book.

de̱ for day dem.pron.; če for East. či̱, čə (conj.)

(4) rā́ǵe̱ for rā́ǵay; sə written tsə; ú̱kṛi for wə́kṛi

(5) ba nṣató . . . kedó ba past I forms with ba indicate duration and repetition (GP § 92.4a).

pa for pə

(6) ná šəm zǵamə́le (East. zǵamə́lay, Kand. zǵamə́lāy) potential phrase

xār is written ṣahr (see 4.2)

u̱m for hu̱m (2 above)

xu̱ for xo, ná for nə́

(7) yára vocative from yār m 2 'friend', colloquially used as intensive and an interjection. Am. English: "oh boy!"

ka . . . ná we, nu . . . ba ná wa (East. nə́ way, Kand. nə́ wāy). Notice the use of the past tense with ba in the conclusion of the unreal conditional clause (GP § 92.4b) xu̲dé̲ for xwdāy, xa for ṣa, de for day 'is' (Kand. dəy)

(9) sóč sóč, also stéṛo stéṛo (13 below); doubled phrases (GP § 101.4a)

(10) rāwā̲́ǵišto written rāwāxisto

sādár written tsādar

(11) ná šwe barābarawú̲le in Kandahar: nə́ swāy (or swe) barābarawə́lāy (GP § 95.4, 3)

(12) rāwṛé past I 'was bringing', rā́wṛe past II 'brought'

rú̲sto for wrústo

(13) ḍoḍái for ḍoḍə́y

(14) láka če for lə́ka či̲ conj. 'as if'

(15) zān written dzān; tar for East. tər prep.

TRANSLATION

(1) The village was completely silent. When Sherdil reached home, then all the members of the household were asleep.

(2) By the side of Rekhmina, Shirinai was also asleep. And when in order to kiss her, he went near Shirinai,

(3) she uttered a sob in (her) sleep, and she made the heart of Sherdil worried.

(4) When Sherdil came to his bed, he was thinking that he should make some arrangement for Shirinai's bracelets.

(5) His mind was getting entangled in every matter and was being torn in two directions:

(6) "If I don't bring the bracelets for Shirinai, then I simply cannot bear this grief, and if I go to the city, this also cannot be done."

(7) Again his mind became entangled: "Well certainly, being by oneself is only all right for God. Were I not alone, this fear surely would not exist for me,

(8) that if I am not (around), then the landlord will turn my family out of the house."

(9) With these (various) thoughts he went to sleep, and when the priest called out (for morning prayers), he was again awake.

(10) He put his shawl on his shoulder, took up the sickle from the platform,and came out.

(11) In fact he could not face Shirinai.

(12) And a short while after the sunrise his neighbor's son was bringing tea for him,

(13) and at his side Shirinai, carrying bread on her head, approaching with tired steps, appeared in the distance;

(14) then it seemed to Sherdil as if hot lead was running through his entire body.

(15) And when he hurriedly went up to Shirinai, then this hot lead had reached his eyes.

UNIT 25

د سرو تعویذ

یوه شپه شمروز یو څو اجرتي قاتلان د جمیلې په کور ورخطا کړل. ډاکه پرېوته. صابره او جمیله دواړه په کښې مړې شوې. شمروز د خپلې ورېرې او د بوډۍ په مرګ د مکر ډېر وير او ژړا اوکړه. پولیس خپل تفتیش کښې ډېر په اخلاص سره کار اوکړو، ولې هېچا هم د ریښتیاؤ شهادت ته غاړه نه کېښوده. او نتیجه دا شوه چه شمروز په یو څو ورځو کښې د خپل مشر ورور په خانۍ کېناستو. خو د ناصر په بچ کېدو ئې په زړه کښې غټه بوغمه پاتې شوه. په خوا او شا کلو کښې ئې ډېر کوشش ورپسې اوکړو، ولې هېڅ پته ئې اونه لګېده.

ماشوم ناصر د خپل وطن نه ډېر لرې یو لوی ښار ته اورسېدو. یوه شپه چه ډېر ستړې شو، نو چرته په یوه باغیچه کښې د یو بینچ د پاسه اوده شو. دا باغیچه د لوی کاروباری تاجر په کور کښې وه. سحر وختي چه د کور مالک سېټهه رحمان د سېل د پاره بهر تلو، نو په باغیچه کښې ئې د خپل کور نه خطا شوې ماشوم اولیدو، چه لا هغه شان بې غمه اوده پروت وه. بنګلې ته لاړو او سره د خپل ښېره بېرته هغې ځائ ته راغلو، چرته چه هغه ماشوم لا هغه شان اوده وه. وایې چه د دې سېټهه یو زوې وه، چه ډېر ښکلی وه او هم لکه د دې ماشوم وه. دوی ته خپل مړ شوې زوی وریاد شو، د دواړو په سترګو کښې اوښکې وې. دواړه ساه نیولی د ماشوم په خوا کښې غلی ولاړ وو، چه په دې کښې ناصر هم له خوبه بېدار شو. اوتر اوتر ئې کتل او بیا په رتهو رتهو په ژړا شو. د سېټهه ښېر ناصر خپلې سینې ته جخت کړو. دواړو ژړل، خو دواړه نه پوهېدل چه د دوئ د ژړا وجه څه ده. سېټهه رحمان ناصر په غېږه کښې اوچت کړو، او سره د خپل ښېره کمرې ته لاړل.

TRANSCRIPTION

da sró tāwíz

(1) yawá špá Šamróz yaw sò ujratí qāti̱lā́n da Jamilé pa
kór warxatā́ kṛel.

(2) d̯ākā́ préwata. Sābí̱ra aw Jamilá dwā̯ra pakè mṛé šwè.

(3) Šamróz da xpéle wreré aw da bu̯d̯é̱ pa márg da mékər
d̯ér wír aw jaṛā́ ókṛa.

(4) pu̱lís xpél taftí̱š ke d̯ér pa i̱xlā́s sara kā́r ókṛo,
wàle héčā hù̱m da rìštiāo šahādát ta g̱ā̯ra né̱ kèxoda.

(5) aw natijá dā́ šwà če Šamróz pa yáw só wrázo ke da xpèl
méšər wrór pa xāné̱ kénāsto.

(6) xò da Nāsér pa bác̆ kedó ye̱ pa zṛé ke g̱áṭa bog̱má pāte
šwà.

(7) pa xwā́ u šā́ kélo ke ye̱ d̯ér koší̱š wàrpase ókṛo, wále
hés páta ye̱ onélageda.

(8) māšúm Nāsér da xpèl watán na d̯èr lére yaw lwé xā́r
ta órasedò.

(9) yawá špá če d̯èr stéṛe šo, no čárta pa yawà bāg̱ičá
ke da yaw bí̱nč da pā́sa udé šo.

(10) dā́ bāg̱ičá da lwé kārubārí tājír pa kór ke wá.

(11) sahàr waxtí če da kór mālí̱k Séṭ Rahmā́n da sél da pā́ra
bahár tlò, no pa bāg̱ičá ke ye da xpél kór na xatā́
šéwe māšúm ólido, če lā́ hág̱a šā́n bèg̱áma udé prót o.

(12) banglé ta lā́ṛo aw sará da xpə́l ṭabára byérta háǥe zé̱
ta rā́ǥlo, čárta če háǥa māšúm lā́ háǥa šā́n udé o.

(13) wā́yi če da dé Séṭ yaw zwé wò, če ḍer xkú̱le o aw hù̱m
láka da dé māšúm wò.

(14) dwí ta xpə́l mə̀ṛ šə́we zwé wàryā́d šo, da dwā́ṛo pa
stə́rgo ke úxke wè.

(15) dwā́ṛa sā̀ niwə́li da māšúm pa xwā́ ke ǥə́li walā́ṛ wu,
če pa dé ke Nāsə́r hú̱m la xóba bè̱dā́r šo.

(16) awtár awtár ye̱ katə́l, aw byā́ pa ráṭo ráṭo pa jaṛā́ šo.

(17) da Séṭ ṭabár Nāsə́r xpə́le siné ta jú̱xt kṛò. dwā́ṛo
jaṛə́l, xò dwā́ṛa nə́ póedə́l če da dwí da jaṛā́ wája
sə́ da.

(18) Séṭ Rahmā́n Nāsə́r pa ǥéga ke učát kṛò, aw sará da
xpə̀l ṭabára kamré ta lā́ṛel.

GLOSSARY

taˁwíz̲ m 1 'locket'

(1) ujratí adj. V 'hired'

qātí̱l m 2 'murderer'

warxaṭā́ kawə́m verb IV 'to send'

(2) ḍāká f 2 'attack'

prewúzəm (prewə́zəm), past prewat- verb II (intrans.)
'to fall down'

məṛ adj. II 'dead'

mə̀ṛ kéẓəm verb IV 'to die'

(3) buḍə́y f 4, f 5 'old woman'

wrerá f 2 'niece'

marg m 1 'death'

mə́kər m 1 'deceit, fraud'

(4) pu̱lís m 'police'

taftíš m 1 'investigation'

i̱xlā́s̤ m 1 'devotion, sincerity'

wále conj. 'but'

riṣtiā́ f 3 'truth'

šahādát m 1 'evidence, testimony'

(5) xāní f 4 'landlordship, ownership'

mə́šər wrór m 1 'elder brother'

(6) bàč kéẓəm verb IV 'to escape'

ǥaṭ adj. I 'big'

boǥmá f 2 'worry, concern'

(7) xwā́ u šā́ adj. V, adv. 'neighboring' (see šā̀ wu xwā́ 20.10)

koší̱š m 1 'effort'

páta f 1 'trace'

lagéẓəm, past laged- verb II (intrans.) 'to be touched, hit'

(8) māšúm m 2 'young child'

lwe for loy

(9) čárta adv. 'somewhere, where'

bāǥičá (also bāǥčá) f 2 'garden'

bịnč m 1 'bench'

da . . . da pā́sa prep.-adv.phrase 'upon'

(10) kārubārī́ adj. 'of business, commercial'

tājī́r m 2 'merchant'

(11) saḫár m 1 'morning'

waxtī́ adv. 'early'

mālī́k m 2 'owner'

xaṯā̀ kéẓəm verb IV 'to be lost'

šān m 1 'manner'

bèǵáma adj. V 'carefree, without worry'

(12) banglá f 2 'bungalow, house'

ṭabár f 'wife'

(14) waryādéẓəm verb IV-A (intrans.) 'to be remembered' (prefix war-)

úṣka f 1 'tear'

(15) sāh f 5 'breath' pronounced like sā

sā̀h niwə́lay adj. IV 'breathless'

ǵə́le adj. IV 'silent' (East. ǵə́lay)

be̱dāréẓəm verb IV-A (intrans.) 'to wake up, become awake'

(16) awtár adv. (also adj. I) 'surprised'

raṭ adj. I 'big (of tears)'

(17) siná f 2 'chest, breast'

ju̱xtawə́m verb IV-A (trans.) 'to bring close'

žā́ṛəm verb I (impers.-trans.) 'to weep'

wája f 1 'reason'

(18) ǵéẓa f 1 'bosom'

uc̆atawә́m verb IV-A (trans.) 'to lift' (uc̆át adj. I 'high')

kamrá f 2 'room'

NOTES

This text is taken from the novel <u>da</u> <u>sró</u> <u>ta'wíz</u> ("The Golden Locket") by Rashid Ali Dehqan (Peshawar: University Book Agency, 1958), pp. 39-40. The author, originally a native of Waziristan, is a well-known Pashto writer, and is program organizer for Radio Pakistan in Peshawar.

The text was transcribed by Jehanzeb Niaz, a native of the Peshawar district, teacher of Pashto at Islamia College near Peshawar. J. Niaz's dialect is almost identical with Khayal Bokhari's as shown in unit 24 (see its Notes), but there is no /ai/ written ئ in his dialect: buḍé̱ (3), xānḛ́ (5).

sro for sró zә̀ro obl. of sré zәr m pl

(1) Jamilá is the niece of S̆amroz.

so written tso

(2) Sābí̱ra is an old female servant of Jamila's.

(3) wír aw z̆aṛā́ ókṛa (Eastern wә́kṛa). The verb agrees with the second noun (z̆aṛā́) only. (GP § 103.4)

z̆aṛā is pronounced jaṛā́ (also 16, 17, below)

(4) "nobody put his neck to the testimony of the truth"
riṣtíā́, plural like singular (GP § 59.1b)
kéxoda written keṣoda; riṣtiā pronounced rištiā́
(5) só wrázo written tso wradzo
xāné̱ written xāney
kénāsto 'sat' for kṣénāsto
(6) Nāṣ̈ér is Jamila's brother and the nephew of Šamroz..
(7) hes written hets
(8) lwe for loy (also 10 below)
xār written ṣār
(9) stéṛe adj. IV for stéṛay (24.13)
(11) sel 'walk' for sayl m 1 (see 4.13)
ṣ̌éwe for šéway
(12) byérta for East. bérta
ze̱ for dzāy; háǥe does not indicate a fem.
o '(he) was' is written we here.
(13) zwe, for zoy, written dzoe in the source
xkú̱le for ṣkélay
(14) dwi for duy
šéwe for šéway
(17) dwā́ṛo jaṛél Notice the impersonal-transitive construction in past I (GP § 83.3a) jaṛél for žaṛél
pòedél for pu̱hedél

TRANSLATION

The golden locket

(1) One night Shamroz sent a few hired murderers to the house of Jamila.

(2) The attack was made. Sabira and Jamila both died in it.

(3) On the death of his niece and the old woman Shamroz hypocritically lamented and wept a great deal.

(4) In its investigation the police did its work with great devotion but nobody was ready to testify to the truth.

(5) And the result became this that Shamroz in a few days settled down as the owner of his elder brother's property.

(6) But concerning the escape of Naser a great worry remained in his heart.

(7) In the neighboring villages he made a great effort concerning him but did not get hold of any trace.

(8) Young Naser very far away from his country reached a large town.

(9) One night when he became very tired, somewhere in a garden he fell asleep on a bench.

(10) This garden was in the house of a great merchant.

(11) Early in the morning when the owner of the house Set Rahman was going out for a walk, he saw the homeless child in his garden, who was still lying asleep in this manner without worry.

(12) He went to his house, and with his wife he came again to that place where that child was still asleep in that manner.

(13) It is said that this Set had one son who was very handsome and also resembled this child.

(14) They remembered their own dead son, and in the eyes of both of them were tears.

(15) Both holding their breath stood silent at the side of the child, when Naser also woke up from his sleep.

(16) He was looking around in surprise, and then burst into (a flood of) tears.

(17) Set's wife pressed Naser to her bosom. Both were weeping, but they did not know what the reason for their weeping was.

(18) Set Rahman lifted Naser up in his arms, and with his wife they went to their room.

PASHTO WORD-INDEX

PASHTO WORD-INDEX

The entries are given only in the following citation forms: direct singular for nouns; direct singular masculine for adjectives; 1st singular present I for verbs.

Personal and uncompounded demonstrative pronouns, personal and most place-names have been omitted.

The references are to unit and sentence. 16.1 means the entry occurs in sentence 1 of unit 16. Usually not more than 4 occurrences are indicated. Ex. 2 means Exercises of lesson 2, 14b means the title of text 14b.

The order of the entries is according to the Pashto alphabet (from right to left!):

ا ب پ ت ټ ث ج چ ح څ ځ

خ د ډ ذ ر ړ ز ژ ږ س ش

ښ ص ض ط ظ ع غ ف ق ك گ

ل م ن ڼ و ه ی ي ې ۍ

On each page read down first the right column from top to bottom, then the left column from top to bottom.

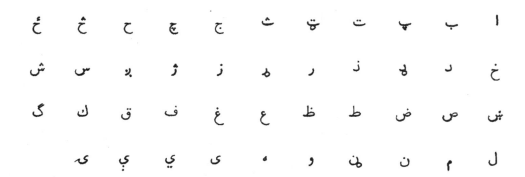

PASHTO WORD-INDEX

اباسم ـ اشتراک

ا

آشنا ـ آهنگر

ایږدم	1.11 4.7 8.3 9.13
ایرانی	16.4

ب

بابا	23.1 23.8
بادشا	6.15,16
بارسوخ	16.16
باربږم	21.1
بازار	10a.1
باسم	2.12 7.16 12.1 18.6
باغیچه	25.9,10,11
بالاخره	9.13
بال بچ	24.8
بالکل	24.1
بام	7.3,5
بانگ	13.3
بانک	24.9
باید	12.1 16.10 18.7 20.4
بجه	14a 14c.2 15b.3
بچ کیږم	25.6
بحثکوم	3.14
بحیره	15c.1
بخشش	4.5
بدلون	8.6
بدن	24.14
برابر	8.9
برابروم	24.11
برج	20.2
برخه	5.7 8.1 10a.1 15c.2
برسبره پر	17.10,13
برغه	23.5
برم	20.9
برمه کاري	18.4,14
برنی	21.5
بریالیتوب	18.12
برید	7.3
بری لیک	17.8
بزرگ	2.4
بزکشي	4.14
بزگر	5.3
بس	23.14 24.7
بشپړ	11.3,15
بل	1.9 6.10 9.6 13.1
بلا	2.12
بلکه	6.9 9.4 13.16
بلي	1.10

بم — پاده وان

پ

پورته کوم — پېښېږم

پورته کوم	1.3 5.13
پورته کېږم	4.12
پوره	8.6
پوښتنه	1.3 1.12 15b 15b.2,4
پولیس	25.4
پولند	15b.2
پوله	13.15
پوه	11.6
پوهنتون	17.18
پوهنځی	17.6,7,9
پوهه	16.10
پوهېږم	12.8 21.11 23.9
په	1.5,9 2.12 3.2 16.3
په اثر	10a.1
په باب	15b.2 18.11
په باره کښې	15b.4
په ... باندې	3.14 12.7
په ...... پورې	16.7
په توګه	9.16 14c.3
په زوره	7.3
په کار	14c
په کارېږم	13.14
په ... کښی	1.2 16.14,16
په ... کښې	2.15 3.1,6,8
په ... کې	2.2 4.9 21.5
په ګډه	5.6
په مجردې چه	20.12
په مقابل کښې	13.8
په نزد	19.6
په هکله	18
پهلواني	14a
پیاله	22a.3
پیپ	14c.1
پیدا	22a.2,3,5
پیدا کوم	12.12 13.3
پیدا کېږم	12.9 15c.3
پیر	2.9
پیره دار	20.11
پیسې	6.18 7.6
پینځه	5.8 9.6 14a 14c.1
پېرم	14c.1
پېژنم	1.2 13.12,13
پېښ	2.12 23.9
پېښه	14b.1 19.2
پېښېږم	3.10 15c.4

تاثير ــ تفتيش

ت

تفحص — جختوم

خاوره — خيال

خير — دم

دنیا	6.10 12.3
دواړه	23.10 25.2,14,15
دوام	9.1 17.3
دود	4.1 9.3
دوره	17.1,6,7
دوړه	15c.2
دوستانه	16.19
دولت	10b.1,3
دومره	6.6 11.2,16 18.7
دونکاچه	24.10
دونه	11.3,9,16
دوولس	16.1
دوه	1.7
دیدار	22a.2
دیدن	21.8
دي	6.7 7.12,18,19
دي	6.12 12.10,13 19.5
دېره	3.12 5.9

ډ

ډاډ	18.13
ډارېږم	8.15
ډاکټر	15b.1
ډاکټري	17.8
ډاکه	25.2
ډرامه	8.5
ډک	14c.1 22a.3
ډکوم	21.8
ډکېږم	8.2
ډګر	18.15
ډم	5.6
ډوډۍ	4.10 5.10 24.13
ډول	3.5 8.2 9.3
ډېر	4.2 6.5,12 13.5
ډېرېږم	8.5

ذ

ذوق	14b.4
ذهن	24.5

ر

راباسم	10a.1,4
رابولم	16.16
راپس	21.10
راپورتاژ	18
راپورته کېږم	2.12

راپیدا کوم — ریښتیا

راپیدا کوم	19.3
راته	21.10 22a.2
راحت	13.13
راځم	1.2,15 2.3 9.16
راداخلیږم	20.13
رارسیږم	20.11 24.15
راروان	24.13
راز	11.2 15b.3
راساً	16.8,13
راښیم	11.6
راغونډیږم	3.14 4.2
راکوزیږم	3.4
راکوم	1.4 7.4,7,12 21.7
رالیږم	9.15
رانتوزم	2.6
راوړم	4.5 5.10 7.11 22a.7
راهیسی	11.8
رایه	16.8
رئیس	1.5 15b.3
رباب	22b.2
رپیږم	23.7
رټ	25.16
رُخسار	22a.7
رخصت	23.2
رسم	3.8
رسوم	17.12 19.7 24.15
رسیږم	9.4 12.5 16.9 19.8
رشوت	13.3
رفیقه	14b.4
رنګ	9.8 17.8 19.3
رګ	22b.2
روابط	16.19
رواج	5.5
روان	8.9 9.9 15c.1
روانوم	8.8
روانیږم	6.17 20.9
روپۍ	7.4,5,7, 13.3
روغ	9.15
رود	21.3
روزم	17.17
روزنه	11.8,9
روژه	22a.3
روغتیا	15b.3
روغ رمټ	10a.5
ریاست	1.4 10b.1
ریښتیا	25.2

ساه — سوځېږم

ساه	25.15
سبا	9.15 21.1
سبق	5.8
سبک	8.7,8,9
سپړېږم	20.8
سپورټ	14a.1 14b.2
سپی	2.9,11
سپين	2.5 11.7
سپين ږيری	5.11 6.3,4
ستايم	16.10
ستر	14b.3
ستر د رستيغ	14c.2
سترګه	5.11 22a.2 23.10
ستړی	24.13, 25.9
ستنه	11.6
سحر	25.11
سخ	23.14
سخت	7.2,8,16,19
سخي صاحب	4.12
سر	2.5 9.5,6,7
سربېره	9.6
سرحد	3.9
سردار	3.3 18.1
سره	4.2 5.1,14 11.3,6
سره سره	19.5
سری	23.11
سړی	1.2,3,12,14
سرې او تودې	13.12
سزا	7.19
سږنی	19.2,7
سفرخرڅ	17.13
سک	16.5
سل	7.4 16.8
سلام عليکم	1.5
سلسله	6.10
سلګی	24.3
سلطان	3.3
سم	8.6
سمدستي	6.1
سنبله	18.1
سنجوم	20.4
سنګر	21.6
سوارلي	20.11
سوچ	24.4,9
سوچه کوم	12.1
سوځېږم	23.7

سور — شی

سور	14c.1 21.9 23.10
سوغات	4.9
سهار	14c.2 15b.1
سیاست	12.7
سیاسی	8.4 19 19.6
سیکه	24.14
سیل	4.13
سیمه	15c.3
سینما	14b.2
سینه	25.17
سیوری	11.8
سپل	25.11

ش

شا	21.5
شاگرد	17.10,17
شامل	16.15
شان	25.11,12
شا وخوا	20.10
شاهي	15b.2 16.6
شپه	2.3 25.1,9
شپږ	17.1
شپېته	16.9
شته	8.10
شخص	16.16,17
شراب	22b.1
شرط	14c.3
شرع	16.6
شرقی	15c.3
شروع	4.7 9.1
شعر	13.7
شق	18.2
شکل	9.8
شل	18.6,8
شمار	4.13
شمال غربی	15c.2
شمالي	15c.2 18 18.1
شمول	12.12
شمېر	15a.2 16.5,8,9
شمېرم	7.6
شورا	16.7,8
شوروي اتحاد	19.3,4
شوری	15b 15b.1,3
شهادت	25.4
شهی	22a.6
شی	8.1 17.10

فصل — کتونکی

کټ — کېږم

کټ 24.4
کچنی 5.8
کړه 21.1
کرا 5.4
کرایه 17.13
کرغه 23.5
کرم 6.1,3,8
کرنه 6.3
کره 7.8
کړم 21.8,10 22a.2,6 22b.3
کړی مړی 24.3
کس 13.14 16.8
کښېنم 3.5 25.5
کښېنوم 20.10
کفیل 15a.1
کلا 20.2,12
کلمه 12.8
کلوپ 14a
کله Ex. 2,8,9
کلی 2.1 5.1,2 24.1
کلیز 19.3,7
کلیوال 5.6,11
کم 7.4 9.4

کمره 25.18
کمزوری 8.10
کمیسیون 15b 15b.1,2,3
کنه 22a 22a.1,2,3
کوټه 24.8
کوچنی 5.8
کوړل 13.15
کور 4.9 5.1,17 7.2
کورس 14a.1
کورگېلی 5.7
کورنۍ 9.14
کورې 2.10
کوزده 9.3
کوشش 25.7
کوښښ 17.3
کوم 2.4,6 9.12 11.3
کوم 1.3,8,9,12 3.2
که Ex.1,2,4 6.6 7.4,19
که څه هم 8.7 11.3,14 13.15
کهول 23.6
کبل 1.4
کېږم 2.10,12 4.1,7,12 6.10

گټه — لغت

لغوی — ماذونبېږم

لغوی	8.5,9
لفظ	12.9
لکه	8.4 11.7 12.4 20.9
لکه چه	7.9 8.3,10 24.14
لګوم	7.16
لګیا	6.1
لګېږم	25.7
لمن	8.2 11.17 21.1
لمونځ	5.8
لنډ	8.6,9 19
لنډ ی	21
لوازم	17.10,13
لور	24.10
لوړ	11.5,7 14b.3 17.4
لوست	11.1
لوستونکی	19.1
لولم	14b 17.4 19.1
لومړنی	17.1,4,9
لومړی	16.3 18.4,5
لوی	3.12 4.11 5.15 10b.2
لوی حاکم	10b.2
لوی حکومت	15a.1
لوی مدیر	15b.1
لوېدیځ	18.1
له	21.8 23.5 24.6
له	4.1 7.2,18 11.3
له امله	17.15
له کبله	20.4
له پاره	4.5 5.15 6.9 14b.4
له ... څخه	1.9 3.8 5.15
له ... سره	7.6 12.3 13.5,13
له ... نه	10a.1,5 22b.3
لیسانس	17.7
لیک	8.10
لیکم	1.7 8.7 11.1 15b.5
لیکوال	14b.3
لیکه	11.11
لیلیه	17.13
لېږم	17.18
لېسه	17.5,6
لېونی	7.16

م

مار — مرواري

موکبرم — ملي شوری

موکبرم	25.2
مونی	11.3
موبرم	13.7
مزدور	9.11
مزدوري	5.5
مسافر	2.2,3,4 5.9
مسئله	16.15,20
مسئوليت	16.13 18.7
مست	22b.1
مستخدم	13.8
مسجد	2.1,2 3.12
مسکين	17.11
مسلمان	16.5
مشاوره	14b.4
مشر	11.8 16.12 19.5
مشر ورور	25.5
مشري	19.4,5
مشهور	3.7 16.2 17.18
مصرف	17.14,19
مصرفوم	17.16
مصور	18
مضمون	8.2,4
مطبوعات	1.4
معارف	17 17.15,17
معامله	5.16
معرب	12.9
معطل	20.10
معلوم	3.12,13 19.7 22b.3
معنا	12.11,13
مفرس	12.9
مفغن	12.9
مفهوم	12.11
مقابله	20.3,5
مقاله	1.6,7
مقررات	16.6
مقننه	16.7
مکتب	5.15 17.12
مکر	25.3
مگر	1.2 8.10 13.3 20.1
ملا	5.6,8,11
ملت	12.4 16.15 19.2
ملك	13.5
ملکي	18.15
ملگری	4.9 6.17 19.2 20.8
ملي	3.1 16.3,7,8
ملي شوری	15b 15b.1,3

ملیون — ناره

ن

ناست — نيم

نیم بسمل — وړمه ورځ

نیم بسمل	22b.4

و

وار	6.15 19.1 21.7
واړه	23.6
والي	4.4
وایم	2.1,7,8 5.1
و... ته	1.3 1.7 11.3 16.11
وجه	25.17
وچ	22b.2
وخت	3.4,10 5.8
وختی	25.11
وداني	15a 15a.1
وراچوم	7.5
وراستوم	9.16
ورباندي	6.2 13.3 22b.2
ورپسی	2.12 25.7
ورتگ	14a.1
ورته	2.7,8 5.1,10
ورڅخه	10a.4
ورځ	4.1 7.1 12.4
ورځپانه	19.1
ورځم	4.12 5.9 14c.2 22a.6
ورخطا کوم	25.1
ورسپارم	16.11
ورسره	9.10
ورښکاره	24.13
ورکوم	5.5,10 6.12 8.10
ورلیږم	9.3
ورنږدي	24.2
ورو	8.5 21.8
ورور	23.4 25.5
وروړم	9.5,11
وروستنی	6.11
وروسته	6.5,9 10a.1
وروسته تر	1.5
وروستو	24.12
وروستی	14c.2
وریادېږم	25.14
وریځ	15c.2,3
وربره	25.3
وړ	14b.1 16.10 18.9
وړاندی	23.9
وړاندی کوم	1.8
وړم	9.8 9.15 18.2
وړمه ورځ	10b.1

همکاري — یې